Lecture Notes in Social Networks

For further volumes:
http://www.springer.com/series/8768

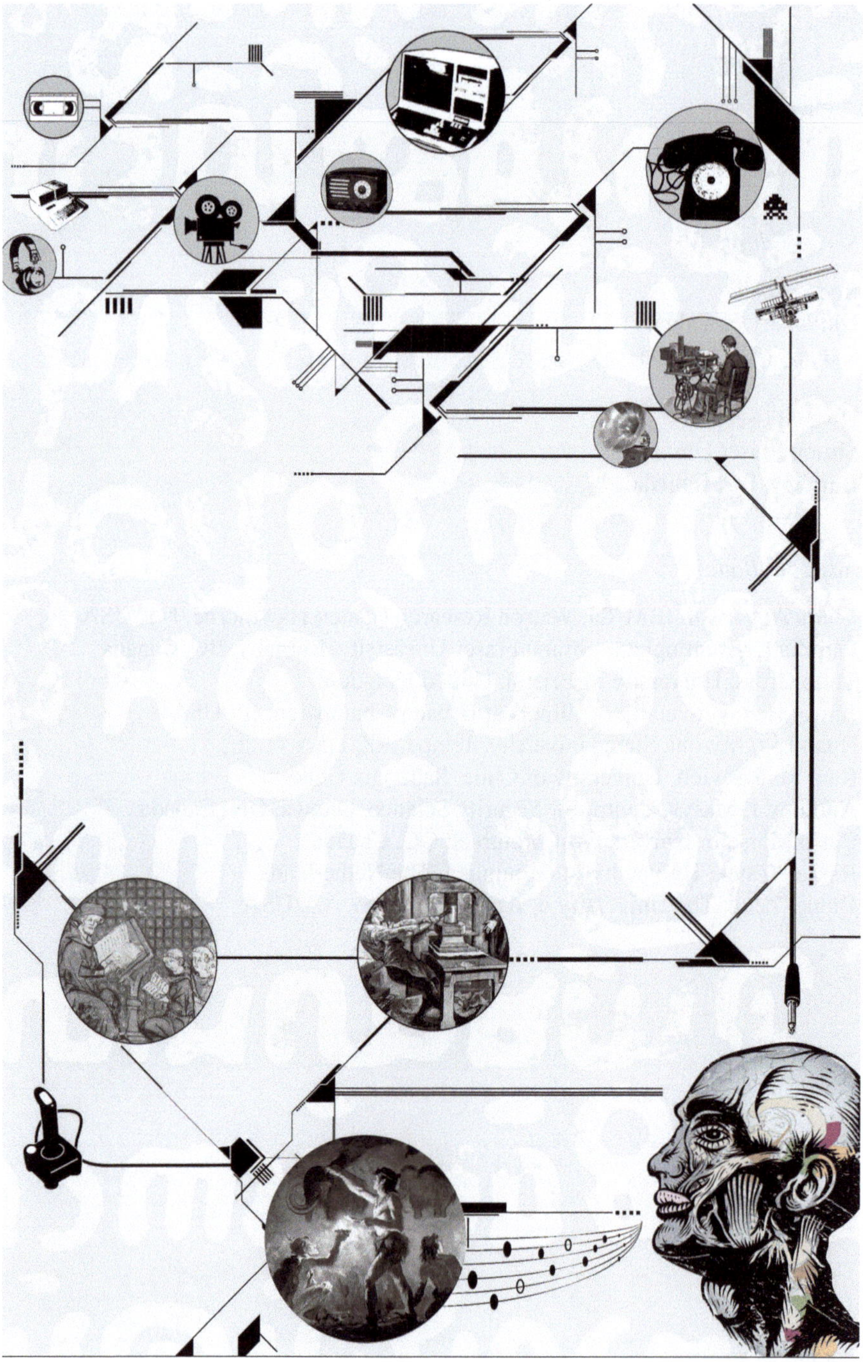

James A. Dator • John A. Sweeney
Aubrey M. Yee

Mutative Media

Communication Technologies and Power Relations in the Past, Present, and Futures

Springer

James A. Dator
Department of Political Science
Hawaii Research Center for Futures Studies
University of Hawaii at Manoa
Honolulu, HI, USA

John A. Sweeney
Department of Political Science
Hawaii Research Center for Futures Studies
University of Hawaii at Manoa
Honolulu, HI, USA

Aubrey M. Yee
Department of Political Science
Hawaii Research Center for Futures Studies
University of Hawaii at Manoa
Honolulu, HI, USA

ISSN 2190-5428 ISSN 2190-5436 (electronic)
ISBN 978-3-319-07808-3 ISBN 978-3-319-07809-0 (eBook)
DOI 10.1007/978-3-319-07809-0
Springer Cham Heidelberg New York Dordrecht London

Library of Congress Control Number: 2014944071

Printed on acid-free paper

Springer is part of Springer Science+Business Media (www.springer.com)

"The bourgeoisie cannot exist without constantly revolutionizing the instruments of production, and thereby the relations of production, and with them the whole relations of society."

—Karl Marx

Preface

To grasp a glimpse at the futures, you must always begin with the past. Understanding the roots from whence we have come and how we have arrived at our present situation with all its guts and glory is foundational to thinking about where we may go in the years ahead. When we first began thinking about the notion of innovation and the technologies of communication we went way back to the beginning and have in fact returned several times to ponder foundational questions like whether Neanderthals had the capacity to speak and how oral societies adjusted to the world of written words. These and other monumental moments in the history of human communication technologies have helped us to think about the ways in which human communication might radically change in the futures. Will we someday soon be part artilect, part human with the ability to program our own internal software and download information to and from our friends? Will we be able to 3D print our clothing, new shoes, or the food we eat? Will synthetic biology allow us to manage our own genetic structures to enable longer, healthier lives? All of these burgeoning technologies appear within grasp and yet there are the looming potentialities of systems collapse with us at the very same moment. Will we be able to create truly clean energy to continue all of these technological advances? Will our population growth and economic fragility conspire to create an even deeper socioeconomic inequity in the future? Will climate change overwhelm our capacity to feed ourselves and will we see millions of climate refugees with no nation to call home creating increased geopolitical insecurity? All of these are very possible realities as well.

This volume is the final product in a stream of presentations, publications, and other activities resulting from a research project based on a proposal titled, "Communicating Power: Technological Innovation and Social Change. Past, Present, and futures." We submitted our research proposal in May 2011 in response to an invited call on "Technology, Innovation, and Society," specifically focusing on "How does technology change the balance of power in society?" We were awarded a small research grant by the University of Hawaii Foundation and agreed to conduct that research for the 2012 calendar year. While we fulfilled the requirements of the grant during that period, we realized we had enough material to write a book on the subject. You are now reading the results of that decision.

In our proposal we stated that, "We propose to examine how communication technologies have contributed to changes in the structure of societies, and hence to the distribution of political power, in the past, and at present, and in four alternative futures. We propose to rely on a survey and analysis of existing studies for our past and some of our present research; on original research on several current instances; and on certain techniques of alternative futures forecasting in order to develop and present the possible four alternative futures." We approached this proposal with some preconceived notions born of years of thinking about these very issues. But as social scientists and futurists, we endeavored to remain open-minded and as unbiased as possible as we carried out our research.

We proceeded as follows. First, we reviewed the proposal, and assigned specific tasks outlined in it to each of us. Dator took responsibility for the theoretical and historical portions from the evolution of human language through to the establishment of television and the Internet. Yee took responsibility for gathering and analyzing information about communication technologies and their impacts from the emergence of social media into the futures. Sweeney took responsibility for research on theories of power and for the development of the interactive game, which was actually co-devised with Aaron Rosa—to whom we owe immense gratitude. In addition to coordinating significant aspects of the game, Aaron made significant written contributions to Chap. 5, which developed from a report published in *The Journal of Futures Studies*. Aaron is also the artist behind the cover image for this monograph. He is a true renaissance man, and we are fortunate to have him as a colleague!

In addition to our individual responsibilities for these various sections of the project, the three of us worked cooperatively on all aspects of the research throughout the course of 2012. We established a pattern whereby we engaged in our research individually on a daily basis, sharing electronically ideas and items we encountered not only as they related to our own *kuleana* (responsibility) but also to each other. Once a week, we met for several hours and discussed what each of us had done since our last face-to-face meeting. At the end of each face-to-face session, we assigned tasks and made commitments for research over the coming week. As the final months and weeks of the project neared, we intensified our individual research, our electronic correspondence, and our face-to-face discussions of ideas and concerns.

The research process was both exhilarating and exhausting. Our weekly meetings were animated discussions of new findings as well as revisions of earlier assumptions. There have been various products of our labor along the way:

1. Presentation of research in progress by Aubrey Yee to the Department of Political Science, University of Hawaii at Mānoa, as part of a masters degree culminating experience. "Communicating Power: Technological Innovation and Social Change in the Past, Present, and Futures"—Honolulu, HI, May 2012. *Link to presentation*: http://prezi.com/wnlwvonipn8t/technology-innovation-and-society-grant-2012/

2. Presentation of research in progress by John A. Sweeney at the University of California Santa Barbara, *Contagion and Control: Speculative Futures Graduate Colloquium.* The presentation was integral in thinking through our research into the futures of communication technology, specifically the affects of new media. Looking at two recent incidents related to viral media, Sweeney charted some trends and emerging issues that became critical aspects of the scenarios for our larger project. Santa Barbara, CA, May 2012.
3. Presentation by John A. Sweeney and Aubrey Yee, "Communicating Power: Technological Innovation and Social Change in the Past, Present, and Futures," Session 15 on "Futures, values and sociological theory, Part II," Research Committee Futures Research (RC07), International Sociological Association, Buenos Aires, Argentina, August 3, 2012. The connections made in Argentina and the feedback received from our conference presentation were an important part of the development and evolution of the final stage of our project and the futures immersive game in particular. *Link to presentation*: http://prezi.com/wnlwvonipn8t/technology-innovation-and-society-grant-2012/
4. Jim Dator, "Communication Technologies and the Futures of Courts and Law," in Sam Muller, Stavros Zouridis, Morly Frishman and Laura Kistemaker (editors), *The Law of the Future and the Future of Law Volume II.* The Hague: Torkel Opsahl Academic EPublisher, 2012. Chapter 3.7, pp. 211–221. Portions of Chapter Two of this monograph are based on that article.
5. John A. Sweeney, Aubrey Yee, Aaron Rosa, Jim Dator, "Emerging Futures, Emerging Futurists." A one-day futures symposium organized by the researchers to facilitate networking and presentations of academic works. Attended by over 30 academics in the field of futures studies from around the world. Honolulu, HI. November 30, 2012.
6. John A. Sweeney, Aubrey Yee, Aaron Rosa, Jim Dator, "Gaming with the Futures" (http://www.gamingwiththefutures.tumblr.com). We developed a portable gaming platform entailing experiential alternative futures to immerse players within a variety of power relations relative to an array of communication technologies. Participants included both undergraduate and graduate students from the University of Hawaii at Mānoa, undergraduate students from Kapiolani Community College, and visiting Futures Studies' scholars and researchers from Australia, Bahrain, Canada, Finland, Germany, and the mainland. In total, "Gaming with the Futures" or "Gaming Futures" (as it was also called) utilized 12 gamers, 8 actors, and 5 facilitators. Honolulu, HI, December 1, 2012.
7. Jim Dator, John A. Sweeney, Aubrey Yee, Aaron Rosa, "Communicating Power: Technological Innovation and Social Change in the Past, Present, and Futures." Report on TIS research and Gaming Futures published in *The Journal of Futures Studies*, June 2013, 17(4), 117–134. http://www.jfs.tku.edu.tw/17-4/R01.pdf
8. Aubrey Yee, John A. Sweeney, Jim Dator, Political Science Departmental Colloquium. Our research was presented to a group of students and faculty as part of a weekly colloquium series in the Department of Political Science, University of Hawaii at Mānoa, April 2013.

Since that time, the three of us have worked on writing, revising, and rewriting our various sections of the book as well as commenting, adding, and editing each other's work. We continued the rhythm with which we began our work: virtual meetings alternating with face-to-face meetings until we produced what you see here. As with all projects of this magnitude and certainly all projects dealing with alternative futures, one of the greatest challenges is knowing when to stop. There will always be more emerging issues, more relevant research, more ideas, and more revisions … especially more revisions. So, while we feel that this manuscript is a complete vision of our ideas, it will never (to us) feel fully completed. It will always be a thought experiment in progress. We hope that it inspires in you some thoughts about how you see the futures, some vigorous debates about the past, and some critical lenses with which to view the present. This is our collective vision, but it is quite surely not the only or the "right" one.

Our thanks to Maury Solomon and Nora Rawn of Springer, for shepherding our manuscript through the publication process. They have been wonderful to work with in every way,

Honolulu, HI
April 1, 2014

James A. Dator
John A. Sweeney
Aubrey M. Yee

Contents

About the Authors

James A. Dator is Professor and Director of the Hawaii Research Center for Futures Studies, Department of Political Science, and Adjunct Professor in the Program in Public Administration, the College of Architecture, and the Center for Japanese Studies, of the University of Hawaii at Mānoa; Co-Chair and Core Lecturer, Space Humanities, International Space University, Strasbourg, France; former President, World Futures Studies Federation.

He also taught at Rikkyo University (Tokyo, for 6 years), the University of Maryland, Virginia Tech, the University of Toronto, and the InterUniversity Consortium for Postgraduate Studies in Dubrovnik, Yugoslavia.

He received a B.A. in Ancient and Medieval History and Philosophy from Stetson University, an M.A. in Political Science from the University of Pennsylvania, and a Ph.D. in Political Science from The American University. He did postgraduate work at Virginia Theological Seminary (Ethics and Church History), Yale University (Japanese Language), The University of Michigan (Linguistics and Quantitative Methods), Southern Methodist University (Mathematical Applications in Political Science).

He is a Danforth Fellow, Woodrow Wilson Fellow, and Fulbright Fellow.

John A. Sweeney is Deputy Director of the Center for Postnormal Policy and Futures Studies at East-West University in Chicago, IL, and a Ph.D. candidate in the Department of Political Science at the University of Hawaii at Mānoa (UHM), where he is also a Researcher at the Hawaii Research Center for Futures Studies. John received his Master's Degree in Religion from UHM in 2007 and a Bachelor's Degree in History of Ideas (magna cum laude) from Kennesaw State University in 2005. In support of his doctoral studies, John is also an Affiliate Researcher at the Centre for Studies on Urban Creativity at Sapienza—Università di Roma in Italy and a member of the Nonkilling Futures Studies Research Committee with the Center for Global Nonkilling.

John has facilitated and designed strategic foresight workshops in conjunction with the East-West Center in Myanmar, Kanu Hawaii, the Hawaii State Office of Planning, UNESCO, and other local and international organizations. He is a member of the World Futures Studies Federation, the World Future Society, and the Association of Professional Futurists. He also serves on the Board of Directors of Kanu Hawaii and the Advisory Board for *Itineration*: *Cross-Disciplinary Studies in Rhetoric*, *Media*, *and Culture*. John's work has been published in *The Journal of Futures Studies*, *Ctheory*, *Futures*, and *East-West Affairs*: *A Quarterly Journal of North-South Relations in Postnormal Times*. He tweets on trends, emerging issues, and all things postnormal at @aloha_futures.

Aubrey Morgan Yee was born and raised on Oahu. Aubrey Morgan Yee is a futurist, business strategist, and consultant. She is currently pursuing a Ph.D. in Futures Studies in the Department of Political Science at the University of Hawaii at Mānoa, where she is also a Researcher at the Hawaii Research Center for Futures Studies. Aubrey is the project director for the Omidyar Group's new initiative—Hawaii Quality of Life—using systems mapping and complexity theory to help nonprofit social change organizations with their strategic planning. She received her undergraduate degree from UCLA in American Studies. Aubrey has co-facilitated foresight workshops for the State Office of Planning on Oahu, the Hawaii Futures Summit, Samsung Corporation, Kamehameha Schools, Oxfam's Asian Development Dialogue Series, the first annual Myanmar Futures Exchange, and a variety of other national and international organizations, institutions, and businesses.

Aubrey currently serves on the board of KANU Hawaii, a grassroots social change nonprofit dedicated to increasing the quality of life in our islands through promoting island values. She also consults as a strategist and writer for Sustainable America. Aubrey and her husband Brady helped to found the Hawaii chapter of After School All Stars, a nonprofit serving Hawaii's at-risk middle school youth by providing free after school enrichment programs. In her scant free time, she enjoys writing, working on her fine art photography, and relaxing with her family in Kaneohe on the island of Oahu.

Chapter 1
Technology, Communication, Power, Society, and Change

1.1 Introductory Concepts

Many people in the modern and postmodern worlds are involved with technology in one way or the other. Some love it and can't wait to use the latest gadgets; others profess to hate technology and strive to live their lives free of it, while most simply take the increasingly ubiquitous nature of evermore sophisticated technology as somehow given, inevitable, unproblematic, and natural. Moreover, there is a vast and growing cache of academic literature about the interrelationship between technologies, individuals, societies and environments.

This study seeks to explicate how communication technologies seem to have contributed to changes in the structure of societies, and hence in the distribution of political power, in the past, at present, and in four alternative futures. This is not a collection of detailed case studies. Rather, we have taken a decidedly macro approach and focused on five periods where such influences were likely to have been both substantial and well-documented: during the emergence of language and speech; during the shift from entirely oral to some handwritten communication; in handwritten, scribal societies up to the invention of the printing press and related technologies; from the printing press to electronic communication technologies; and ending with potentially emerging modes of communication.

For information on the past and present, we relied on the extensive and growing literature about the four historical periods. However, since our focus is so wide, our analysis seldom is able to go very deep. Thus, we alternate between broad, sweeping, though often well-documented statements to a few detailed, and indeed sometimes very personal, examples. The latter are especially prevalent once we get to electronic communication technologies that have impacted our daily lives and about which we have shared our speculations publicly before. Our discussion of potential future technologies and impacts is based on theories and methods of futures studies developed over the last 4 decades in the Alternative Futures program of the Department of Political Science of the University of Hawaii at Mānoa, as will be discussed later.

J.A. Dator et al., *Mutative Media: Communication Technologies and Power Relations in the Past, Present, and Futures*, Lecture Notes in Social Networks, DOI 10.1007/978-3-319-07809-0_1,

A great deal of our research effort was a survey of the literature on technology *per se*, and especially on technology as an agent of individual, social, and environmental change. Our intention here is not only to develop a theory of technology and its possible role in such change to guide our own research but also to enable us to refine or reject a tentative theory of technology and technologically induced change that we had developed over previous decades. At the outset we needed to make it clear that our main interest is to learn if, and if so, how, a new level of communication technologies *per se* serves as an agent of social change. We are only secondarily interested in how the information and ideas promulgated through the new technologies might also cause change. This is a distinction that the Canadian philosopher of media, Marshall McLuhan, intended to highlight by his dictum "the medium is the message" [32, 33].

We discovered in our research not only that many students of communication technologies and social change do not make this distinction clearly, if at all, but also that they more often comment on the substance of the message rather than on the impact of the medium itself. In presenting the results of our research here, we usually rely on scholars who study the impact of new communication technologies *per se* on modes of thought and behavior, and then try to make the distinction apparent in our discussion of the findings of others. To be sure, it is not always easy or perhaps even possible to unambiguously separate message from medium, but we endeavor to do so, if only to show the ways in which the two are deeply interconnected and, as it were, the immense effect the latter has on the former.

1.2 What Is "Technology"?

We looked at "technology" from two perspectives. One perspective follows Charles Singer in his masterful multi-volume work, *A History of Technology*, that took him 2 decades to complete. He states that technology is best understood as "how things are commonly done or made … (and) what things are done or made" [38]. Somewhat earlier, Lynn White, Jr., [43] wrote: "Broadly speaking, technology is the way people do things. (In a certain sense, there is even a technology of prayer.)"

As Paul Boyer observes, this definition provides "a broader view of technology as ways of 'making and doing things' that, at its most expansive, encompasses all ways of shaping the real world—natural and social—to human ends. Technology so understood signifies a thoroughly social process that touches all human beings, and whose history is inevitably bound up with questions of power and authority." [6]

Thus, our definition of technology is "how humans do things," or, "how humans get things done." The importance and utility of this broad definition will be made apparent later.

The second perspective of our work understands technology as media—as intermediating processes between whatever "objective" real world may be "out there" for humans to perceive and interact with, and our inner "consciousness" of that world and of ourselves. As Walter Benjamin argues, "technology is the mastery not of nature but mastery of the relation between nature and humanity." [2, 5] That is to say, humans never (except perhaps as newborn infants) perceive the world directly. We create the world through media as much as the world is created for us through the media and the technologies we inherit. In short, humans are *prosthetic becomings*. This understanding is increasingly more prevalent among a range of thinkers and, as one might imagine, raises numerous socio-political issues—many of which have deep existential implications. As Stiegler observes, "The evolution of the 'prosthesis,' not itself living, by which the human is nonetheless defined as a living being, constitutes the reality of the human's evolution, as if, with it, the history of life were to continue by means other than life." [40, p. 50] Calling into question the very limits and possibilities for conceiving of life itself, Stiegler gives voice to the notion that humans are porously open systems, which is to say that humans always perceive, understand, and address the world through various media, beginning with language and speech, which has both liberal and "conservative" aspects—in other words, an implicit (and clearly explicit) politics [17]. We thus here seek to understand how the media influence our understanding of the world while also influencing our understanding of ourselves, personally and interpersonally.

1.3 Three Views of "Technology," Plus One

One of the purposes of our research was to test our long-standing contention that both popular and academic beliefs about technology fall into one of three basic categories. The first widely and often uncritically shared perspective is that *technology is neutral*. Technology does not impact society in any important way. Technologies can make our lives better, or can be misused to make them worse, this view maintains. It is entirely a question of how humans use technology—a matter of human agency and not of any essential feature of technology. This view is well captured by the insistence by many gun enthusiasts in the United States that "Guns don't kill people. People kill people." Guns can be used for anything. It is up to humans to decide to use them to kill people or not.

A variation of this view is that while technology is neutral *per se*, technological research and development aimed at improving the economy and the lives of ordinary humans is a good thing, and should be increased. Technological innovation is routinely said by decision makers worldwide to be essential for national security and individual/national wealth. Most formal education at all levels everywhere presently is aimed at increasing the number and skills of scientists, technologists, engineers, and mathematicians (the so-called "STEM" academic subjects) and related disciplines so that they can develop new tools for the benefit of humanity. Although any technology can be used for evil, the intention of technologies that are being invented and diffused as a consequence of scientific research are done so in order to improve human welfare and national strength, it is repeatedly said. Many people most directly responsible for the creation and spread of new technologies—policymakers, financiers, educators, scientists, engineers, designers, entrepreneurs, marketing specialists—espouse this view. Their intentions are noble, they say, and they accept no responsibility for how their creations, intended for good, are subsequently used. Michael Thad Allen and Gabrielle Hecht quote, but do not support, the belief that "technology did not inevitably lead to an Orwellian social order, any more than it did to a democratic utopia." [3, p. 20]

In contrast, a second view, sometimes more widespread than at other times, is that *technology is inherently evil* or at least profoundly alienating. As Fuller observes, "The world populace identifies technology with (1) weapons and (2) machines that compete with them for their jobs. Most people therefore think they are against technology, not knowing that the technology they don't understand is their only means of exercising their option to 'make it' on this planet and in this life." [16, p. xxvii] This view, as Fuller implies, often maintains that humans once enjoyed a healthy, pre-technological existence, or at least lived in societies where technologies were "on a human scale" that complemented but altered neither what it means to be human nor the natural environment within which humans evolved. Proponents of this view often argue that with every new technology, humans have become increasingly alienated both from their true nature and from the natural world around them, which successive technological developments have progressively destroyed. They often argue that humans should stop further technological development and "return" to some stage when humans, their technologies, and their environments were and again will be in dynamic balance—in a condition of "sustainability" perhaps.

Just as we will demonstrate later that some people greet each new technology as a step towards paradise, so also there are those who see new technology as a step towards hell, often because of its mass-eroticizing potential. Filippo de Strata, a late fifteenth century Benedictine friar and—importantly—a copier by hand of ancient manuscripts, wrote:

> Through printing, tender boys
> and gentle girls, chaste without foul stain,
> take in whatever mars the purity of mind or body …
> Writing indeed, which brings in gold for us,
> should be respected and held to be nobler
> than all goods, unless she has suffered
> degradation in the brothel of the printing
> presses. She is a maiden with a pen, a
> harlot in print.

De Strata's lament is cited by Lewis Lapham [26], who offers a supremely eloquent mediation on what he considers to be the dehumanizing tendencies of everything from television to the Internet.

A third view, much less widespread and popular, but well represented in the scholarly literature, is that *technology is neither neutral nor evil. It is transformative*. Humans have never been "without technologies," and progress, whether individually or collectively, is a direct result of increasing technological development. "Technology is therefore no mere means," Heidegger said. "Technology is a way of revealing." [22, p. 12] Humans are, indeed, defined by their interactions with the environment and other people via some medium, some technology. Individual and social characteristics are defined by biological, environmental, and technological limits and capabilities by which humans build cultures, societies, institutions, and values [7]. These factors and their interrelationships may remain relatively stable until something disturbs them. Agents of change may be military conquest, natural climate change, or newly acquired knowledge or beliefs. Often the change agents are new technologies *per se* that permit new behavior and thus challenge and destroy old institutions and the old values that were based upon the old technologies, eventually creating new values and institutions, which will be transformed themselves by yet newer technologies.

The bumper-sticker expression of this view is yet another dictum of the Canadian philosopher of media, Marshall McLuhan: "We shape our tools and thereafter our tools shape us." [32, 33] Perhaps a riff on Churchill's sentiment, "we shape our buildings, and afterwards our buildings shape us," McLuhan's adage affirms that the ultimate power rests with those who do the building, so to speak, but the line between builder and building, which is to say between humans and technology, is often blurred. When health problems prohibited the German philosopher Friedrich Nietzsche from continuing his work in the mid 1800s, he acquired a Hansen Writing Ball, which was the first typewriter to be produced commercially. Noting the impact this: thing" had on his work, Nietzsche intimated in an 1882 personal correspondence that, "our writing tools are working on our thoughts." [25, p. 200] As Nietzsche's typewriter literally mutated his work, there is another perspective to be considered concerning how humans view technology.

While our research was initially guided by the third view, we have now concluded that there is *a* fourth and better way to understand technology and its role as an *actant of change*. We now prefer to say that technology is mutative, and our deployment of Latour's concept emphasizes the dynamic ways in which technology intersects complex networks of relations, connections between a variety of things, human and otherwise [27]. That is to say, technology does change individual and hence social behavior in profound ways, but that change is neither transformative in a positive sense, nor demonic, nor neutral—it is simply what it is. Thus, it is like a mutation in biological evolution, the utility and continuation of which depends on whether the mutation makes its possessors more apt, or at least gives them a fighting chance, for survival. Noting the systemic repercussions of technological adaptation and enhancement, Lem observes:

> Every technology is actually an artificial extension of the innate tendency possessed by all living beings to gain mastery over their environment, or at least not to surrender to it in their struggle for survival. Homeostasis—a sophisticated name for aiming toward a state of equilibrium, or for continued existence despite the ongoing changes—has produced gravity-resistant calcareous and chitinous skeletons; mobility-enabling legs, wings, and fins; fangs, horns, jaws, and digestive systems that enable eating; and carapaces and masking shapes that serve as a defense against being eaten. Finally, in its effort to make organisms independent of their surroundings, homeostasis implemented the regulation of body temperature. In this way, islets of decreasing entropy emerged in the world of general entropic increase. [28]

While life's struggle to live is readily apparent in Lem's big-picture perspectivism, this dynamic is also apparent in Nietzsche's transition "from arguments to aphorisms, from thoughts to puns, from rhetoric to telegram style," which was due, in no small part, to his new technological companion as much as his ill health [25, p. 203]. When Nietzsche says that his writing tool is working on his thoughts, he is literally giving voice to the mutative capacity of technology, which, as McLuhan later noted, makes "the medium is the massage" a more apt expression for the dynamic ways in which media condition our prosthetic becoming [32, 33]. The advent of McLuhan's mutative aphorism may be due to the error of a typesetter, who mistakenly turned "message" into "massage." Thus, mutations enable new challenges as much as opportunities, and attending to both equally lies at the heart of our research.

We encountered many examples of statements about technology illustrative of the belief that technology is neutral (and/or intends good, though can be used for evil), or that it is demonic, inevitably destroying essential processes and values. Jennifer Daryl Slack and J. Macgregor Wise [39] put the issue this way: According to the dominant view, "first, technology is the central defining characteristic of what it means to be human at any particular time. We move through ages: Stone Age, Bronze Age, Iron Age, Industrial Age, Electronic Age, Information/Computer/ Digital Age. Each of these 'ages' carries with it an image of cultural life that is dramatically different from the others. Second, technology is seen as the causal agent of these ages." They continue, "Third, and this point is a bit more subtle, the driving force, or goal, of each of these ages is to perfect these technologies and this stage of development. In this way, technology is the end product, the ultimate effect, and the *raison d'etre* of the age." [39, p. 3]

They then say, "we would like to flip this formulation around and reposition culture as a more central actor in the technological drama, although perhaps its role is subtler. The technological drama typically unfolds in majestic style with one act following another, featuring waves of innovation, revolution, and change. But in each act, culture is up there on stage: a voice in the discovery of human needs and wants, the methods to meet our needs and wants, and setting and investing in priorities, and in practices of manufacture, distribution, and use." [39, p. 3] They often cite the "guns don't kill people" contention throughout their book to illustrate different points and reformulations of the phrase to reflect different views of causality.

It should be clear in what we write below that we do not take the view of "technological determinism" that Slack and Wise state is widespread. That is one reason, as we explain later, that we make the hardware, software and especially orgware distinction that we do—as well as the other distinctions we will discuss below.[1] That is also the point behind McLuhan's phrase as we understand and use it: "We shape our tools and thereafter they shape us." It is our intention here to tease out the role of "we" as shapers, as well as the ways "we" are subsequently shaped.

[1] In our lengthy discussion of various aspects of "technology" in this chapter, we make many distinctions. One distinction is between hardware, software, and orgware. The latter term, coined by the cyberneticist G. M. Dobrov in 1979, refers to the people and institutions (ORGanizations) needed to make the hardware and software of technology function. We explain the concept in detail later in this chapter.

Slack and Wise devote several chapters to elucidating the views of groups who argue that technology is demonic: the Luddites; notions of "appropriate technology" in E. F. Schumacher, *Small is Beautiful*, and Ivan Illich, *Tools for Conviviality*; The Unabomber; Jacques Ellul, *The Technological Society*; Lewis Mumford, *The Myth of the Machine*; and Herbert Marcuse, *One-Dimensional Man*. We agree those certainly are classical examples of the demonic view of technology.

Slack and Wise end their book with an extended analysis from what they call "A Cultural Studies approach to technological culture." [39] They

> develop a way of understanding technology that foregrounds the interconnectedness with which things appear, are developed and have effects. While the approach we develop relies on the theoretical concepts of articulation and assemblage, it owes a great debt to many scholars who have proposed alternative approaches to conceiving the interconnectedness of technology culture. For example, in his book Technology as Symptom and Dream, Robert D. Romanyshyn defines technology as 'an enactment of the human imagination in the world.' Andrew Feenberg, in Critical Theory of Technology, defines it as "a process of development suspended between different possibilities." Langdon Winner, in The Whale and the Reactor, defines technologies as 'forms of life.' Elizabeth Grosz has recently put it particularly elegantly. She writes in her article titled, "The Thing:" "Technology is that which ensures and continually refines the ongoing negotiations between bodies and things, the deepening investment of the one, the body, in the other, the thing." [39, p. 98]

Although these are phrases we do not use, the underlying perspectives of Slack and Wise are very much in keeping with our understanding of the interrelationship between "technology" and "society" (or "culture"). More accurately, our understanding, if not our mode of expressing it, is very much in keeping with theirs. Their elaborate discussion of different notions of causality (pp. 101–114) and of the related concept, agency (pp. 115–124), and of identity (which in effect considers who the "we" in McLuhan's formulation typically are and are not) is congenial with ours as well.

Nonetheless, we often get the feeling that they are accusing the emperor of having no clothes even though there is no emperor in sight who claims he is clothed. Who are the "technological determinists" they are discrediting? They do not say clearly. One scholar who holds a generally positive (and also broad) view of technology, Arnulf Grübler, says: "All the numerous technology studies of the twentieth century share one conclusion: it is simply wrong to conceptualize technological evolution according to a simple linear model, no matter how appealing the simplification. Technology evolution is neither simple nor linear. The four most important distinctive characteristics are instead that it is *uncertain, dynamic, systemic,* and *cumulative.*" [20, p. 21] Although Slack and Wise seem intent on making sure that no one believes in technological determinism, or that technology and culture can be viewed separately, they offer example after example of what appears to be "soft determinism" (in their formulation), and often do seem to treat technology as though it were a "tool" separate from culture. Moreover, like many other things we have read that are written by recent scholars, their views seem to be too heavily influenced by recent electronic technology and not by technology and culture in other places and times. That is one reason why we have endeavored to cast our gaze widely in order, we hope, to penetrate more deeply as well.

1.4 Three Kinds of Technology: Physical, Biological, and Social

Most people when they think of "technology" think only of what we here call "physical" technology—a specific tool or piece of hardware, such as a hammer, a car, or an iPad. That is one *kind* of technology, and it is a kind especially important in the world some of us live in presently. But for most of history, and many parts of the world now, biological and social technologies were and are far more pervasive and influential than physical technologies. Remember our definition of technology as "how people do things." or "how humans get things done"? Humans need oxygen, water, energy, minerals, vitamins, and roughage to live and function. They need to remove waste and toxins from their bodies. Humans explore their environment and need ways to do that—to see, hear, feel, touch, move towards/away from things. They seek to reproduce. They experience a variety of emotions and try to enhance or inhibit them sometimes. Humans historically and typically now receive oxygen by breathing the air around them; they eat in order to get energy, minerals, vitamins and the rest. They remove wastes and toxins by urinating, defecating, sweating. They have eyes to see, ears to hear, fingers to touch and manipulate, legs to walk, arms and legs to swim. They engage in heterosexual intercourse to reproduce. And so on. Ultimately, our experiences of the world are mediated, and mutated, by our bodies, which are porous open systems that are dramatically shaped by environmental factors on a variety of scales.

When Jaroslav Flegr began researching Toxoplasmosis (hereafter toxo) twenty years ago, he did so for decidedly personal reasons. Having always felt that something was plaguing him, Flegr's groundbreaking work on the parasite led to some pretty startling, albeit contentious, propositions. Theorizing the dramatic effects of toxo on our porous humanity, Flegr claims, "the 'latent' parasite may be quietly tweaking the connections between our neurons, changing our response to frightening situations, our trust in others, how outgoing we are, and even our preference for certain scents" [31]. As with Flegr's research on toxo, a flurry of recent studies points toward the potency and perils of our extraordinary sensitivity to nonhuman phenomena on a variety of scales. As McAuliffe reports, "In a 2011 study of 20 European countries, the national suicide rate among women increased in direct proportion to the prevalence of the latent Toxoinfection in each nation's female population" [31]. Correlating atmospheric lead levels, which skyrocketed during the post-WWII boom in the US and elsewhere, with an increase in crime in urban centers, Rick Nevin, an adviser to the National Center for Healthy Housing, authored a report arguing, "Toddlers who ingested high levels of lead in the '40s and '50s really were more likely to become violent criminals in the '60s, '70s, and '80s" [14]. On a more positive note, the National Bureau of Economic Research recently published a working paper contending that, "the iodization of salt in the United States in the early 1900s raised the I.Q. scores of some populations by as much as 15 points—a full standard deviation—in the span of just 10 years" [19]. While critics have been quick to point out the difference between correlation and causation, which is to say that likeliness is not the same thing as assurance, the many and varied questions raised by these studies, and the plethora of media coverage surrounding them, have brought the nonhuman to the fore of public awareness and scrutiny, although some have been keen to the inherently relational nature of what it means to be human for some time. In short, the human in inextricably yoked to the nonhuman.

Noting the evolutionary necessity of nonhuman things, Latour observes, "There is no sense in which humans may be said to exist as humans without entering into commerce with what authorizes and enables them to exist (that is, to act)." [27, p. 192] In line with Latour's thesis, a recent study has shown that intestinal bacteria, which varies by weight in most people somewhere between 3 and 5 lb, actually co-evolves with its host, which is also to say that we have co-evolved with it, and the article goes on to claim that medical developments, such as the increasing utilization of antibiotics, is killing off vital bacteria and fostering an autoimmunity epidemic [9]. Our co-evolutionary symbiosis with nonhuman things has a long history, and Wrangham argues that the very advent of "*Homo erectus*" is a direct result of our capacity to control fire [1] and subsequently cook our meals, which "changed our bodies, our brains, our use of time, and our social lives." [47, p. 2]

However, some of the things our bodies, and the variety of nonhuman things inside them, do can be done better, or as well as in some circumstances, by physical technologies. A current example is artificial insemination, or so-called "test-tube babies," which replaces sexual intercourse as a way for some people to reproduce who either cannot do so or prefer not to do so (or at least do not want sexual intercourse to do it). Indeed, some futurists say that all of the human functions that are currently performed by biological technologies might well be performed entirely, or optionally, by physical technologies in the foreseeable futures.

Similarly, we have done, and still do, many things via social technologies. We socialize infants, care for the elderly, regulate sex, and provide comfort, shelter, and identity for humans via the social technology called "the family." We provide knowledge and status via education in school buildings. We find salvation from sin and triumph over death via religion. These are all social technologies. And they, too, are increasingly being replaced, marginalized, or redefined by physical technologies, MOOCs in contrast to classroom-based education being one current hot topic.

Indeed, a key to understanding how technology serves as one agent of social change is to study what happens as physical technologies begin to duplicate, challenge, and replace very long-standing social and biological technologies. In order to do that, we need to distinguish three *aspects* of technology.

1.5 Three Aspects of Technology: Hardware, Software, and Orgware

Just as many people only think of physical technologies and ignore social and biological technologies, so also many people think of technology only as a piece of hardware—a "pen" for example that is used for writing (or used to be). But on first encounter, how do you know it is a pen, instead of an ear or fingernail cleaner, a weapon, a hair clip, or half of a pair of chopsticks?

In order for a pen to be a pen (or an ear cleaner, weapon, hair clip or chopstick) it needs software and orgware. Most people understand the concept of software now, since computers have popularized the term. Software specifies instructions for using hardware. Different software will cause the same hardware to operate very differently from the way it operates with other software. Software that enables a pen to be used for writing is quite different from that which enables it to be a hair clip.

On the other hand, the concept of orgware is almost completely unknown. Although we will cite some examples from our review of the literature that demonstrate understanding of the distinction and the necessity of comprehending both hardware and software, we saw examples of, but no specific reference to, the term "orgware" or anything like it. Orgware is a word invented by the Soviet cybernetician and futurist Gennady Dobrov to describe the organization that is necessary to create, maintain, use, repair, and improve both hardware and software [13]. It designates the humans (and/or artilects) who envision, create, and maintain the hardware and software, and, very importantly, for whom the hardware and software provides a job and personal identity Because most people overlook orgware as an aspect of technology that is every bit as vital as hardware and software, technological transfer (passing one kind of technology from a place where it is being used and diffused to another place where it does not yet exist) often fails because adequate provision for orgware is not included in the transfer. This has often been the case when economic development specialists have sought to transfer technologies from "developed" to "underdeveloped" communities, only to see the transfer fail because no or insufficient attention was given to the creation of culturally as well as technologically appropriate orgware.

Indeed, social conflict between new and old technologies occurs primarily within the orgware and not over the hardware or software *per se*. It is in the orgware that cultural and social values are embedded. People derive the fundamental meaning of their lives from their role within the orgware. They are dependent upon the continuation of certain hardware and software for their identity as well as their livelihood. Orgware is where human agency most clearly effectuates the operation of the technology in certain directions and not others.

Consider eating. Food is the hardware and there are many rules about what food is and is not. Pork is favored by most Chinese while forbidden for Muslims, in China and elsewhere. Insects that are cooked and savored in Thailand are exterminated with extreme prejudice by most French persons who nonetheless relish snails that many Americans regard as slimy and repulsive. Many a tourist has choked down three fingers of poi at a Hawaiian luau, but few then bring bags of it home to add as a staple to their daily meals.

Recipes provide software for food preparation, but it is mainly over how to eat "properly" that conflicts occur. Is it OK to eat food with one's hands? If so, both hands, or only one? If one, which one? Is it OK to put your elbows on the table? Is it OK to "slurp" your food, or should food be ingested quietly and chewed thoroughly before being swallowed discretely? What about belching and farting?

Who should prepare food and who should not? That is an orgware question. Once upon a time, and still in many cultures, it was only women who were allowed to prepare food at home (and only men who could prepare it in restaurants). It was especially the duty of mothers and grandmothers to prepare food for the family. Few men would consider that their right or obligation, and few mothers and grandmothers would permit their husbands or sons, or any man, to usurp one of their most defining roles. Although this seems to be changing in many places, even where women "go to work" in numbers equal to men, they are often still expected to come home and prepare supper (or at least to pick up something to eat to bring with them on their way back home). And it is women who clean up and wash the dishes afterwards. Even though many women may complain about this extra work on top of their outside employment, they may also feel guilty that they aren't the kind of skilled and creative cooks their mothers or grandmothers used to be.

In some parts of the world, however, home cooking (typically "starting from scratch") has become a hobby that men monopolize, relegating women entirely to the role of passive though ebullient eaters of their culinary delights (and to cleaning up the mess men make in the process, of course).

However, who really cooks meals "from scratch" any more? And just when does "scratch" begin? With the raising, killing, plucking, preparing (combining with other ingredients from one's own garden), and cooking of the chicken? With buying a whole chicken, along with fresh potatoes, tomatoes, herbs, etc., at a market—or many different markets—and bringing them home to prepare, combine, cook and serve? With buying a complete frozen chicken dinner and putting it in the microwave? With picking up KFC on the way home and putting the bucket on the kitchen counter? With no one eating a home, certainly not together, but with everyone gulping fast food while rushing around?

This may seem trivial, but there are probably more fights within families and between roommates over what food to eat, who and how to prepare it, and how to eat it than over anything else. Future cooperation between Russian cosmonauts and American astronauts floundered at least once over what an American claimed was too much smelly borscht and gross table manners on a Russian spacecraft [13].

Or consider designer and test tube babies versus babies produced via heterosexual intercourse. It is the software and especially the orgware surrounding intercourse—who does it with whom, where, when, how, towards what ends, and (very importantly) who gets to make the rules—that is the root of the controversy more than the hardware itself. Certain religious groups have too much power at stake over sex and many other things to allow doctors (much less would-be parents) to decide what is permissible child conception and birth and what is not.

Although orgware has much to do with culture and values, it is also the case that existing technologies create certain prejudices and bias toward existent technological trajectories. Commenting on the potentiality for humans to develop truly artificial organs before such technologies came to be, Lem notes:

> Whether we use transplants or substitute organs made from abiological substances will always be decided by the state of the knowledge and technology at a given time. It will probably be easier to replace certain organs with mechanical ones, while others will need to

> wait until transplant technology has developed far enough. Importantly, any further development of biological and abiological prosthetics will be dictated not only by the needs of the human system but also by the needs of new technologies. [28]

The "needs of new technologies," as Lem puts it, speaks to the diffuse and reciprocal ways in which orgware comes into existence and evolves, and, perhaps most importantly, intersects with hardware and software.

Although clearly exhibiting a "neutral" or indeed "sublime" view of technology, Grübler explicitly acknowledges the existence and important differences between hardware and software. He also describes, but does not name, what Dobrov called "orgware":

> What is technology? In the narrowest sense, technology consists of manufactured objects like tools ... and containers. Their purpose is either to enhance human capabilities ... or to enable humans to perform tasks they could not perform otherwise .... Engineers call such objects 'hardware.' Anthropologists speak of 'artifacts.' But technology does not end there. Artifacts have to be produced. They have to be invented, designed, and manufactured. This requires a large system including hardware ... factor inputs (labor, energy, raw materials, capital), and finally 'software' (know-how, human knowledge and skills). Thus technology includes both what things are made and how things are made. Finally, knowledge, or technique, is required not only for the production of artifacts, but also for their use. Knowledge is needed to drive a car or use a bank account. A typewriter, without a user who knows how to type, let alone how to read, is simply a useless heavy piece of equipment. Institutions, including governments, firms, and markets, and social norms and attitudes, are especially important in determining how systems for producing and using artifacts emerge and function. They determine how particular artifacts and combinations of artifacts originate, which ones are rejected or which ones become successful, and if successful, how quickly they are incorporated in the economy and the society." [20, p. 20]

1.6 Six Phases of the Technological Life-Cycle

It is also necessary to distinguish the *phases* of the life-cycle of technologies in order to understand where in the life-cycle technology is most likely to serve as an agent of social and environmental change. The six phases are *invention, development, diffusion, maturity, obsolescence,* and *death.*

For most of human history, the invention of new technologies was rare, unsought, unfunded, an unintended byproduct of some other activity, done by marginal, lazy people idly whiling away the time, or by educated people who had a lot of time on their hands, such as the village shaman or priest, just fooling around. Inventions and innovations were often considered dangerous and unwelcomed. Most inventions went nowhere. Something was invented, some folks played with it until it was forgotten, with no lingering influence on society at all. Classical Greek history is full of things that were treated as toys or interesting but trivial items, and whose potential practical utility was not recognized until thousands of years later, when the hardware was invented again.

So the mere invention of a new technology has for most of history seldom been the occasion for significant social or environmental change occurring. However, by now, the circumstances of invention have altered completely. The change began during the seventeenth century, and became established in the first third of the nineteenth century with the invention in Germany of the research university, and then most dramatically during and after the Second World War with the invention of invention itself, via "R & D" (research and development) programs through which governments began spending considerable sums of money on basic research, and businesses on applied research. Endless new inventions and discoveries that are then developed so as produce better military and commercial products and processes has become the overwhelming norm—indeed, the hallmark—of a "developed" nation. All faculty members (including those in the humanities) in "Carnegie Level One Research Universities" in the United States are now expected to discover or invent things that can eventually be turned into money-making and/or death-dealing technologies.

Still, even now, not much social or environmental change is likely to result immediately from a new invention. Most new inventions are fragile and flimsy things. Their utility and impact is heavily dependent on their being repeatedly tested, improved, discarded, revived, and revised through a process known as "development"—the "D" of "R & D." Explaining his theory of *combinatorial evolution* with regards to technological development, Arthur writes:

> Early technologies form using existing primitive technologies as components. These new technologies in time become possible components—building blocks—for the construction of further new technologies. Some of these in turn go on to become possible building blocks for the creation of yet newer technologies. In this way, slowly over time, many technologies form from an initial few, and more complex ones form using simpler ones as components. The overall collection of technologies bootstraps itself upward from the few to the many and from the simple to the complex. We can say that technology creates itself out of itself. [4]

Although Arthur emphasizes the ways in which our tools shape us, or themselves via certain technological trajectories, the role of human choice and action remains key. Thomas Hughes "demonstrates that invention is not a matter of a sudden flash of inspiration from which a new device emerges 'ready-made.' Largely it is a matter of the minute and painstaking modification of existing technology." [4] From tinkering to prototyping, humanity's seemingly intrinsic proclivity to play with things should not be overlooked, and, as MacKenzie and Wacjman, argue "the authors of this process are normally anonymous, certainly not 'heroic inventor' figures, and often skilled craft workers, without formal technical or scientific training. It is probably best seen as a process of collective learning rather than individual innovation." [29, p. 8]

Even so, development now generally occurs in a lab or in narrow segments of society. Social and environmental impact doesn't begin to happen until the diffusion stage, which is typically done through command (military) or commercial (advertising and marketing) processes. The diffusion process often begins either with restricted military use of a technology that is only later "transferred" to commercial arenas (the so-called "dual use" or "spin-offs" of a technology), or begins initially as a toy and/or a new opportunity for pornography(?) before it is picked up for broader commercial exploitation and expansion.

MacKenzie and Wajcman observe that "A technological system … is never merely technical; its real-world functioning has technical, economic, organizational, political, and even cultural aspects." [29, p. 11] They, too, critique the idea of "technological determinism" favored, as we have seen, by many critics—the notion that technological change follows an autonomous logic that asserts that "once the necessary constituent elements are present ... there is a sense in which an invention must occur: 'Given the boat and the steam engine, is not the steamboat inevitable?' asked Ogburn and Thomas." [29, p. 8] Of course it is not inevitable, MacKenzie and Wajcman reply, as the example of the non-existence of sailing railroads—and many other possible technologies—makes clear, they say.

Concerning the role of the economy, they observe that "if technological systems are economic enterprises, and if they are involved directly or indirectly in market competition, then technological change is forced on them. If they are to survive at all, much less to prosper, they cannot forever stand still. Technical change is made inevitable, and its nature and direction profoundly conditioned by this." [29, p. 12] Nonetheless, "economic calculation and economic 'laws' are, after all, specific to particular forms of society, not universal ... ." [29, p. 13] In different economic systems that do not stress unbridled market competition, but that seek to preserve certain social or environmental values, for example, technological development might be constrained, rare, and guided by those values.

Institutions of the state and governments are also involved in shaping technologies. MacKenzie and Wajcman point out that "the single most important way that the state has shaped technology has been through its sponsoring of military technology. War and its preparations have probably been on a par with economic considerations as factors in the history of technology." "Military interest in new technology has often been crucial in overcoming what might otherwise have been insuperable economic barriers to its development and adoption, and military concerns have often shaped the development pattern and design details of new technologies." [29, p. 15]

As a technology diffuses, now in various forms with varying hardware, software, and orgware configurations, it eventually reaches maturity or saturation. Eventually, "everyone" has some form of it. There are no new markets or uses. Old varieties may be replaced with new models, but in the world we live in now, much more common is that a new technology is developed specifically to replace the old, which is now obsolete, a collector's item at best, until it dies out entirely except in a few museums or "backward" communities.

It is often the case that the social and environmental effects of a technology fade as well. Whales return in numbers once they are not hunted for their oil. Trees grow when they are not cut down to make charcoal for ink. Smog subsides as internal combustion engines vanish. But sometimes the effects of the old remain in the new technologies that replace them: women, enlightened and liberated by reading (and writing) the books made abundant and cheap by the printing press, may remain liberated, if perhaps not enlightened, as radio, movies, television, the Internet, and Twitter marginalizes books and magazines.

As Grübler observes, "Invention is the first demonstration of the principal, physical feasibility of a proposed new solution." [20, p. 23] He continues, "Innovation is defined succinctly by Mensch as a point when a 'newly discovered material or a newly developed technique is being put into regular production for the first time, or when an organized market for a new product is first created.'" [20, p. 23] Finally,

"Diffusion is the widespread replication of a technology and its assimilation into a socioeconomic setting. Diffusion is the final, and sometimes painful, test of whether an innovation can create a niche of its own or successfully supplant existing practices and artifacts." [20 p. 24] Grübler also exhibits a figure that shows the time lag between invention and innovation of a sample of 140 major innovations introduced in the period 1850–1970, with most taking from 10 to 60 years. It then takes more time for diffusion to begin, and even more before the technology is powerful enough to cause significant alterations in human behavior and hence social change [20, Figure 2.1 on p. 27]. However, as a consequence of the institutionalization of R & D, the time between invention and diffusion and then major impact for many technologies has shortened.

Diffusion typically follows an S-shaped temporal pattern. The basic pattern is essentially invariant, although the regularity and timing of diffusion processes vary greatly [20] p. 65]. In fact, technology in a broader sense often displays some kind of a series of overlapping S-curves from origin and rapid growth to maturity. At maturity, the specific technology, with its hardware, orgware, and software, may indeed decline and die, but the function the technology performed may not cease. That does happen. Each technology may reach its "limits to growth" and die. But perhaps more often than not, especially recently, a new technology emerges "just in time" to replace and surpass the old.

That is one of the reasons there are such arguments now over the future of our current way of living, made possible only by the discovery and utilization of cheap and abundant oil a little over 100 years ago, now reaching depletion. Will we find equivalent replacements in time, as we have done in the recent past? From human and other animal labor, running water, wind and wood, to coal, to whale oil, to petroleum—the march forward of new energy sources seems inexorable. But is it? There are many alternatives to oil in principle, but there may be none in reality that aren't themselves dependent on oil in many ways not easily apparent to many observers. This is the "net energy" problem: if you don't get more energy out than you put in, you are in a losing situation. The truth about the present and future potential of oil and its replacements is in grave dispute. The truth is literally a matter of life and death. Will other energy supply systems come along, just in the nick of time, and take over more or less effortlessly from the magnificently complex petroleum system, or not? Will the S-curve of energy soon come to an end, or are new energy sources about to emerge that will reach their takeoff stage before the oil S-curve collapses, enabling the S-curve of energy, *per se*, to continue onward and upward?

1.7 The Scope of Technology: Single Technologies, Clusters of Technologies, Levels of Technologies

There is a final distinction that needs to be made in regard to technology as an agent of social and environmental change: the negligible impact that most *specific new pieces* of hardware, with their software and orgware, are likely to make; the greater impact of *clusters* of related new technologies; and the profound impact of interrelated clusters of new technologies that can be called a new *level* of technology. The most substantial, widespread, and lasting change occurs when old levels fade as new levels emerge.

Wu et al. observe that often "new technologies were initially developed for a different function from that which they ultimately served with greater economic and/or social effect." And that "technological change should not be conceived of as the consequence of one-off innovations, but rather as a long-term process that involves not only technological improvements but also the adaptation and change of economic habits and negotiations over cultural norms." [48]

Grübler offers a taxonomy of technological change that is similar to this perspective: incremental improvements; radical "new combinations" (that change a specific process dramatically, such as the Bessemer steel process); changes in technological systems (such as the movement from steam engines to electric motors); clusters and families (e.g., the automotive industry not only automobiles, but also oil discovery, refining, distribution; the public road system; legal systems; insurance industries; health and medicine; suburbanization) [20, pp. 41–45].

1.8 Six Eras of Social Organization

The importance of this distinction is perhaps best understood by reference to the idea that humans have gone through six major eras of social organization so far, with a seventh era possibly emerging.

In the first, extremely long era, *Homo sapiens, sapiens* lived very much like other primate and *homo* species in very small, nomadic bands. This was followed by the emergence of nomadic, but somewhat larger and better-organized hunting and gathering tribes. Then between 8,000 and 5,000 years ago, sedentary human settlements, a few of them of impressive size and durability, emerged. Some of those societies later developed into very large empires with all of the marks of advanced civilization.

The next phase was the end of feudalism in the seventeenth and eighteenth centuries and the rise of modern, industrialized nation-states during the nineteenth century, seguing now into the sixth and current era of "information societies" only a few decades ago first in North America, parts of Europe, and Japan. Some futurists see evidence that the next era is that of "dream societies" where neither land, nor material production, nor information is the basis of wealth and power, but rather the design and creation of aesthetically appealing icons, dreams, images, and invented identities that motivate and guide human activities. However, as Dator and Seo, observe, "Other futurists doubt a dream society will ever happen, given the environmental, resource, economic, and cultural challenges which humanity is not only refusing to address but also is continuing to exacerbate." [10]

There are of course other ways of looking at human history, and many people would not use that specific set of six categories at all. But if we adopt it for our purposes here, then what are the bases of each of the six eras, and, most importantly, what leads to the emergence of each new era from the old one? One answer obviously is technology, with communication technologies often used as one of the major examples, though many other technologies played major roles as well. We showed above that some "cultural" critics dispute both the categorization and especially the rationale of labeling them by their putatively defining technologies.

The major focus of our research for this project was to see if, and if so, how, changing communication technologies influenced power relations in those six eras and the alternative futures. We will present and discuss our findings here after considering some of the other concepts that guided our research.

So, in summary, we define technology as "how humans do things"; we note that there are three "views" about technology in the literature (that it is neutral, demonic, or transformative), but that a fourth view seems more accurate—that while technology is neither neutral nor demonic and often is not transformative, it clearly is mutative; that there are three *kinds* of technology (physical, biological and social, though most of the literature only discusses the physical); that there are three "aspects" of technology (hardware, software and orgware, though the literature focuses on hardware primarily, software less, and orgware not at all as such); that much of the literature does distinguish six "phases" in the life-cycle of technologies (invention, development, diffusion, maturity, obsolescence, and death, with major social and environmental change occurring in the diffusion and maturity phases); and that significant social and environmental change does not occur from a single new technology. Clusters of technology exert more influence, with profound impact coming from changing levels of technology such as those that propelled societies from hunting and gathering to agriculture, to industrial, to information, and potentially to dream societies, to collapse, or to something entirely beyond our current ability to imagine.

1.9 Technology, Social Change, and Age-Cohort/Generational Analysis

Another perspective that guided our research is that of age-cohort analysis (also called generational analysis)—that is, the sociological and not demographic version of age-cohort analysis [21, 30, 34, 41]. Age-cohort analysis helped reinforce our understanding that any impact of technology on humans and the environment occurs over time, and almost never instantly, on the first emergence of a new technology or technological system. Not only does the technology itself need to mature, and its use to diffuse geographically, but also it takes several generations of immersive use with supporting social institutions and values before it becomes so ubiquitous that the technology becomes essentially invisible and effectively "natural" for most individuals. It is at this stage that profound and lasting change occurs, if it occurs at all.

We also noted that the pace of any technologically induced change was typically very slow for most of human history, both in terms of the number of new technologies introduced into society at any one time, and the time between the emergence of one disruptive technology and the emergence of another. Thus substantial change in the past was typically both rare and episodic. A new technology or technological system might appear, causing considerable agitation, but after a period of adjustment societies and the environment would typically settle down for a long period of stability based on the new normal produced by the integration of the once-new with old technologies.

However, during periods of very rapid technological change, such as the last several hundred years, each new age-cohort is born into a mix of technologies, social institutions, and values that are different from those of cohorts often only slightly older and younger than they are. As Prensky notes, "There are so-called 'technological natives' and 'technological immigrants,' but those who are haughty 'natives' for a while soon find themselves struggling 'immigrants'—or complete outcasts—as new technologies come along that become completely natural for the new natives born into them." [35]

We will illustrate and explain this phenomenon historically and at the present time, as well as use it in our forecasts of alternative futures.

1.10 Perspectives on Power and Technology

Central to our research is the issue of what "power" is in society, how it is created and changed, and thus if and how society is changed as new technologies change the relationship of societies erected upon older technologies. Although much has already been written about power, specifically its social implications and dynamics, a central aspect of our research was to understand critical perspectives on how power operates.

Manuel Castells says that "[p]ower is the relational capacity that enables a social actor to influence asymmetrically the decisions of other social actor(s) in ways that favor the empowered actor's will, interests, and values. Power is exercised by means of coercion (or the possibility of it) and/or by the construction of meaning on the basis of the discourses through which social actors guide their action. Power relationships are framed by domination, which is the power that is embedded in the institutions of society." [8, p. 10] Affirming the intrinsically relational nature of power, Foucault argues, "power [...] is a name that one attributes to a complex strategical situation in a particular society." [15, p. 93] Implying that broad definitions of power fail to account for the nuances of unique socio-political contexts, as well as the ways in which power always-already presumes resistance, Foucault's examination of "power relations" provides a lens to view power as a productive force—one whose fluidity determines its efficacy. Foucault continues:

> Power's condition of possibility, or in any case the viewpoint which permits one to understand its exercise, even in its more "peripheral" effects, and which also makes it possible to use its mechanisms as a grid of intelligibility of the social order, must not be sought in the primary existence of a central point, in a unique sovereignty from which secondary and descendant forms would emanate; it is the moving substrate of force relations which, by virtue of their inequality, constantly engender states of power, but the latter are always local and unstable. [15, p. 93]

Along with Foucault's elucidation of power as being intrinsically relational, we sought to understand how power relations, even if elastic and brittle, subsist, and this is where we found the strongest resonances between power and technology, specifically communication technologies. Situating the programmatic intricacies of TCP/IP, or what he calls "protocol," as the systemic guide that governs certain actions and limits others, Galloway argues, "It is important to remember first that the technical is always political, that *network architecture is politics*." [18, p. 245] Pairing Foucault with Galloway and Castells, we see power as indicative of relational dynamics within a given politico-technical context, which is also to say a force for navigating as well as mitigating change within a given field of socio-technical interactions. Power relations, then, have as much to do with the ability one has to shape available choices (actor-network relations) as it does with the actual capacity to make a choice (agency). Within a diverse array of socio-political contexts, we discovered that there are views of power that seem to mirror attitudes towards technologies, and so we use the same four-part structure for conceiving of power relations.

Many political scientists argue that power is to politics what wealth is to economics—its very lifeblood. From this perspective, power is a necessary and proper measure of the ability to get things done. Power is neutral. It is how you use it that matters. As Deutsch observes, "In simple language, to have power means not to have to give in, and to force the environment or the other person to do so. Power in this narrow sense is the priority of output over intake, the ability to talk instead of listen. In a sense, it is the ability to afford not to learn." [12, p. 111] From this perspective, the "legitimate" authorities of a polity need power to achieve their goals. Power, thus, is necessary and normalized within a certain socio-technical context. Mere "power relations," then, are intrinsically formulaic and affirm the status quo, even if some people—perhaps many—find them questionable, if not detestable. As the old saying goes, "The devil you know is better than the devil you don't." When mere power relations are enacted, both content and form remain relatively stable, predictable, and normative. This dynamic is evident within the ascendency of America's two-party system, whose perpetuity is about the only thing both Democrats and Republicans, as well as the organizations and entities that give sizable financial contribution to both, seem to agree upon now.

To others, however, power is indicative of oppression and coercion. Power is evil and used by the powerful solely to dominate the powerless. There are ample historical examples of this, and the goal of all revolutionaries is to wrest power from those who have it and to vest it in themselves, and in laws of their making ("law" in this view being a vehicle by which the victors of a power struggle embed their victories into what then becomes the ground upon which later power struggles take place). *Demonic power relations*, as it were, are an enactment of control. In most social contexts, they are sustained through various programs, taxation, entitlements, etc., and at times a lack thereof, but it is also the case that demonic power relations can be visceral and tangible, perhaps in the form of a military strike or police action. Demonic power relations thrive upon hierarchy and, as is perceived by some, the inherently exploitative nature of politics and governance in general. North Korea's stringent social norms and repressive laws are one of the clearest examples of entrenched demonic power relations.

And yet, power can also be transformational. Indeed, transformational change cannot occur without something causing it, and that thing or things must have power of some kind, even if only presumed and imagined. While emergent and transformational technologies certainly can sustain existing power structures, they also can thwart them, providing opportunities for new and different power relations to arise while challenging the normative conceptions of power within a particular context. *Transformative power relations* are those with progressive intents and aims, and many of these efforts have been driven by impassioned public movements, such as the women's suffrage and civil rights campaigns of the twentieth century, which is to say that it is often those with less power demanding equality that can initiate and foment transformative social change. While women having the right to vote and desegregation are undoubtedly progressive social advancements, the glass ceiling for women's pay and the incarceration statistics for African-American males demonstrate that truly transformative change is the most difficult to enact and measure, which is to say that transformative power relations are the most subjective.

Finally, *mutative power relations* are those in a state of flux, even if only presumed and potentially desired. Although such events and actions are often brought about by crises, such as the looming catastrophes related to global warming, mutative power relations suggest the potentiality for radically new forms of governance and interrelations, and the diffuse effects of climate change have already sparked a few unheralded socio-political mutations. In New Zealand, a river was recently granted equal rights under the law to protect it against further degradation [37], and widespread news coverage of a CIA-backed feasibility study on geoengineering has sparked public debate on the controversial solution to climate change [46]. Viewing power as a field of experience with decidedly practical and material ramifications, we describe socio-political power as an ongoing process of exchange that is fundamentally inscribed within both applied and emergent technologies incumbent to various contexts. As such, understanding the impacts of access and dominion over such technologies is integral to ameliorating the flow and tenor of power within specific socio-political contexts.

As an artifact of relational ecologies, power ultimately centers on the creation and conscription of affects, or embodied modes of sensation and behavior. Power relations, then, exist as one perceives things to be powerful, and one modifies, at times even unconsciously, human behavior in accordance with prevailing power relations. This fits with Ranciere's framing of politics that we use to explore the interstices of power, politics, and technology. Distinguishing between politics and policing, or the maintenance of a particular social order, Ranciere offers a broad lens with which to examine political phenomena. He explains, "Politics revolves around what is seen and what can be said about it, around who has the ability to see and the talent to speak, around the properties of spaces and the possibilities of time." [36, p. 13]

Although this definition of politics is expansive, it succinctly encapsulates the myriad levels at which power can and might operate within a given social context, which is to say that politics has as much to do with creating choices as it does with making them. Thus, politics, as with power, can, and ought to, be seen as a product of certain technologies (software, hardware, and orgware) as well as a force that can and might foster technological invention, development, and diffusion. Policing, on the other hand, refers to the norms, behaviors, and structures that maintain a particular political order.

Since our research is as equally interested with both the politics and policing enabled by various technologies, our analysis illuminates not only the way in which new technologies could and have been used to overthrow existing power structures and create new ones, but also, and perhaps more convincingly, the fact that such overthrows and new structures are often temporary—that during the time it takes a new technology to become normalized within a society, successors of the old regime recover from the shock that allowed power to be wrested from their ancestors and find ways to regain positions of power via the new technologies.

This dynamic is taken up with great vigor by Majid Tehranian in *Technologies of Power: Information Machines and Democratic Prospects* [42]. Tehranian starts from the premise that information technologies are not neutral, but neither is their influence on power unidirectional. He was writing at a time (late 1980s) when there were high hopes that emerging electronic communication technologies would enable electronic democracy (though he prefers the term “communitarian democracy”). At the same time, Tehranian fully acknowledged the many forces working against that hope in his time. We have frequently seen this kind of optimism expressed as each new technology emerges, such as the “Arab spring” that once was proclaimed as being ushered in by social media.

Arguing that there are four contending perspectives on the relationship between then-current and emerging information technologies (IT) and the concentration or decentralization of political power, Tehranian provides a critical lens with which to view perspectives on technological development, particularly in relation to Ranciere’s politics and policing distinction.

		Yes	No
IT leads to power concentration	Yes	Technostructuralism	Technophilia
IT leads to spread of power	No	Technophobia	Technoneutralism

According to Tehranian, technophiles “believe that the present technological revolution [in IT] has already inaugurated a ‘post-industrial information society’ with higher productivity and plenty at the world centers that will eventually trickle down to the peripheries.” [42, p. 4] Countries such as the United States would cease manufacturing any but the most technologically sophisticated products. Instead, they would produce “information.” This followed from the observation that “advanced” industrial nations (the centers) of the time ate very well, but were hardly engaged in agricultural and food production at all. They imported their food from the “developing” nations. Dirty industrial products would be produced in the developing countries (the peripheries), who would become richer in due time. Prophetically, many of the processes Tehranian discusses as constituents of “technophilia’ were in fact subsequently instituted in the United States and elsewhere, leading over the intervening decades to the “hollowing out” of industry, the outsourcing of many manual and mental jobs overseas, the rise of finance, banking, and high tech entrepreneurial ventures as the major avenues towards wealth and power, with the ensuing gap in wealth and power between the 1 % and everyone else.

In contrast, technophobes "point to the threats that increasing robotization and computer-assisted design and manufacturing hold for rising structural unemployment and socioeconomic dualism; to the perils that the new databases pose for political surveillance and individual privacy; to the dangers that homogenization of culture by media monopolies present for cultural autonomy and diversity." [42, p. 5] The fears of technophobes as well have certainly amplified over the passing years, not only since the 2008 financial collapse but also since revelations about the extent to which the US government and most private electronic communication organizations spy on citizens and customers nationally and worldwide.

Technoneutrals, on the other hand, "typically tend to be the consultants, who have few theoretical pretensions and considerable interest at stake not to alienate their clients. They often assume a neutral position with respect to the question of effects ..." [42, p. 5] Lack of theoretical grounding and a convenient belief in the neutrality of technology is also now well confirmed and persistent among those most enthusiastic of new technologies, particularly those who profit from the correlative buzz and bubbles engendered by such practices.

Finally, technostructuralists "argue that technologies are by themselves neither good nor bad, nor neutral! This is because they developed out of institutional needs (in the case of IT, primarily military and business needs), and their impact is always mediated through institutional arrangements and social forces, of which they are an integral part." [42, p. 6] This position resonates with our research as well. Tehranian says his book "assumes a technostructuralist perspective. However ... it can be demonstrated that the current technological revolution in informatics promises some democratic outcomes in world development." [42, p. 6]

At the same time, Tehranian concedes that "telecommunication also abstracts and distantiates. Media realities are by their very nature distorted realities. Telecommunication provides the opportunity for the senders of messages to reconstruct reality to suit their own purposes." [42, p. 13] That most certainly is true, as our survey will attest, and by no means unique to telecommunications. On the one hand, all media, including talking and writing, "distort" reality, and, on the other hand, many social forces strive to use media to distort perceptions to suit their purposes.

Compare the world that one language expresses with the world another, very different, language constructs. Many of the things "naturally" discussed by two native Japanese speakers in Japan are extremely difficult to express, if they can be accurately expressed at all, in English. A good example of this are the different (and increasingly demanding) reciprocal obligations between humans conveyed by the Japanese words, *giri, gimu* and *on*. All three refer to nuances of obligation and responsibility for which there is no English equivalent, in word or practice. Similarly, the distinctive aesthetic concepts, *wabi* and *sabi*, express a Japanese emotional preference for plain, old, imperfect, transitory things for which there is no word in English, and precious little empathy felt by native speakers of English-only.

On the other hand, the subtleties of the world conveyed by even the simplest English prepositions (on, in, of, by, for, at, etc.) that are used perfectly by native

English children at a very early age without any formal instruction are a huge stumbling block for almost all non-native speakers trying to use them correctly in English. Try explaining why you have to say "I am going *at* noon *on* Sunday *in* March," and that using those same three tiny little two-letter words in a different order in that same sentence is "wrong." All media "distort" reality in order make the vastness, complexity, ambiguity, and uncertainty of "reality" comprehensible and expressible by mere humans.

As an example of using technology to construct a specific view of reality, Michael Thad Allen and Gabrielle Hecht, state, "human power rides upon the history of things." [3, p. 3] Noting the centrality of technology in forging the political, they observe, "Technology is central to human history; everywhere it shapes and is shaped by political, cultural, social, and economic change." [2, p. 3]

Reflecting on the contributions of Thomas Parke Hughes, Allen, and Hecht explain that he demonstrated "how America went from being nature's nation to being technology's." [3, p. 5] America was founded as a geographically vast nation with tiny concentrations of populations separated by great distances and little in the way of modes of transportation connecting them. The technologies and customs were those of the agricultural era with hints of modernity here and there—primarily in their novel structures of governance. Within less than 50 years after its founding, the United States was becoming an industrial society, so that from the Civil War through the Cold War, it became increasingly enamored of technology as applied science. Arguing the immense, yet underlying, effect technology had upon political developments in the twentieth century, Allen and Hecht contend, "Thus, faith in the transformative, democratizing powers of technology not only provided the logic behind the arms race and the space race, it also undergirded Cold War geopolitics in its broadest forms." [3] This "faith" still persists in the rhetoric and actions of those in governmental and economic power in the United States today, including presidents from Reagan through the Bushes to Clinton and Obama. Hughes, however, makes it clear that there was nothing inherent in "technology" that produced this faith, and as a useful political tool, it was socially constructed by those in power who benefited by making it seem so. Again, Allen and Hecht explain:

> 'Technology'—especially when used narrowly to refer to complex machines—is itself a power-laden term. Going back to the United States in the nineteenth and the early twentieth century, for example, we can see that while skills middle-class boys developed to design machinery were considered technological by educators and the public, skills developed by girls (such as sewing or cooking) were not. Similar conceptions endure today, when—in most contexts and for most people— 'technology' denotes the latest machines and professionally vetted expert knowledge. The Amish, for instance, are popularly portrayed as anti-technological, but we could more legitimately argue that they enthusiastically embrace Renaissance technologies. [3, p. 13]

The above is a very good example of the fact that while "the medium is the message" in many instances, certain people can also sometimes give meaning to a medium that is not actually inherent in the medium but can be made to seem so. This is the median position of a medium between a medium and its message, if you will—whereby a message gives a medium powers it does not have absent the compelling power of the effective and repeated message.

1.11 What Is Communication?

Communication is typically defined as the act or process of sending messages through a channel to a receiver, and, often, of receiving a message back through the same or another channel to the sender. Communication is thus an interactive and decidedly social act, whether it involves humans, animals, plants, bacteria or (if it is not stretching the term "social" too much) genes, chemicals, photons, electrons, and other particles. As Wiener observes, "Birds communicate with one another, monkeys communicate with one another, insects communicate with one another, and in all this communication some use is made of signals or symbols that can be understood only by being privy to the system of codes involved." [44, p. 74] Thus, in order for communication to be communication, the receiver must recognize the channel and understand the message, which is also to say distinguish the signal from noise. Although I may not understand a message sent to me in Finnish, depending on the context I might get the basic point even though I do not understand the system of codes itself, strictly speaking. Receiving, interpreting, and responding to feedback lies at the heart of communication, and the capacity for control, or the ability to govern or regulate signal-to-noise, is thus a crucial dynamic within communicative systems on a variety of levels.

Some scientists are deeply immersed in trying to figure out how and what cells communicate, in order to use that information to improve the health of humans, plants, and other animals—and perhaps to serve as the basis of new post-electronic communication technologies. Others are trying to determine if life elsewhere in the galaxy is trying to send messages to us. Even if "contact" is made, communicating may be either very difficult or totally impossible, even if we decide a message is being sent. Communication can take place in a variety of modes and be received by a variety of receptors. These are the technologies associated with communication. Biologically, the modes might be gestures (and the receptors eyes); speech (and the receptors ears); heat (and the receptors fingers); smells (and the receptors noses), reproduction (and the receptors genitals), and so on. The main focus of this monograph is on how changing modes, channels, and receptors change the kinds of messages sent, and thus the behavior and beliefs of humans in societies.

It is sometimes difficult to distinguish communication from transportation. Transportation is often defined as the movement of things from one place to another. Here also, there are various modes of transportation serving different or competing purposes. However, a lot of transportation turns out to be primarily for the purpose of communication. A great deal of social conflict today is precipitated by the fact that we can often now communicate without transporting ourselves closer to the person with whom we wish to communicate. Noting that most of the "rush hour" traffic congestion in modern cities was because of people going to and from central places in order to communicate with each other (and if not then, surely shortly thereafter, by sending messages to people sitting 3 ft from them via electronically linked computers and social media), President George H. W. Bush said "Sometimes the best transportation policy means not moving people, but moving their work … a trend known as telecommuting … . Think of it as commuting to work at the speed of light." [49, p. 5] Indeed, one way to interpret the evolution of communication technologies is at the expense of transportation technologies. Again, Wiener observes, "If the seventeenth and early eighteenth centuries are the age of clocks, and the later eighteenth centuries and nineteenth centuries constitute the age of steam engines, the present time is the age of communication and control." [45, p. 39]

As we will see, with each change in levels of technology from the emergence of speech onward, humans have been able to extend their communicative grasp over both time and space, which is also to say their control, although the signal-to-noise problem remains consistent, if not resistant, given the ubiquity of communication technologies today and those that might come tomorrow. Now, with what appears to be the rapid emergence of 3-D printing, even the use of transportation for the shipping of products from factories to warehouses, to stores, to consumers may be vanishing away, or at least being "put in its place." With the emergence of nanotechnologies, not only the manufacture of products but also the provision of raw materials and the removal of industrial, commercial and consumer waste may mutate since "everything" will be raw material for new products, and nothing a waste. If advances in teleportation, on the one hand, and brain-to-brain (or AI-to-brain) communication, on the other hand, continue, almost all transportation may come to an end and everything might become a process of communication alone.

1.12 What Is "Society" and What Is "Social Change"?

Margaret Thatcher is famous for proclaiming, "[T]here is no such thing as society. There are individual men and women, and there are families." [24] Whether she meant it as absolutely as she stated it is doubtful. Her point seems to have been that too many citizens of the UK rely on "society" to take care of them, and do not take care of themselves as all people should—and can—in her view. Nonetheless one view of the human condition is that "society" is an abstraction that is used to force free individuals to conform to the will of others—whether it be the will of strong men, or wise men, or the Common Man—and not to follow their own individual will and desires. Many libertarians and anarchists make a similar argument.

Expressions of strong individualism have been very popular in the United States since the earliest days, with colonial era slogans such as "Give me liberty or give me death!" attributed to Patrick Henry, or "Don't tread on me" on the yellow Gadsden's flag with a coiled solitary rattlesnake about to strike, or even the much earlier motto on the royal coat of arms of the British monarch—in French!—*Dieu et mon droit*, that has sometimes been appropriated in the United States as "God and my right(s)." The national anthem of the United States proclaims that America is "the land of the free and the home of the brave."

At the same time, most Americans seem more than willing to give up their individual rights and freedom for collective protection when their lives appear to be threatened, such as when the events of September 11, 2001, transformed most

Americans into willing collectivists whose private lives American security agencies may surveil with complete impunity. But this embrace by Americans of community protection is not new. Strong appeals were made to unity and community in the struggle for American independence as well. Benjamin Franklin published a cartoon of a snake—the same snake as on the Gadsden's flag?—cut into eight pieces labeled with the abbreviations of the names of eight of the American colonies above the words "Join, or die." On the same point, Franklin also advised the colonists that "We must hang together, gentlemen, or else we shall most assuredly hang separately."

The first US Congress of 1782 put the phrase, *E pluribus unum* (Latin for "One out of many") on the official seal of the United States, expressing the fact that the United States became one nation by uniting thirteen separate nations. The philosopher Thomas Hobbes described life in the "State of Nature" as being a condition of a war of all against all (or of each against each) so that life for each individual was "solitary, poor, nasty, brutish and short." In order to have community, peace, prosperity, and civilization, these solitary poor, nasty and brutish individuals gave up their "freedom" to the "Leviathan"—to the all-powerful state—knowing that, without an all-powerful apparatus controlling everyone, violence and anarchy would break loose again. This view that humans will return to the violent chaos of nature without powerful governments strongly influenced the writers of the American Constitution, in part because the conditions of life for many Americans under the earlier, short-lived "Articles of Confederation" seemed to confirm Hobbes' analysis, leading many Americans to agree reluctantly to greater central control, within a novel tripartite and federal arrangement that divided and separated "political power," than they might otherwise have been willing to do.

Anthropologists overwhelmingly agree that Hobbes' analysis of the state of nature is completely wrong. Earliest humans did not live alone in miserable conditions. Much was lost as well as gained with the rise of civilizations compared to when humans lived in small, homogenous, nomadic, egalitarian groups of families, called bands. As we will see later, convincing evidence shows that many humans lived peacefully together for tens of thousands of years in small communities amid "subsistence affluence" with plenty to eat, ample materials for shelter and clothing, and abundant time for leisure and communal activities.

At the same time, we must acknowledge the existence of the philosophical and epistemological position called *solipsism* that maintains that all we can be sure of is ourselves and our minds, that everything that appears to be "outside" of our minds might very well be projections of something entirely within them. In this case, neither society nor anything else objectively exists other than in my imagination. However, there is something very convincing about there being a physical reality "out there" independent of me because of the difficulty I have in completely controlling it, and because of its ability to do considerable mental and physical harm to me against my will.

And that brings up another matter. There is renewed discussion of the (im)possibility of "free will." Some argue that recent developments in brain sciences demonstrate that believing is seeing, and that our mind appears to "decide" to act well before we consciously make a decision. Others maintain that we live in a completely deterministic world in which our every act, apparently freely decided by us each passing moment, has in fact been programmed "from the beginning" (an awkward phrase if "time" itself may not be an objective, "real" property of nature, but only a construct of a mind in a biological body that is aware it was born, is maturing, and will die).

Nonetheless, in spite of these and similar possibilities, we adopt here the position that *"society" does exist as the personal and interpersonal environment within which we all live*. We acknowledge the unique and personal basis from which each individual perceives and interacts with the constituents of society, while also emphasizing society's broad communal and largely (to each individual) predetermined base. We each are born into a society that has strong determinative features so that even our own idiosyncratic ideas and behaviors are shaped by those features in interaction with our unique but inherited biological body. Even those of us who seem to be "alone" find that our mode of being solitary is shaped by aspects of the society from which we are now separate.

Within the broad embrace of "society" there are many "cultures" based on different languages, histories, cosmologies, and institutions, themselves composed of "communities" of varying kinds (including families) in which "individuals" with thoughts and behaviors very much their own exist while also being profoundly influenced by the features of the individuals, communities, and cultures of the society around them.

So, yes, society does exist.

1.13 But Does Society Change? What Is Change and What Is Stability?

These are the more difficult questions. The answers are strongly linked to the question of time and to the scale at which humans, individually and collectively, perceive things. Consider the analogy of the sequence of water from a stagnant pool, to a flowing stream with standing wave-patterns, which at one point goes over a waterfall. I step into the stream and change the wave-patterns, but when I step out, the patterns return. I dam the stream and permanently alter the flow and wave patterns. I heat the stream and change the water into steam and the sand into glass.

Where does "change" occur in this analogy? We maintain it is when I step into the stream onward. Thus, even the waterfall manifests stability rather than change. It is a matter of the integrity of the system. Even though the stream flows rapidly, it retains systemic patterns. It is only when the patterns of the system are altered that change occurs and a new system emerges, or there is a return to a previous pattern.

But there is also an issue of scale. At the scale of normal human observation, neither the pool of water nor the flowing stream is "changing." But if I use a microscope, I may notice great change within the subsystems of the "stagnant" pool. And from the Moon, even the heating of the stream and streambed may be an inconsequential detail in the overall stability and change of the Earth of which the stream and my actions are but tiny parts.

Evolution is change. Development is change. The persistence over time of a set of forms and relationships is stability, even if the relationships are highly dynamic. Is change normal or abnormal? Do we need to explain why society changes, or why it does not change more? Wars have been fought over this issue. The philosophy of dialectical materialism behind communism assumes that social change is normal and continuous in the famous waltz of history: from thesis, to antithesis, to synthesis, which becomes a new thesis, provoking its antithesis, which creates a new synthesis, and so on forever (or until somehow history stops when the perfect communist society is achieved).

On the other hand many social scientists in capitalist societies assume that while the interaction of the components of a functioning society is dynamic, the system itself is stable—like the flowing stream. For a capitalist system to change into something else must therefore be explained and resisted. The reason for change from capitalism to something else, according to many social scientists, is unanticipated and unwelcomed. The free market of capitalism is natural to all humans. Once a capitalist system is established, its change must be viewed as pathological, malicious, and subversive. Only external forces or agents can change a capitalist society. If change or threats of change are observed, we must find and destroy the outside subversive elements fomenting the change. A properly functioning capitalist society should not change, even though its internal parts must sometimes experience "creative destruction" so that newer and better parts that will make the system function even better can take their place. Thus, a capitalist society may "go over the waterfall," but it should then retain or recover its natural capitalist form and functions.

Concerning whether change is internal and normal or external, there thus seem to be three views:

1. Change is *endogenous*. Societies are somehow in a perpetual dynamic equilibrium that can occasionally go astray. There is some kind of a "social DNA" similar to the DNA that drives biological birth, growth, and death. Indeed, societies may follow a natural cycle of birth, maturity, senescence, and death, just as organisms do. Sometimes the DNA mutates randomly, and if it is adaptive to the environment it may be sustained. If not, it will be naturally rejected.
2. Change is *exogenously imposed* similar to the way a disease attacks an otherwise healthy body, or by processes such as revolution, invasion, and education (the latter being a process by which one teaches in order to change the learners regardless of their desire to learn and change).
3. Change is *exogenously sought* in the way that a system operates through positive or negative feedback processes, by gaining new information, or by actively seeking change through purposeful innovation and learning. Elementary students go to school because their elders want education to change them. Graduate students go to school because they want what they learn to change them.

We conclude that society does exist and does change, and we will now discuss various ideas about what "causes" society to change, and what parts may not change, may resist change, or may change easily. With this we move uneasily into the field of macrohistory, which is vast in time and expanse and could easily take us far afield from our main task here.

1.14 What Is "Cause"?

There is first of all the issue of "cause." If we say that society changes, whether endogenously or exogenously, then we often seek to explain why society changes, typically asking, "What causes social change?" To do so is to enter into an arena where scientific, philosophical and religious terminologies and explanations are extensive and often conflicting. For our purposes, we will for the most part adopt Hume's formulation that says:

1. The cause and effect must be contiguous in space and time.
2. The cause must be prior to the effect.
3. There must be a constant union betwixt the cause and effect.
4. The same cause always produces the same effect, and the same effect never arises but from the same cause [23].

However commonsensical this may seem there are numerous potential pitfalls. The very first statement—that the cause and effect must be contiguous in space and time—is problematic when dealing with a dynamic system such as "society," where influences often take so much time to mature that the initial cause may be very difficult to determine to the exclusion of other possible causes. Causes of change in society are seldom like the impact of one billiard ball hitting another, since the impact passes through humans, and often generations of humans, before it is fully manifest as a "change" in society.

This is one of the reasons that age-cohort analysis is useful, since it provides an explanation for the delayed impact technology typically has on society. Moreover, the change we expect from a new technology is a change in human behavior first, and then a change in the views that humans have of themselves and their environments as a consequence of their changed behaviors. New technologies allow people to behave differently from the way they were able to behave with old technologies. However, these changes in behavior are seldom seen in the first mature generation that experiences them, since the influence and presence of old technologies is persistent in them. But generations born with the once-new technology experience it as a "natural" and powerful part of their environment, without the direct, once-exclusive experience of behavior enabled or thwarted by older technologies. However, if a new technology does not become established and dies out, then, as Hume's third principle implies, old behaviors based on old technologies may re-emerge, or newer behaviors based on newer technologies may arise.

Another danger with taking Hume's formulation too literally is that it begs the question of cause vs. correlation. Generations of social scientists have learned to be very cautious in implying cause to correlation. Even what seem to be very "obvious" causes may later prove to be correlations, the cause(s) of which lie elsewhere. This is most certainly the case with any attempt to say that technology causes any specific social change, and cannot be said so about any specific piece of hardware (without the consideration of software and especially orgware), or of physical technology (without the consideration also of competing social and biological technologies).

Thus, since we have not looked specifically for other possible "causes" for the effects we observe, but have relied on the research of others, readers should understand that whenever we say technology A causes behavior B (which we seldom do), we are at the same time admitting that there may be some other cause(s) which we fail to see yet. By frequently documenting and emphasizing in our analysis the differential impact of a technology in different cultures and places, we seek to make clear the fact that software and especially orgware are at least as important as the hardware itself in causing or thwarting social change.

Although we will discuss our understanding of futures studies later, in order to anticipate the futures of society, or its parts, we have come to learn that we need to understand the existence and operation of three overarching processes: *the push from the past, the pull from the futures,* and *the friction of the present.*

Factors from the past that push society into its futures include deep, lingering cultural myths, beliefs, and practices; old images of the futures that once were alive, new, and vigorous; and deeply ingrained, ongoing, long-running trends (such as established technologies, population growth (or decline), environmental conditions, climate stability or change, resource utilization, etc.—what we call "the drivers" from the past).

Factors from the futures that seem to lure, entice, or pull society forward include emerging issues (such as possible new technologies, lifestyle preferences, resource and environmental challenges, etc., that are just beginning to be seen and felt, and are not yet established trends or problem/opportunities); new generations of humans who express new behaviors and values; and new images of the futures resulting from the emerging issues and behaviors.

Factors of friction in the present include the major entrenched social institutions such as government, commerce, military, education, religion, etc. (hardware); the laws and practices that create and sustain them (software); and all the people whose daily lives depend on them (orgware), most of whom either deny or try to prevent substantial change in the institutions, while some try to cause the institutions to change, or to create new institutions (sometimes successfully, other times not).

These three factors—push, pull, and friction—are always in contest against one another, so that some social and environmental dynamics and possibility of change is always ongoing. However, when the forces pushing from the past and/or pulling from the futures become too strong for the frictional forces of the present to resist, substantial social and environmental change occurs, and a new normal may be established as the overall dynamic process continues. Such change usually happens when new levels of technology replace established levels; age-cohorts come into power; and/or major disruptions occur, such as war, profound disasters, climate change, or similar permanently wrenching processes. We live in a world where the drivers from the past and the pull of the futures are especially strong, and so social and environmental change of one kind or another seems permanently ongoing.

References

1. Adams RM (1996) Paths of fire: an anthropologist's inquiry into Western technology. Princeton University Press, Princeton
2. Agamben G (2004) The open: man and animal. Stanford University Press, Stanford, CA
3. Allen MT, Hecht G (eds) (2001) Technologies of power: essays in honor of Thomas Parke Hughes and Agatha Chipley Hughes. MIT Press, Cambridge
4. Arthur WB (2009) The nature of technology: what it is and how it evolves. Free Press, New York
5. Benjamin W (1978) Reflections: essays, aphorisms, autobiographical writings. Harcourt Brace Jovanovich, New York
6. Boyer P (1968) Technology, http://www.encyclopedia.com/topic/Technology.aspx
7. Cashmore AR (2010) The Lucretian swerve: The biological basis of human behavior and the criminal justice system. Proc Natl Acad Sci 107(10):4499–4504
8. Castells M (2009) Communication power. Oxford University Press, New York
9. Chung H et al (2012) Gut immune maturation depends on colonization with a host-specific microbiota. Cell 149(7):1578–1593
10. Dator J, Seo Y (2008) Korea as the wave of a future: the emerging dream society of icons and aesthetic experience. In: Hoare J et al (eds) Korea: the past and the present: selected papers from the British Association for Korean studies. Global Oriental, Folkestone
11. Dator JA (2012) Social foundations of human space exploration. Springer, New York
12. Deutsch KW (1963) The nerves of government: models of political communication and control. The Free Press of Glencoe, New York
13. Dobrov GM (1979) The strategy for organized technology in light of hard-, soft-, org-ware interaction. Long Range Plann 12(4):79–90
14. Drum K (2013) America's real criminal element: lead. http://www.motherjones.com/environment/2013/01/lead-crime-link-gasoline
15. Foucault M (1978) History of sexuality, vol I, An Introduction. Pantheon, New York
16. Fuller RB (1981) Critical path. St. Martin's Press, New York
17. Furniss G, Gunner E (2008) Power, marginality and African oral literature. Cambridge University Press, Cambridge
18. Galloway AR (2006) Protocol: how control exists after decentralization. MIT Press, Cambridge
19. Gonzalez RT (2013) Adding iodine to salt may have helped boost America's I.Q. http://io9.com/adding-iodine-to-salt-may-have-helped-boost-americas-i-880854738
20. Grübler A (1998) Technology and global change. Cambridge University Press, Cambridge
21. Hastings D, Berry L (eds) (1979) Cohort analysis: a collection of interdisciplinary readings. Scripps Foundation for Research in Population Problems
22. Heidegger M (2008) Basic writings: from being and time (1927) to The task of thinking (1964). Harper Perennial Modern Thought, New York
23. Hume D et al (2010) A treatise of human nature, vol 1. Oxford University Press, Oxford
24. Keay D (1987) Interview with Margaret Thatcher. http://www.margaretthatcher.org/document/106689
25. Kittler FA (1999) Gramophone, film, typewriter. Stanford University Press, Stanford
26. Lapham L (2012) Word order: The Internet as the toy with a tin ear, http://www.laphams-quarterly.org/ magazine/means-of-communication.php
27. Latour B (1999) Pandora's hope: essays on the reality of science studies. Harvard University Press, Cambridge
28. Lem S, Zylinska J (2013) Summa technologiae. University of Minnesota Press, Minneapolis
29. MacKenzie DA, Wajcman J (eds) (1999) The social shaping of technology. Open University Press, Buckingham [Eng.]
30. Mason WH, Fienberg SE (1985) Cohort analysis in social research: beyond the identification problem. Springer, New York

31. McAuliffe K (2012) How your cat is making you crazy. http://www.theatlantic.com/magazine/archive/2012/03/how-your-cat-is-making-you-crazy/308873/
32. McLuhan M (1964) Understanding media: the extensions of man. New American Library, New York
33. McLuhan M, Fiore Q (2001) The medium is the massage. Gingko Press, Corte Madera
34. Norman R (1965) The cohort as a concept in the study of social change. Am Sociol Rev 30
35. Prensky M (2001) Digital natives, digital immigrants. Part 1. On the Horizon 9(5):1–6
36. Rancière J (2009) The future of the image. Verso, New York
37. Shuttleworth K (2012) Agreement entitles Whanganui River to legal identity. http://www.nzherald.co.nz/nz/news/article.cfm?c_id=1&objectid=10830586
38. Singer C (1979) A history of technology, vol 1. Clarendon Press, Oxford
39. Slack JD (2005) Culture+technology: a primer. Peter Lang, New York
40. Stiegler B et al (1998) Technics and time, vol 1, The fault of Epimetheus. Beardsworth R, Collins G (trans.) Stanford University Press, Stanford
41. Strauss W (1991) Generations: the history of America's future, 1584 to 2069. Quill, New York
42. Tehranian M (1990) Technologies of power: information machines and democratic prospects. Ablex, Norwood
43. White L Jr (1940) Technology and invention in the Middle Ages. Speculum XV:2
44. Wiener N (1965) Cybernetics: or, control and communication in the animal and the machine. MIT Press, Cambridge
45. Wiener N (1989) The human use of human beings: cybernetics and society. Free Association, London
46. Williams R (2013) CIA backs $630,000 study into how to control global weather through geoengineering, http://www.independent.co.uk/news/world/americas/cia-backs-630000-study-into-how-to-control-global-weather-through-geoengineering-8724501.html
47. Wrangham RW (2009) Catching fire: how cooking made us human. Basic Books, New York
48. Wu X et al (2012) Early Pottery at 20,000 years ago in Xianrendong Cave, China. Science 336(6089):1696–1700
49. Transportation Implications of Telecommuting (1990) U.S. Department of Transportation | Research and Innovative Technology Administration, National Transportation Library

Chapter 2
Communication Technologies and Power Relations in Five Historical Periods

2.1 Language, Speech, and Power

The purpose of this study is to discover if, and if, in what ways, changes in communications technologies have influenced, strengthened, and/or changed relations—primarily power relations—between humans, and between humans and their environments. We started our quest "at the beginning"—when the first humans interacted via the first communication technologies—in order to determine a base from which to note the power changes, or lack of them, that subsequent communication technologies wrought.

Thus, our inquiry started by researching literature about modes of communication (such as gestures, touching, sounds, and images) in the early *homo* family that existed prior to *Homo sapiens*, as well as the emergence of speech in *Homo sapiens* (or, others would say, which emergence led to and became a defining mark distinguishing *Homo sapiens sapiens* from other *Homo sapiens*, as well as from the other *homo* species, especially *Homo neanderthalensis*, depending on one's interpretation). This also led us into a brief inquiry into the literature on communication among other animals, and, most importantly, to a consideration of the evolution of language in humans.

Even though other animals communicate, and may have language, human language seems to have greatly enhanced the emergence of the mind from the brain by providing the brain with something through which to develop increasingly useful concepts. At the same time, changes in the larynx, vocal tract, tongue, and lips of humans enabled them to do something that some (but by no means all) experts feel no other animal or *homo* species could do then and still cannot do, which is to produce the sounds for the vowels *i, a*, and *u*, and in general use the physical structures of the skull to develop and communicate ideas and concepts orally and aurally effectively and in ways that enriched language and mind in the process.

This ability to think, talk, and act in certain ways appears to have set humans off on a trajectory about 100,000 years ago that enabled them to become, in an evolutionary eye blink, the kind of globally dominant animal that humans are now.

J.A. Dator et al., *Mutative Media: Communication Technologies and Power Relations in the Past, Present, and Futures*, Lecture Notes in Social Networks, DOI 10.1007/978-3-319-07809-0_2,

If human dominance is to some significant extent due to language, then that seems to be Power with a capital P.

One aspect of the debate about that trajectory lies squarely at the intersection of our research interests. Could Neanderthals speak? Or at least speak as well as humans do? If not, is the apparent extinction of Neanderthals about 30,000 years ago, and the subsequent emergence of *Homo sapiens,* as the only surviving *homo* species due, to some important extent, to the fact that humans could reason and speak (more effectively)? Did language and speech enable humans to organize themselves so they could respond to the changes in the natural environment, impacting them more effectively than could Neanderthals? Did humans successfully use their ability to think and speak specifically to organize themselves so as to eliminate Neanderthals? [3, 10, 24, 33, 35, 38].

If so, then this is one of the most dramatic and earliest examples of how new communication technologies changed power relations among the *homo* family. Evidence suggests that Neanderthals were more muscular than humans; their skeletons were more massive; they were hairier and thus perhaps better protected against the cold; they appear to have had larger brains; they may have had a better sense of smell; their gestation period perhaps was for 10–12 months instead of 9; they seem to have matured faster after birth and were fully adults by age 15. But they may have had shorter lifespans as well. Nonetheless (if they were a separate species of *Homo sapiens*, which itself is disputed), Neanderthals seem to be extinct, and humans reign solitary and supreme.

Why? The ability of humans to speak may be the, or at least one, reason. Early evidence suggested that Neanderthals might have lacked the physical ability to produce the range of vowels and consonants that humans could—the shape and placement of their larynx and related structures made it impossible [3, 42]. Neanderthals might have been "smart" enough to produce human-like speech, but not physically able to do so. And thus the superior ability of humans to think, plan, discuss, organize, and act may have enabled them to adapt successfully to environmental changes while Neanderthals did not—indeed, perhaps humans acted affirmatively to eliminate Neanderthals.

Or not. Although this issue is seldom the main focus of research on the evolution of humans, language, and speech, there has been some heated discussion of it in the literature. During the 1970s, there seemed to be enough evidence to support the hypothesis that Neanderthals did not have the physical apparatus to speak at all. Now, expert sentiment [10] seems to be that they both spoke and heard in the same range as humans, but that humans seem to have developed a greater repertoire of abilities and behaviors that enabled them to survive in adapting to the rapidly changing environmental conditions to which Neanderthals could not—or in any event, did not—adapt.

In an impressive survey of data about human and Neanderthal co-evolution during transition from the onset of the last glacial maximum at the end of the Pleistocene period to the warmer and more stable Holocene period, Clive Finlayson lists 14 features that both modern humans and Neanderthals possessed in varying degrees at the beginning of the transition: "almost total dependence on mammalian herbivore meat; fat deposition; storage, food sharing; trade; large home, annual and inter-annual ranges; large group size; within-group division of labor and operation as teams; reliable-type technology; large-range, projectile, technology; tool re-use; complex social structure including kin-and non-kin altruism; rapid development and transmission of technological ideas; [and] behaviors that transmitted information not directly experienced by all group members—symbolism and complex spoken language" [24, p. 134].

After a careful evaluation of the evidence, Finlayson concludes that humans and Neanderthals utilized or altered these factors in ways that enabled humans to survive while Neanderthals went extinct about 30,000 years ago or so. He concludes in the last paragraphs of his last chapter, titled provocatively, "The Survival of the Weakest":

> Moderns have continued the trends towards increasingly complex technologies and social system, having conquered even the most inhospitable of environments. Cultural and social diversity is the hallmark of human societies across the Earth today yet nobody seriously attempts to equate these differences to biological differences. Nobody, rightly, suggests that we are observing different species of humans. Yet, looking at similar evidence of cultural and social diversity in the Pleistocene there are still those who equate these to biological differences, the product of mutations that made us something apart from the rest of nature. It is just another version of the antiquated view of humans at the top of the evolutionary pyramid. If anything, I hope to have shown in this book that we are the product of chance and a great deal of luck. We are here because, in scrambling for survival in the margins of the world of other humans, we became increasingly inventive and kept finding ways of hanging on and then taking over when others that had been better adapted than ourselves vanished as circumstances changed. That we are here today is the end result of a series of chance events that kept us in the running. It could easily have gone the other way ... [24, p. 208]

Finlayson seems to be expressing a "mutative" view here: "We are the product of chance and a great deal of luck" by which we apparently fortuitously made use of the 14 features he listed above to survive and thrive in ways Neanderthals did not and other species could not.

Similarly, in *Adam's Tongue: How Humans Made Language, How Language Made Humans*, Derek Bickerton adopted the concept of "niche construction" to explain the origin of human language. He goes to great lengths to show that human language did not evolve smoothly from earlier *homo* communication modes, such as gestures and cries; still less did human language evolve step by step from the communication modes of other animals. Though not unrelated to these earlier features, human language and speech are aspects of evolution initially largely related to what he calls the "need" for humans to cooperate in order to scavenge for food more effectively [1].

Humans initially used "iconic" imitation of animals and the environment to obtain cooperation. Through repeated use and enhancement, these became "categories," and then "concepts" with symbolic words that emerged, pidgin-like, until it became "possible to build merged, hierarchical sentence structures" [1, p. 245]. While stressing the biological basis of speech, Bickerton repeatedly states that "biological developments don't mandate new behaviors—they merely make them possible. Whether these possibilities are exercised is a matter of choice, entirely up to us"—again, a mutative perspective [1, p. 246].

Bickerton does not discuss the Neanderthal question directly in this book, but does refer to Neanderthals as "a species of almost equivalent abilities" with those of Cro-Magnons [1, p. 246]. While having a biological, evolutionary basis, "niche construction" requires willful constructors: "The pathway of runaway niche construction moves with a powerful current, but not necessarily an undivertable one. The very notion of niche construction asserts the autonomy of the organism, the power latent in species to influence their own destiny. Our niche gave us language, language gave us intelligence, but only the wise use of that intelligence can keep us free and fully human" [1, p. 249]. Nonetheless, one does not need to advocate intelligent design, evolutionary "progress," or that "man" is the Crown of Creation to observe that somehow humans do seem to have used language and speech so as to think, plan, discuss, organize, and act more efficiently and effectively than was possible before the emergence of language and compared to those without human language. We are not able to say anything with any confidence about how power relations among humans were impacted by this, but it seems clear that language did enable the hairless ape to do things, to itself and to its environments, that were impossible to do so fully before the acquisition of language and speech, and that this set humans on the niche-creating trajectory we are still on, to our ultimate triumph or tragedy.

However, speech was not the last new communication technology that humans used for these purposes.

2.2 Governance and Power in Oral Societies

It clearly is difficult, if not impossible, to know for certain what life was like "in the state of nature"—in the tens of thousands of years humans are believed to have lived in small nomadic hunting and gathering oral societies. No written or other clear records remain from that time, since writing apparently was unknown, and if there were other modes of recording and preserving information, they appear not to have survived or are currently undiscovered or unrecognized. Archaeologists, anthropologists, linguists, and others have tried to reconstruct the structures and processes of early societies by examining what physical evidence remains from the past, on the one hand, and by studying what are assumed to be (and are a rapidly diminishing number of) currently existing societies that might serve as examples of the way all humans once lived.

The latter activity is especially fraught with many political as well as methodological and substantive difficulties. What was once bravely called "political anthropology" has been under attack in recent years as the work of biased, paternalistic, and ethnocentric people, largely from the west, who brought all of their western prejudices and feelings of superiority with them [26].

So it is with great trepidation, here also, that we attempt to characterize the social and power relations within and between non-literate, oral societies. We rely initially on the recent work of Ted Lewellen, since he has been involved in the study of political anthropology for a long time and has tried to respond to criticisms in later versions of his earlier work [37].

Lewellen says that "in most non-state systems, power is fragmentary and temporary, dispersed among families, bands, lineages, and various associations … . Although politics is constant in such societies as individuals seek support for leadership positions, public decisions are made, and territory is defended, it is not manifested in either a monopoly on coercive force nor in any form of centralized economic system based on taxes or tribute" [37, p. 22].

According to Lewellen, for almost all of humanity's past, humans lived in small nomadic bands of between 25 and 150 people. Most of them were biologically related to each other. They knew and spoke the same language—their most powerful medium of communication—and thus shared the same basic view of the world that had been passed down by repeated imitation and word of mouth. There were slight divisions of labor based on the most obvious gender or age differences, but for the most part everyone, from the youngest to the oldest, and whether male, female or other, did whatever each could do without any fixed status distinction. For the most part, everyone "knew" what to do on the basis of tradition, but when decisions needed to be made, issues were jointly discussed and solutions agreed upon by consensus. The clichéd question of many a cartoon—aliens from a spaceship asking a group of Stone Age people to "take me to your leader"—would have been utterly meaningless. There were no "leaders" in any organized, hierarchical, hereditary way. The groups were economically, politically and socially self-sufficient, peaceful, and egalitarian—what one person had, everyone had. No one accumulated wealth while others went wanting. Being nomadic hunters and gatherers of their food and utensils, both private and public property was unknown. There were no fixed territorial boundaries. Even though there was internal conflict, murder was rare, while organized killing between groups was so rare as to be essentially nonexistent, some recent arguments to the contrary notwithstanding [50].

This mode of social organization seems to have persisted for many tens of thousands of years. If so, we humans have lived far more of our lives in these social conditions than in any subsequent ones—especially those of the very recent industrial or informational present. We are in some psychological and perhaps even biological ways predisposed for life in small, intimate, like-minded familial groups where (in effect) "everybody knows your name."

Although there are disagreements within the anthropological discipline about terminology and boundaries, Lewellen designates the form of social organization that developed after the band as the *tribe*. "Tribes are uncentralized egalitarian systems in which authority is distributed among a number of small groups; unity of the larger society is established from a web of individual and group relations. Because these groups rely on domesticated food sources, they are more densely populated and usually more sedentary than are hunting-gathering bands. As with bands, there is little political or economic specialization, except for a division of labor along age and sex lines, and there is no religious professionalization" [37, pp. 26–27].

After providing several examples of tribes, and characteristic of many others, Lewellen points out that "throughout Melanesia certain big men attain significant political authority through wealth, generosity, and courage in war. Although these leaders may exercise chieftain-like authority, their position is inherently unstable, because it is dependent on their ability to buy followers thorough gift giving and loans. A bad crop, an inability to gather sufficient pigs for a lavish feast, or a failure in battle can quickly shift authority to a contender with better luck or skill" [37, pp. 27–28].

The next development in early forms of governance after tribes were *chiefdoms,* which are marked by higher population density and complex centralized authority. In contrast with both bands and tribes, "chiefdoms have relatively permanent central agencies of government, typically based on collection and redistribution of an economic surplus (often including a labor surplus). A position of chief, unlike that of headman of a band or lineage, is a position of at least minimal 'power'—that is, the chief has access to a certain amount of coercion. The chief may be the final authority in the distribution of land and may be able to recruit an army. Economically, he is the center and coordinator of the redistribution system. He can collect taxes of food or goods, some of which will be returned to the populace, creating a new level of group solidarity in which a number of specialized parts depend on the smooth functioning of the whole" [37, p. 33]. Lewellen gives pre-contact Hawaii as an especially impressive example of a large, complex, forceful, and prosperous chiefdom system [37, p. 34].

The next step in social organization, according to Lewellen, is the *state,* which has many of the features we now recognize as political forms and processes. "States are generally large, complex societies, encompassing a variety of classes, associations, and occupational groups. Occupational specialization, including a full-time political bureaucracy, unites the entire group in a web of interrelated dependencies. Because of the vast range of individual and class interests within a state, pressures and conflicts unknown in less complex societies necessitate some sort of rule of impersonal law, backed by physical sanctions, for the ongoing maintenance of the system" [37, p. 36].

Lewellen does not discuss orality or any modes of communication, or suggest that they are in any way related to the organization or emergence of bands, tribes, and states. However, Madden, Palimi, and Bryson [39] offer an example of how reliance on oral communication only influences the social and political structures and processes of non-literate societies. The study by Madden et al., is based on research into the Kope people in Papua New Guinea, who first encountered westerners briefly in 1930 but did not have extensive contact until after the Second World War.

They conclude that oral communication "can be regarded as performing three main functions:

1. Defining tribal identity through history and mythology
2. Preserving social networks
3. Promulgation of practical skills, including hunting, house-building, agronomy" [39, pp. 5–6]

In discussing "tribal politics" Madden et al., say that "leadership among the Kope has never been hereditary; leaders were chosen on merit. The tight network of family connections helped to make the biases and motivations of aspiring leaders common knowledge, and their skills would have been on display to all [39, p. 6]. The main role of the tribal leader was to represent his tribe in inter-tribal negotiations.

In consequence, the most important skill for a chief was oratory. He would need to be well versed in local history and politics, but not only was his knowledge important, so too was the skill with which he presented it" [39, p. 7].

In this regard, it is instructive to cite Rosalind Thomas, who pointed out that "the most important factor in oral tradition is the way the tradition is passed on. This includes several elements: the precise nature and form of the transmission, for example, whether the tradition is passed on in poetic or other fixed form; the group which transmits it, whether a family, dynasty or whole community; and why it is being transmitted (e.g., for status or honor)" [53, p. 6]. Noting the importance of mnemonic professionals, Thomas continues, "For instance where we find traditions kept by professional memorizers who lay great stress on strict accuracy because they are responsible for dynastic traditions, we may expect fairly accurate transmission over a long period" [53, p. 6].

In another study that demonstrates the complexity and sophistication of knowledge that can be achieved by oral communication alone, Carol Fleisher Feldman "reports that among the Ilongot of the Philippines there are thirteen oral genres, each identified by a distinctive genre name, that are divided by the Ilongot into three main categories: straight speech, crooked speech and language of spells. There are three genres of straight speech: news or gossip'; stories about the recent past; and myths or stories about a more distant past. There are genres of crooked speech: riddles' children's rhymes' songs, performances—usually of a daring kind; and oratory. Finally there are five genres of spells: boasting about headhunting prowess; highly conventionalized and formalized boasts and pronouncements, curses, invocations in the service; of healing by layman; and such invocation known only to shamans" [22, p. 50].

Madden et al. list the roles of oral communication in the Kope as:

Induction—the passing on of the knowledge and skills needed to make a person a fully contributing member of the tribe.

Dissemination—the spreading of news and stories.

Presentation—the ability to select and express information in a way that best suits the "interests of the representative and those of his family, or of the clan he represents."

Organization—the sharing of information to co-ordinate group activities, such as hunting, warfare and trade.

Interpretation—the ability to derive information.

Preservation—the retention of tribal history, culture, and expertise by the elderly [39, pp. 9–10].

Regarding our interest in communication and power, Madden's point about "presentation" seems especially important. Whoever is the communicator is able to some extent to shape information so as to further the interests of the communicator's family or clan. Then, as now, the ability to set the agenda of a meeting is an exercise of significant power.

As Lewellen said of pre-state societies generally, Madden et al. also affirm that the "Kope were of necessity generalists. Age and sex played a part of the roles a

Kope may be able to fulfill, but all members of the tribe had an understanding and appreciation of every task, making them well able to judge whether or not they were being adequately performed" [39, p. 12].

Madden et al. focus on the various ways in which information is acquired, stored, and shared in an oral society, and the impact those modes have upon the social structure of the Kobe society. Speaking, reciting, remembering via various mnemonics, including music and dance, were key. "It is widely acknowledged that, in pre-literate cultures, hearing was the sense most commonly associated with the exchange of information." However, seeing is important too: "[C]olour and imagery commonly play a part in pre-literate cultures, not only in ritual but also in the exchange of information." The use of body paint and wearable ornaments to show status, and of physical markers to delineate the boundaries of regions was common: "When a society becomes sufficiently stable, it begins to manipulate the landscape by producing permanent structures." However, even then, memory and living speech were essential: "As a means of transmitting information from generation to generation, [physical artifacts] were only effective when reinforced by rituals, or 'social acts of remembering' that imbued them with meaning … . If such mnemonic rituals and rhymes are suppressed or prevented … after a few generations the communal memory will be lost, and with it, the meaning assigned to the material representations of that culture" [39, pp. 19–21]. As we shall see, this is exactly what happened when literacy emerged, especially when oral tribes encountered literate empires.

2.3 Governance and Power in Scribal Societies: Tallies, Tokens, and Thought

Apparently only a few thousand years ago, and for the first time in human history, symbols began to be used, at first not to convey abstract ideas or emotions but rather to designate items, identify who owned them, how much they were worth, and perhaps where they were going. For about a thousand years or so, what eventually became writing was nothing but markers, labels, lists, or tables. But these pale scratches made communication across time and distance easier than it had ever been before, bestowing power and privilege on those who knew how to make and interpret the symbols. Enos [21] describes the process in detail. He states that no symbols have been found "from the first half million years of human occupation of the Middle East" [21, p. 19]. And, "The first archaeological material attesting to a symbolic tradition in the Middle East belongs to the epoch of Neanderthal man, the Mousterian period, as late as 60,000—15,000 BC … . Fragments of ochre [with] no indication of how the red pigment was used" and "funerary paraphernalia displayed in burial sites" have been found. For example, flowers were deposited in a grave at Shanidar Cave, about 60,000 BC. At Qafzeh, Israel, a child's tomb was furnished with animal antlers [21, p. 19].

Bone fabrics from the Paleolithic period (15,000–10,000 BC) have been found with engraved parallel, V, or X-shaped markings. Iconic symbols representing animals have also been found from this period. Enos points out that "the function of these two categories of symbols—iconic and linear, or naturalistic and geometric—can only be hypothesized." "Marshack proposed that the notched bones were lunar calendars, each incised line recording one appearance of the moon … . Andre Leroi-Gourhan reviewed the animal images as referring to the numinous, each species representing one manifestation of a complex cosmology. If these interpretations are valid, we can for the first time identify the use of both symbols and signs" to communicate ideas and information [21, p. 21]. However, great care must be taken in imputing meanings into ancient artifacts. While it probably is true the images were fashioned so as to communicate ideas and information, unless we have other, corroborating data we should be very reluctant to assume we can be sure what those ideas and information actually were. They may be numinous. They may be profane. They may be sexual. They may be whittling. They may be Jungian. They may just be "art" with no other purpose than to be.

Enos does seem correctly to summarize the importance of these signs and symbols for the evolution of human consciousness and social organization: "The Paleolithic tallies are an impressive step in the evolution of technologies for the communication and manipulation of data". Their major significance was to promote abstraction:

> The signs translated concrete information into abstract markings. They removed the data from their context […]. The signs separated the knowledge from the knower, presenting data—as expressed by Marshall McLuhan—in a 'cold' and static visual form, rather than the 'hot' and flexible oral medium which involved voice modulation and body language. As a result, graphic signs not only brought about a new way of recording, handling, and communicating data, but an unprecedented objectivity in dealing with information. [21, p. 22]

This "cold," seemingly objective character of graphic signs (and written communication) is one of its most distinctive features, giving writing the impression of being unbiased and authoritative in ways speech seldom if ever can in comparison.

At this point, further innovations in human symbolic communication seem to have stagnated for a while. Enos states that "there is no evidence for any major modification in the use of symbols during the Mesolithic period [10,000–8,000 BC] in the Middle East" [21, p. 22].

However, the Neolithic [8,000–6,000 BC] brought big changes. This was the period when many extensive sedentary communities based on true agriculture arose. Many clay tokens have been found that were used to convey important information about agricultural possessions and products. Enos makes clear that "tokens were never found in sites where hunting and gathering was the base of food procurement, but are part and parcel of the first agriculturalists' tool kits. Second, the timing of their appearance and their geographical extension in the eighth millennium BC precisely coincides with the time and region involved in experimenting with the domestication of plants and animals. Third the first tokens stood for products of the farm. Fourth it appears logical that a lifestyle based on planning a harvest and hoarding food for survival would incite record-keeping. Fifth, and finally, it also makes sense that a socioeconomic system based on the redistribution of commodities would require a device for record-keeping in order to control goods … . Symbolic meaning emerges as cultures evolve to a point that such forms of manifesting meaning are needed and valued" [21, pp. 24–25]. This latter point is probably true, but it is not inevitable that a culture will decide it "needs" symbols; that the medium will be clay; that the need or medium will become permanent; or that the medium will evolve into something better at expressing, preserving, and transmitting desired meanings.

However, in this case, Enos declared that these clay "tokens are the link between tallies and writing" [21, p. 25]. He continues, "While tallies were meaningless when out of context, the tokens could always be understood by anyone initiated into the system. The cone, for example, stood for a small measure of grain and could only have this one meaning." "The tokens were 'word signs.'" "The greatest novelty of the tokens was in that they formed a system" [21, p. 26]. They "enhanced logic and rational decision making by allowing the scrutiny of complex data" and "presaged Sumerian pictographic writing in form and contents" [21, p. 27].

2.3.1 *The Emergence of Writing and the Transformation of Oral Societies*

As systems of writing emerged, they began to enable forms of social organization the world had never seen before: organized religion and priests in place of free-floating spirituality; formal education and teachers instead of amorphous beliefs and skills based on observation and imitation; terrifying hierarchical authorities of many kinds including, eventually, rulers, bureaucrats, judges, and jailers instead of peaceful, equitable, small groups within an environment of "subsistence abundance," as Marshall Sahlins has so convincingly described typical band and tribal life.

Handwriting and reading was a profoundly mutative technology. Even though most people did not know how to read and write, formal life eventually became for the first time based on written rules that were interpreted and enforced by power-wielding authorities. Wherever writing developed, rigid, rule-based, remote, enforceable "objective" government emerged in place of flexible, functional, direct, participatory governance typical of oral societies. Most importantly, writing enabled thoughts to be frozen, codified, and made mandatory across time and space. Vast empires capturing huge numbers of people spread in large part because of the power of the written word and the power that the word gave those who interpreted and enforced it.

By preserving written law and religious scriptures, and by empowering scribes and priests charged with further preserving, interpreting and enforcing legal and religious words, for the first time the past could effectively control the future, squelching the spontaneous and easy adaptation to changing times and needs which the eternal present of oral societies made possible. Although it might seem to one living in an oral society that norms and mores were eternal, in fact they were frequently highly ephemeral and fleeting. Old norms were often quickly forgotten when they proved dysfunctional and new ones easily adopted in ways that made them seem eternal.

Walter J. Ong focuses especially on the changes in the ways humans think, behave, and believe that are the consequences of literacy, compared to orality. Indeed, Chapter Four of *Orality & Literacy* is starkly titled, "Writing Restructures Consciousness." The opening sentences make the point very clear:

> In recent years certain basic differences have been discovered between the ways of managing knowledge and verbalization in primary oral cultures (cultures with no knowledge at all of writing) and in cultures deeply affected by the use of writing. The implications of the new discoveries have been startling. Many of the features we have taken for granted in thought and expression in literature, philosophy and science, and even in oral discourse among literates, are not directly native to human existence as such but have come into being because of the resources which the technology of writing makes available to human consciousness. We have had to revise our understanding of human identity. The subject of this book is the differences between orality and literacy. Or, rather, since readers of this or any book by definition are acquainted with literate culture from the inside, the subject is, first, thought and its verbal expression in oral culture, which is strange and at times bizarre to us, and second, literate thought and expression in terms of their emergence from and relation to orality. [43, p. 1]

Ong states that "our understanding of the differences between orality and literacy developed only in the electronic age, not earlier. Contrasts between electronic media and print have sensitized us to the earlier contrast between writing and orality" [43, p. 3]. We will see that the interest in the social impact of the printing press that motivated the greatest pioneering scholar of them all, Elizabeth Eisenstein, was piqued by reading *The Gutenberg Galaxy* by Marshall McLuhan, who is rightly viewed as the founding father of media studies, and especially of the impact of television on contemporary societies.

Jack Goody is also one of the main sources for information about the impact of writing on oral societies [27–30]. In *The Logic of Writing and the Organization of Society*, Goody devotes separate chapters that show how writing led to organized religion with a powerful priestly class; strengthened and expanded formal economic systems; created powerful centralized governing systems with controlling bureaucracies; created rigid, remote, "law" and lawyers, while banishing flexible, customary, participatory conflict decision-making; and created other new institutions with their newly privileged social classes, such as in education and the arts, that led to what we call "civilization"—life in cities where the few literate elite ruled in their interest over the far more numerous peasants and other agrarian workers who provided food and other staples at the beck and call of the literate elite.

In Chapter One, "The Word of God," concerning the creation of organized religion, Goody states that "in the beginning was the Book, but it was the priest who read and explained it. Hence religions of the Book are often associated with restrictions on the uses and extent of literacy. In the extreme case the priests are the one category of persons able to read at all: in other words the division between literate-illiterate corresponds to that between priest and laity" [29, p. 17]. Once things are committed to writing they are difficult to remove, and often difficult to add to as well. "It is not of course that writing prevented any change. In some spheres of knowledge a permanent record was a condition of future development. But in other spheres and to different degrees writing made change a question of deliberate reform rather than of continuous adaptation" [29, p. 30] as was the case in oral societies where freezing ideas and practices was much more difficult and on-the-spot modifications of previous norms was common. "To write down a prayer is to fix it in a particular way so that it becomes essential to repeat, for example, the Lord's Prayer in the exact words in which it had been written, even if we scarcely understand them, rather than invent our own variation that may be more appropriate to the times and occasion" as was typical of oral societies that could and did change its sacred words occasionally [29, p. 38].

However, on a point we will see made many times subsequently, Goody also makes clear that "given literate expression, even dissent established its own tradition. One role of the intellectual was to develop and to preserve alternative views of the world (that is, ideologies), the accumulation and further diffusion of which were largely a function of the intervention of writing since it prevents skepticism and speculation from being totally absorbed in the dominant cultural ethos; that is to say, writing may provide even the opposition with a semi-permanent platform" [29, p. 31].

So, with literacy also came the emergence of religions, usually, though not always, featuring jealous and vengeful solitary male gods (whereas manifold fertility goddesses and other spirits had coexisted relatively peacefully before) and the systematic, organized use of killing to gain, control, and extend property (whereas property, whether land or goods, was a useless impediment to the life of hunting and gathering societies, though it became the basis of power and dominance for civilized empires). Writing ended the free floating though perhaps deeply and personally held spirituality of earlier times as well. Although spirituality apparently flourished for millennia before the invention of writing, once writing emerged, god—or his prophets—insisted on writing things down to see that beliefs and practices became fixed and unchanging forever. Fluid personal and tribal spirituality gave way to rigid organized religion with revealed holy texts that only carefully trained persons could read or interpret properly. So while in fact in the beginning was *not* the Word, from about 5,000 or so years ago onward, the Word—the written word properly recited and interpreted—has reigned supreme over transitory personal and oral spirituality. When one Word clashed with another Word, the matter was typically resolved by fighting, killing, and burning the books that contained the evil Words.

As Andreas Feldtkeller comments:

> The act of writing down a religion makes a difference: metaphorically speaking, to write down a religion means to draw a line through the field of religious practice between what is to be preserved and what is to be rejected. To convert something into a written code is to preserve it: an important motive for religious writing, therefore, is to safeguard a certain form of religious practice from the everlasting stream of change, and to take care that this form will be known and practiced, if possible, forever. On the other hand, the same act of writing is also an act of rejection: other forms of religious practice will not be chosen for preservation; they may even be explicitly excluded from what the written form recommends as practice. [23, p. 9]

Of course (and until very recently), even after the invention of writing, most humans could not write or read. Those were abilities possessed by only a handful of persons in any civilized society. Even many rulers and military commanders—and certainly common folks—could not read or write and had to rely on the professional scribes—often religious priests—who could. The effect of this was to make the Word even more mysterious and the influence of those who could read and explain the Word almost magically powerful. Books were scarce—often unique—because they were each laboriously handwritten. The most important books had to be copied over and over in order that the Truth could be passed down to later generations and passed over so as to govern people physically far from the center of power. As a consequence, mistakes, omissions, and new material often found their way into the copies. But that fact was generally unknown since texts located in different places were seldom brought together and compared.

A vivid example of this process can be found in Japan, where the writing of the *Kojiki* and *Nihongi* ended the dominance of the tribal beliefs of earlier people and imposed the beliefs of the ruling clan as supreme. Fujii Sadakazu has discussed the role of Fieda no Are as an intermediary figure between the time that orality and chanters who memorized oral tradition flourished in Japan and the time when they were marginalized and eventually destroyed by the power of the written word (though written words often were memorized and recited aloud as though they were still oral chants) [17, p. 40]. Writing similarly led to the spread of various Buddhist sects and Confucianism in medieval Japan [34].

Along with all other researchers in this area, Goody emphasizes that "the construction of the text, which is in any case something other than the transcription of discourse, can lead to its contemplation, to the development of thoughts about thoughts, to a metaphysic that may require its own metalanguage" [28, p. 38]. *Decontextualization* is inevitable with writing, leading to classification and the easy, repeated study and interpretation of old texts. One certainly can do abstract thinking in oral societies by having set phrases attached to people and events, and by other mnemonics, but it is so much easier—apparently inevitable—to decontexualize (to separate portions of the text from its original time, place, purpose, and promulgator) once hand-writing is established.

Indeed, J. Peter Denny [14] states, "although the effects of literacy upon human thought are large, they are often misconstrued and exaggerated. Western thought, to which literacy is a big contributor, is widely believed to be more reflective, more abstract, more complex, and more logical than thought in preliterate agricultural and hunter-gatherer societies. The available research, however, shows that these beliefs are wrong and that Western thought has only one distinctive property separating it from thought in both agricultural and hunter-gather societies—decontexualization. Decontextualizing is the handling of information in a way that either disconnects other information or backgrounds it" [15, p. 52].

Nonetheless, we believe the evidence does show that the ability to decontexualize thought via writing is by no means inconsequential. It does, as the title of Goody's first book on the subject suggests, lead to "the domestication of the savage mind" as much as the "decontextualization" of teosinte by early humans in what is now Mexico eventually led to maize and thence centuries later to American hybrid sweet corn.

Concerning the part writing played in the establishment of economic systems, Goody states that "the early role of writing in exchange (effectively, commerce), and the role of writing in the management of the economic affairs of the temple and the palace" is crucial [29, p. 45]. As we have noted before, Goody makes clear that "early writing in Mesopotamia was employed for bookkeeping rather than recording myths and rituals" [29, p. 49]. And, "Writing was, in effect, originally an instrument for the communication of orders," declared Leclant, "rather than for the registration of ideas. It is absolutely essential for organization and command" [29, p. 65]. Making a point similar to that of Enos, above, about the emergence of signs and symbols, Goody says that "it is clear that such administrative tasks would be enormously facilitated by writing: a bureaucracy of this scale would seem to be difficult to manage without some form of externalized record-keeping…", though the extensive pre-contact Hawaiian polities, spread across many islands, appear to have done so without writing [29, p. 66].

In *On Writing and Government*, Goody considers the impact of writing on the creation and expansion of formal, external, rigid bureaucratic management of people and ideas in contrast to the personal, interactive mode of oral societies. Indeed, he says that "obviously the whole constellation of modern political institutions and behaviour is part of a developing tradition in which changes in the mode of communication play an important role" [29, p. 87]. "The limitations that oral communication place on the organization of the polity is what I want to examine in the course of this chapter, arguing that writing is critical in the development of bureaucratic states, even though relatively complex forms of government are possible without it" [29, p. 91]—again, of which Hawaii is probably the most elaborate example.

Goody observes that "whoever controls the calendar, the mode of reckoning time … . acquires a power that extends throughout the social system, reaching into each of the domains of politics, religion, law, and the economy" [29, p. 95]. In this regard, it is important to note that the ancient Japanese word for government and administration (called *seiji* today) was *matsurigoto*—doing what was necessary so that the rituals and festivals (*matsuri*) necessary for ensuring bountiful food (among other things) were properly performed (*goto*) at the proper times of the year. Rice growing (unlike, say, potato or wheat farming) demands considerable and continuing cooperation among many people to succeed. Thus obtaining and managing such cooperation was such an essential task that *matsurigoto* was used to describe all government and administration up until very modern times in Japan. Keeping the calendar and other written records was a fundamental duty of government. At the same time, Goody again notes, "writers have influenced political systems throughout the history of the written word, not only by administering and supporting these regimes but also by extending the range of criticism and opposition" [29, p. 119].

Importantly for our study, Goody contends that "writing remains a significant factor since it constitutes an important dimension of power at any level. The composition of the agenda and the written report structures the decisions a committee makes; those who read and study the papers are in a position to exercise power. The taker of minutes is not simply a service role but one that can influence the decisions made" [28, p. 122]. It is important to recollect that we learned above that the ability to set the agenda by the person most adept in remembering and reciting the tradition also gave that person considerable influence in oral societies.

As Goody notes, "One aspect of the introduction of writing is the greater precision it gives to orders from above and to pleas from below. It is less easy to evade an order that has been committed to writing and carries an authoritative signature" [29, p. 124]. Hence, a written "order" is decontextualized—stripped from the authority of the person reciting the order in an oral society and placed in the words and signature on the document from which the person is reading—in a literate, scribal society.

Writing makes governance and other influence possible for increasingly larger and more complex congregations of people, over vastly broader areas of space, and even over many generations through time, down to the present in the case of many of the world's philosophies and religions still powerful today. Indeed, as we will see, each new level of communication technology from speech onwards enables greater and greater complexity of thought, and organization of a greater number of people over expanding arenas of space and time.

It is in the creation of law that Goody makes clearest the role of writing in destroying the forms, processes, and distribution of power in oral societies and in creating new ones. He explains, "[B]y creating a text 'out there,' a material object detached from man (who created and interprets it), the written word can become the subject of a new kind of critical attention" [29, p. 129]. He continues, "The very fact that laws exist in written form makes a profound difference, first to the nature of its sources, secondly to the ways of changing the rules, thirdly to the judicial process, and fourthly to court organization," as he shows in detail [29, p. 134].

As we saw before, in oral societies, rules and procedures can persist or quickly change depending on their utility at the time. "But once committed to writing, 'customs' cannot just fade away. So although writing greatly increases the amount of information held in store, and in this sense enhances the potentialities of the human mind, it also makes the problems of erasure much more difficult … " [29, p. 136] On this, Goody quotes the very influential early legal scholar, Henry Sumner Maine's *Ancient Law*: "'When primitive law has once been embodied in a Code, there is an end to what may be called its spontaneous development.'" [29, p. 138] Any act to change what is written in the law becomes to some extent an act of conscious rebellion. It is seldom easy to do. The process of changing rules in an oral society may in fact be both unnoticed and unintended "so that rules that are no longer applicable tend to slip out of the memory store. But write down the norms in the form of a code or statute and you then have to make deliberate and conscious efforts to effect any alternation" [29, p. 139].

Goody makes very clear the way in which the medium of writing itself becomes an agent of change: "[T]he difference between implicit and explicit reasoning, between the contemplation of the text and the pondering of the utterance, between the capacity to review a statement visually as well as internally, by eye as well as by ear, while in some respects small, is of fundamental importance for the development of what we think of as reasoning. Reading permits a greater distancing between individual, language, and reference than speech, a greater objectivity which increases the analytic potential of the human mind" [29, p. 142]. Furthermore, "Writing affects not only the sources of law and reasoning in law but also the organization of law. The relationship of law to society becomes formalized with the advent of writing" [29, p. 142].

Once writing is used, and a set of persons—judges, prosecuting and defense lawyers, clerks, librarians and the like—emerge who know how to read and write, judgments in current disputes based on precedents (decisions in past, similar disputes) become possible in ways it never was in oral societies. A legal profession arose with knowledge of the past and terminology to describe it that few other people could attain. As Goody explains, "Legal norms no longer reside in the memory of each and every individual (at least of every elder) but may be literally buried in documents to be disinterred only by specialists in the written word" [29, p. 144]. And, "The long-term implications of such dissociation of law and custom, which is at the same time a differentiation of the two realms with the written word usually being given priority, are radical for the development both of society and of the individual" [29, p. 144].

Writing changed everything. But it did not create peace out of presumed primitive chaos. Before there was writing, there was order, but no law. As Stanley Diamond makes clear: "Custom—spontaneous, traditional, personal, commonly known, corporate … is the modality of primitive society; law is the instrument of civilization, of political society sanctioned by organized force, presumably above society at large, and buttressing a new set of social interests … " [15, p. 120]. And, "In Maitland's words, 'the king has a peace that devours all others.'" [15, p. 130] "Thus the law against homicide was not a 'progressive' step, as if some abstract right were involved which the state, coming of age, finally understands and seeks to establish. Anti-social conduct is exceptional in small kinship groups … " […] Crimes of violence were rare, and murder virtually unknown" [15, p. 134]. "Law and order is the historical illusion; law versus order is the historical reality" [15, p. 140].

These conclusions are vivid evidence of the way changing communication technologies change societies and the instruments and distribution of power in them. Moreover, almost all of the above is evidence of how the medium, and not the message *per se*, is the agent of change, though once the media become widespread and entrenched, the messages sent through them become powerful in and of themselves.

David Olson makes similar points but also shows that even well after literacy was widespread and controlling in many areas, "a man's word" and community traditions still had powerful legal force that didn't wane fundamentally until the late medieval period in Europe, decisively ending as a result of the impact of the printing press, as we will show later. Olson writes that "until the twelfth century complaints were delivered orally; the breach of law was stated, and compensation was demanded. The defendant replied to the charge and the local 'doomsman' indicated the type of validation to be used to decide the case. This decision was not a matter of weighing the evidence in the attempt to arrive at an abstract 'truth.' Rather it was a matter of fairness, of allowing some clue to indicate the defendant's innocence or guilt. This of course, is trial by ordeal. The innocent, it was assumed, could survive some horrible ordeal; the guilty would perish by ordeal, lose the duel, or whatever. A physical sign, losing the duel, was a sign of guilt" [42, p. 152].

In England, written documents did not become more important than oral memory and testimony until the twelfth and thirteenth centuries. Olson "detailed how the scrutiny of written documents and records came to provide the evidential bases permitting legally competent judges to pronounce on innocence or guilt of the accused … . The fundamental tenet of the late Middle Ages … was the identification of objectivity with a text. As a consequence … questions also began to be asked about the validity of hearsay testimony, oral family record, and collective memory" [42, p. 155].

Citing Michael Clanchy's *From Memory to Written Record, England, 1066–1307*, Ivan Illich shows how oral commitments and physical experiences were more and more replaced by written agreements. "Formerly, you solemnly walked with the buyer around the property that you wanted to sell: Now you learned to point it out with your finger and had the notary describe it … . Surprisingly, even serfs carried seals, to put beneath their dictation" [31, p. 283].

"For a millennium," Illich continues, "Christians recited their prayers as they picked them up with the community, with great local and generational variants. Sentences were often so corrupted that they might foster piety but certainly did not make sense. The twelfth-century Church synods tried to remedy this state of affairs. Their canons imposed on the clergy the duty of training the laity's memory by having the repeat the *Pater* and the *Credo*, word for word, as they are in the Book. When the penitent went to confession, he had to prove to the priest that he knew his prayers by heart, that he had acquired the kind of memory on which words could be engraved. Only after this memory test could he proceed to the examination of another spot of his heart, henceforth called his conscience, in which the account of his evil deeds, words, and thoughts had been kept. Even the illiterate 'I' that speaks in confession now perceived through new, literate, eyes, its own 'self' in the image of a text" [31, p. 284].

Goody concludes that "the great civilizations of the Ancient Near East ([and also] of India or China for that matter) … possessed and utilized one critical invention of mankind in the sphere of communications, namely writing, whose use was not simply cosmetic but penetrated deeply into many areas of social life, permitting the development of new forms of social organization and new ways of handling information" [29, p. 182]. Importantly, Goody adds that he does not "claim that the introduction of writing immediately or necessarily leads to the changes I have singled out. The written tradition is cumulative, it builds up over time" [29, p. 182].

Moreover, as we will see about printing, it is always possible for a culture to resist or at least postpone the introduction of writing so as, in effect, to preserve the behavior, values, and institutions of an oral society that writing would otherwise destroy. But when all is said and done, the influence of writing on society was profoundly mutative. People who learn and teach by writing think differently from those who do not know how to read and write—even in scribal societies. But in a literate society, even the "illiterate" think and act differently from the way everyone thinks and acts in societies where writing is not known at all. The very structure of society in a scribal society is different from that of an oral society in ways so fundamental as to impact even the modes of through and actions of the illiterate.

Surely, then, literacy is a good thing. Better than the ignorance of orality. Painful as the transition from orality to literacy might be for those who experience it, surely the subsequent benefits of civilization make it all worthwhile. This belief is ingrained in every literate person in modern societies: to be able to read is an unqualified good. To be illiterate is unqualifiedly bad and must be rectified. People of a certain age might remember the tale of Albert Edward Foreman, as told by W. Somerset Maugham in "The Verger" [40]. Foreman was fired from his low paying job as verger—a kind of janitor—at St. Peter's, Neville Square, when—shockingly—it was discovered that he could neither read nor write. Maugham then goes on at length describing Foreman's struggles to survive until he had in fact become quite rich. A bank officer suggests to Foreman that he transfer the money he has in a low interest-paying savings account into products that will earn him much more. But Foreman is hesitant. The banker assures him:

> You needn't have the least anxiety. We'll make you out a list of absolutely gilt-edged securities. They'll bring you in a better rate of interest than we can possibly afford to give you.
>
> A troubled look settled on Mr. Foreman's distinguished face. "I've never 'ad anything to do with stocks and shares and I'd 'ave to leave it all in your 'ands," he said.
>
> The manager smiled. "We'll do everything. All you'll have to do next time you come in is just to sign the transfers."
>
> I could do that all right, said Albert uncertainly. "But 'ow should I know what I was signin'?
>
> "I suppose you can read," said the manager a trifle sharply.
>
> Mr. Foreman gave him a disarming smile.
>
> Well, sir, that's just it. I can't. I know it sounds funny-like but there it is, I can't read or write, only me name, an' I only learnt to do that when I went into business.
>
> The manager was so surprised that he jumped up from his chair.
>
> That's the most extraordinary thing I ever heard.
>
> You see it's like this, sir, I never 'ad the opportunity until it was too late and then some'ow I wouldn't. I got obstinate-like.
>
> The manager stared at him as though he were a prehistoric monster.
>
> And do you mean to say that you've built up this important business and amassed a fortune of thirty thousand pounds without being able to read or write? Good God, man, what would you be now if you had been able to?
>
> I can tell you that sir," said Mr. Foreman, a little smile on his still aristocratic features. "I'd be verger of St. Peter's, Neville Square. [40]

The following excerpts from "The Song of Lawino" by Okot p'Bitek of Uganda vividly reveal the way some people still living in largely oral cultures feel about the imposition of literacy:

> Listen, my clansmen,
> I cry over my husband
> Whose head is lost.
> Ocol has lost his head
> In the forest of books.
> When my husband
> Was still wooing me
> His eyes were still alive,
> His ears were still unblocked,
> Ocol had not yet become a fool
> My friend was a man then …

My husband was still a Black man
The son of the Bull
The son of Agik ... .
The papers on my husband's desk
Coil threateningly ... .
They are tightly interlocked
Like the legs of the giant forest climbers
In the impenetrable forest.
My husband's house
Is a mighty forest of books,
Dark it is and very damp,
The steam rising from the ground
Hot thick and poisonous
Mingles with the corrosive dew
And the rain drops
That have collected in the leaves ... .
O, my clansmen,
Let us all cry together!
Come,
Let us mourn the death of my husband ... .
For the Prince
The heir to the Stool is lost!
And all the young men
Have perished in the wilderness!
And the fame of this homestead
That once blazed like a wild fire
In a moonless night
Is now like the last breaths
Of a dying old man!
...
Bile burns my inside!
I feel like vomiting!
For all our young men
Were finished in the forest,
Their manhood was finished
In the class-rooms,
Their testicles
Were smashed
With large books! [45]

2.3.2 A Note on Women, Literacy, and Power

Belinda Jack, in *Woman Reader,* writes: "Women's access to the written word has been a particular source of anxiety for men—and indeed some women—almost from the very beginning ... . For much of history it was this fear of women assuming greater power that caused the most unease" [32, p. 1]. She adds that concerns about reading have to do with "the ultimate secrecy of reading: no-one outside the reader can know what is going on in the reader's mind, or indeed body, and no-one can know what difference the reading experience may make to his or her thoughts or behaviour. Lone reading is an inherently antisocial activity and the onus on women has been, and often remains, to be sociable and to facilitate easy human relations. Reading is intensely private and literally self-centered" [32, p. 6].

Here again, Jack focuses on the medium as the massage and not on the message that women are reading—the very act of reading is subversive of women's "proper" role. But the message is important, too. Although Jack says that reading induces hidden thoughts, it is what reading might do to a woman's body that is the more subversive. This raises the specter of the eroticizing potential of new media that we noted above about the printing press vs. the hand-copied book. The woman reader both thinks and feels, and might act on her feelings provoked by the private nature of reading in ways she might not while listening in public where such provocative images are not likely to be shared in the first place.

In probably all communities, writing was initially restricted to a very small number of people. Even after writing was known we have seen that most people still lived entirely within the lingering oral society. In fact, the ability to read and write often did not initially bestow much power or prestige on those who were literate. Indeed, early writers were seen more as servants than as masters. Jack points out that "Scribes were readers for the illiterate," functioning "as notaries, accountants, archivists, secretaries and bureaucrats. But more interestingly, they also acted as paid readers, working for their non-literate patrons and superiors." At the present time, "literacy seems to us so fundamental to authority and power … that it is hard to understand a society in which the literate, including some women, were seen merely as servants or craftspeople in an otherwise almost exclusively oral culture … . The deity responsible for the protection of scribes was not a god but a goddess, Nisaba. Her symbol or attribute was a stylus, suggesting that writing and recording were the scribe's primary activity" [32, p. 28].

Geoffrey Roper says this about women and writing in Islamic societies:

> Inevitably in traditional society, most scribes, whether professionals or amateurs, were male. Yet there exist a surprising number of references to women performing this role. Some caliphs and other rulers employed female servants or slaves as calligraphers or as secretaries. Poets and writers also sometimes employed bondwomen to transcribe their works; other Muslim women were themselves poets or scholars who produced their own MSS. Even some fine Qur'āns are known to have been copied by female calligraphers, and in tenth-century Córdoba there were reported to be 170 women occupied in writing Qur'āns in the Kufic script. Much later, in sixteenth-century Iran, a traveller claimed that 'the women of Shiraz are scribes … in every house in this city the wife is a copyist.' (Būdāq Qazwīnī, quoted in Déroche, 192) With all due allowance for exaggeration, these references indicate that book production was by no means an exclusively male domain in traditional Muslim societies. [47]

Nonetheless, as literacy spread, Belinda Jack notes that concerns about its influences increased as well. "In Japan, in the early seventeenth century, the rise of print culture caused anxieties about the increasingly affordable reading material available to women" [32, p 3]. "What has been deemed 'acceptable' women's reading, on the other hand, has often been the same across time and space. In ancient Rome, women's literacy was tolerated or even encouraged provided it constituted a moral training (including strictures on virginity or marital fidelity), or led to women more able to fulfill their role as teachers, particularly of their sons, or if it made them more competent managers of sometimes large households" [32].

Similarly, it is worth noting, concerning literacy and orality in Africa, that "Herbert Chimhundu argues that the gender behavioural patterns embedded in Shona oral art forms are primarily ones that urge conformity to established roles for women and emphasize virtues such as docility, kindness, and generosity and qualities of beauty, fitness and known ancestry. They discourage independence and participation in public life for women and to do this often call up the oppositional images of women as mothers, *madzimai*, and women as prostitutes, *mahure*. The latter is an image associated with women and urban life which runs through Shona written literature" [25, p. 13]. And, "Language is seen by Chimhundu as a conservative factor especially as it is articulated in proverbs and various song genres" [25, p. 13].

A key difference here is the fact that oral admonitions are public utterances whose contents are known and thus can be corrected or supported, while books and pamphlets are read in private, and perhaps in secret, with their content secret and undisputed as well.

"At the same time," Belinda Jack continues, "there was a widespread awareness that literate women were proof of their father or husband's social status, as they were evidence of the family wealth that had provided both tutors and, more importantly, the leisure time necessary for reading. These same criteria applied to women's reading in Europe and the New World in the nineteenth century. Being seen to be reading the right kind of book became something of considerable social importance" [32, p. 4].

From ancient times on, when not altogether convinced or charmed by their reading, some women readers have been prompted to write, modifying a vision or proposing a radically different one. Some of the most fascinating traces of women's reading are in their rewritings, often of works by men [32, p. 11].

2.3.3 A Note on the Korean Alphabet and the Redistribution of Power

Writing was introduced into Korea from China, and with it came both writing in Chinese and writing Korean with Chinese characters. The Korean language is not particularly suitable for writing with Chinese ideographs, and so for Koreans to learn how to read and write at that time was a very long and difficult process that only a few of the ruling elite mastered. To the extent most official written governmental, commercial, and religious affairs were in Chinese or Chinese-written Korean, only a few people were able to understand and communicate in the official medium. Official writing was "Greek" to the ordinary Korean, and so governance was carried out in an unintelligible code beyond the comprehension of most Koreans. This also meant that Korean society, its governance and most profound thoughts, was easily dominated by China. The only "real" culture was Chinese, most elite Koreans believed. Korea had no "culture," except in imitation of the Chinese. That belief both enabled China to easily dominate Korea and for Koreans to feel worthy of domination because of their backwardness.

All of this changed after the Korean alphabet was invented and introduced by King Sejong in 1443. Ki-Moon Lee states that "The Korean alphabet is not an ordinary writing system. The history of world writing is in general a story of borrowing the writing system of a neighboring people, changing it a little, then employing this adapted system to record a new language … . The Korean alphabet, however, is a distinct exception to this generalization. As a completely new creation, it was unquestionably an 'invention.'" [36, p. 19].

S. Robert Ramsey says that "unlike other great reformers in history, Sejong did not enforce use of the new script, nor did he punish those officials who had openly opposed it. It took over a hundred years before *han'gul* [the new alphabet] took root in Korean society, and then largely among those at a remove from social and political power, such as women and Buddhists. Nonetheless, we can imagine that this fate would have pleased him. More than once he urged men of learning to teach the people; as he interpreted Confucian thought, it was education that brought out the basic goodness of human nature. He believed that everyone, including women and girls, should be given the ability to read and write, and for that purpose his script reform succeeded admirably" [45, p. 26].

There was initially great opposition to the new mode of writing. Since the creation of writing different from Chinese characters on the one hand meant, politically, the loss of special privilege and on the other, culturally, the estrangement from China, it is not at all surprising that the memorial submitted to the King by the Ch'oe Malli faction in opposition to the new writing system pointed out exactly these two things:

> Although from ancient times customs and local usages have differed within the Nine Isles, there has never been a case of one of them separately making a script based on the local speech. Only types like the Mongolians, Tanguts, Jurchen, Japanese, and Tibetans have their own graphs. But these are matters of the barbarians and not worth talking about. It has traditionally been said, 'Change the barbarians using Chinese ways'; we have never heard of changing towards barbarousness. Through the successions of ages, China has always regarded our country as having the bequeathed customs of Kija, but in matters of culture, literary and material, and in ritual and music, we have rather taken after China. To now separately make the Vernacular Script is to discard China and identify ourselves with the barbarians. This is what is called 'throwing away the fragrance of storax and choosing the bullet of the praying mantis.' This is most certainly a matter of great implication for our civilization!
>
> If you put the Vernacular Script into practice, then it will be the Vernacular Script that clerks will exclusively study. They will have no regard for learning. The clerks and the officials will diverge from one another and form two classes with respect to writing. If those who are to become clerks can gain positions with the Vernacular Script, then those who advance afterwards will see that it's like this and regard knowledge of the twenty-seven-letter Vernacular Script as enough to establish themselves in the world. Why should they have to strain their minds and labor their thoughts going through the study of 'Nature and Patterns' [in Song Learning]! After several decades of this there certainly won't be very many people who know characters. They might be able to use the Vernacular Script in their application to clerkly matters, but if they don't know the writings of the sages and worthies, 'they won't study, their faces will be to the wall.' They will be blind with respect to right and wrong in the Pattern of things. They will be futilely expert in the Vernacular Script. But what use can be made of that! The Culture of the Right which our country has amassed and accumulated will gradually come to be swept from the earth. [36, pp. 25–26]

To this strong line of reasoning, King Seong replied in part, "The sounds of our country's language are different from those of the Middle Kingdom and are not confluent with the sounds of characters. Therefore, among the ignorant people, there have been many who, having something they want to put into words, have in the end been unable to express their feelings. I have been distressed because of this and have newly designed twenty-eight letters, which I wish to have everyone practice at their ease and make convenient for their daily use" [36, p. 27].

The change of script helped produce the change in society that King Seong wanted. Seldom has the reality of shifting power as a consequence of shifting communication technologies been so clearly revealed!

2.4 The Printing Press, Governance, and Power

The next big mutative step in communication and governance was the printing press. Though a printing press was known first in China and Korea, and played a role in forming the political economy of those cultures, it was the printing press (and auxiliary developments) of Gutenberg and others in Europe from the mid-fifteenth century that is the better example of how changing communication technologies revolutionized power within long-established societies. In terms of the content it produced, the printing press enabled the spread and success of the Protestant Reformation, the flowering of old Greek and Roman knowledge as new knowledge that energized the Renaissance, the creation of the Westphalian nation-state system, the cosmologies of Copernicus, Bacon, and Newton and other ideas and technologies of the modern scientific-industrial revolution, culminating in the maturing of theories of "democratic" governance of Hobbes, Montesquieu, Locke, Rousseau, and others.

But, as we have shown with other communication technologies, probably the more important impact of the printing press is in ways of thinking and perceiving oneself, one's community, and one's world.

Among the first scholars to discuss the mutative role of the printing press was Elizabeth Eisenstein whose, *The Printing Press as an Agent of Change: Communications and Cultural Transformations in Early Modern Europe*, was a stunning eye-opener when I first encountered it shortly after its publication. Coming a decade after my engagement with the person and ideas of Marshall McLuhan (initially his book, *The Medium is the Massage,* Bantam Books, 1967, and an amazing phonograph album based on it) and my writing of "Non-verbal, non-numerical models and media in political science," *American Behavioral Scientist,* May 1968 [11], Eisenstein's work [19] led me to redouble my research in the line of inquiry that has led to this very moment of writing [12, 13]. From a more conventional mode of scholarship than that of McLuhan that I first knew, Eisenstein confirmed, deepened, and broadened my understanding of the role that changing communication technologies played in social change generally. I was not the only one. When I returned to her work for this current project, I discovered that there were scores of scholars who had been as influenced by her as I had been. She was the object of almost fulsome praise, adoration, and defense, as well as the object of some unseemly vitriolic scholarly criticism. However her admirers seem to vastly outnumber her detractors.

We have relied here mainly on the second edition of her more recent volume, *The Printing Revolution in Early Modern Europe,* where she says, "I have written a review essay to serve as an 'afterword' to this edition. It discusses some of the questions posed and issues raised since the publication of *The Printing Press as an Agent of Change* 25 years ago and provides references to recent studies in order to supplement the selected reading list, which has been retained from the first abridged edition" [20].

Eisenstein herself acknowledges that it was reading McLuhan's *The Gutenberg Galaxy* that set her onto trying to understand the social impact of the printing press [20]. She expected to find a vast literature to master but found almost nothing. She was especially astounded to see how few historians, writing their histories of Europe or the world, do anything more than mention the printing press in passing, giving it little or no special importance. Some historians of the period don't mention it at all: "To my surprise, I did not find even a small literature available for consultation. No one had yet attempted to survey the consequences of the fifteenth-century communications shift" [20, p. xv].

It needs to be said at the outset that Eisenstein [18–20] is a tireless advocate of the view that changing communication technologies change power relations in societies, meaning not just the printing press, but most emphatically that. She repeats that point over and over in her writing, always also expressing amazement that so many scholars of history fail to notice it. This leads them to puzzle over many aspects of late medieval/early modern European history that she believes can best be understood by referring to the impact of the printing press: "The advent of an 'industrial' society is too often made responsible for conditions that were shaped by the momentum of an ongoing revolution in communications" [20, p. 112]. She continues, "To leave printing out of the picture is not only to conceal significant links but also to overlook important disjunctions" [20, p. 300]. Additionally, she argues, "One cannot treat printing as just one among many elements in a complex causal nexus, for the communications shift transformed the nature of the causal nexus itself. It is of special historical significance because it produced fundamental alterations in prevailing patterns of continuity and change. On this point one must take strong exception to the views expressed by humanists who carry their hostility to technology so far as to deprecate the very tool which is most indispensable to the practice of their own crafts" [20, p. 308].

In exhaustive detail (that has spurred many scholars to go into even more detail in elaboration of her pioneering work) she demonstrates over and over again that "Intellectual and spiritual life, far from remaining unaffected, was profoundly transformed by the multiplication of new tools for duplicating books in fifteenth-century Europe. The communications shift altered the way Western Christians viewed their sacred book and the natural world. It made the words of God appear more multiform, and His handiwork more uniform. The printing press laid the basis both for literal fundamentalism and for modern science. It remains indispensable for humanistic scholarship. It is still responsible for our museum without walls" [20, p. 309].

The printing press was also one of the key drivers for the emergence of copyright and intellectual copyright law. As May and Sell observe, "Many of the legal innovations that laid the foundations for later copyright laws were first developed in the late fifteenth and early sixteenth century as the extensive Venetian publishing industry oscillated between boom and bust" [41, p. 57]. Although copyright and intellectual property (IP) has a long and storied history, it was not until the 1700s that specific legal frameworks emerged giving birth to the "author." Noting the critical importance of the 1710 Statute of Anne, Rose explains, "This act was, in part, a legislative extension of the long-standing regulatory practices of the Stationers' Company, the ancient London guild of printers and booksellers. Yet there were two major innovations: the statute limited the term of protection (the guild copyrights were perpetual) and authors were legally recognized as possible proprietors of their works (previously only members of the guild could hold copyrights)" [48, p. 4]. Rights of and for "authors," which was certainly driven by the development and diffusion of the printing press, has only become more complicated as new technologies blur familiar lines. But, did the printing press change power relations?

In a point very important for our interest in understanding if and how changing communication technologies change power relations in society, Eisenstein clearly states that "when referring to printing as 'an agent of change,' I had in mind that historical change, in and of itself, is indeterminate, always contingent on numerous factors and usually compatible with movement in diverse directions. Thus the increased availability of vernacular Bibles to readers at large, the provision of polyglot versions to a scholarly elite, and the reactions of Roman churchmen to both developments did not point Western religion in any one direction. But however contradictory these three developments were, they shared in common the fact that they represented change" [20, p. 333]. Indeed, very big social change. Our research in this project strongly corroborates Eisenstein's contention here.

Similarly, Eisenstein emphatically denies advocating any kind of "technological determinism." She writes: "'To describe the printing press as an agent of change,' writes Michael Warner in an influential critique, 'is to make the mistake of privileging a particular technology over culture and worse, to assume that technology is prior to culture.'" [20, p. 356] We have shown above that this charge is frequently made by scholars who stress the importance of culture over technology to explain social stability and change. Eisenstein vigorously rejects Warner's allegation, replying that her repeated use of "scribal culture" and "printing culture" shows she understands that technology and culture are tightly interwoven. Indeed, all her examples show how culture (and human decisions) affects how printing impacts specific societies, and vice versa—perhaps similar to the way the environment influences how and if certain genes are expressed. Which is more important, biology or the environment? Neither, since each is engulfed in and in some ways causative of the other. So also with technology and culture.

At the same time, she stresses that printing was "*an* agent, not *the* agent, let alone *the only* agent of change in Western Europe" [20, p. xvii]. Moreover, "the notion that [social change] could ever be reduced to nothing, but a communications shift strikes me as absurd" [20, p. xix]. Similarly, she makes clear that impact was made by more than the hardware of the printing press alone. "We will take the term 'printing' to serve simply as a convenient label, a shorthand way of referring to a cluster of innovations (entailing the use of movable metal type, oil-based ink, wooden hand-press, and so forth)" [20, p. 14]. Eisenstein is here indicating at the importance of other hardware that facilitated the printing press.

However, we will show that Eisenstein does not specifically discuss any examples of the software or orgware surrounding the printing press, without which the printing press alone would have had little or no impact at all. We take this to demonstrate the utility of the broader definition of technology with which we began this monograph. By focusing on the hardware alone, the greater influence of the technology, in its software and orgware, may go unnoticed, and thus the impact of the technology overall be considerably unrecognized and thus unappreciated. This omission can be particularly important when one wishes to "transfer" a technology from one culture to another. Again, by focusing only on hardware, the profound influence of software and orgware of the technology will not be noticed, and the impact of the transfer be much different—for good or ill—from what was anticipated.

So in what ways did the invention and rapid diffusion of the printing press broadly understood impact Europe? It is difficult to know where to start, the places and mode of impact are so numerous. Let's again emphasize the distinction between the impact of the *substance* of what is being communicated from the impact of the *form* of communication itself—the distinction between the impact of the message vs. the impact of the medium. We will start by considering the impact of some of the messages.

The vital role that the printing press played in the Protestant Reformation has been frequently commented on. However, "although the anti-Turkish crusade was thus the 'first religious movement' to make use of print, Protestantism surely was the first fully to exploit its potential as a mass medium … . Luther himself described printing as 'God's highest and extremist act of grace, whereby the business of the Gospel is driven forward'" [20, p. 165]. "The art of Printing will so spread knowledge, that the common people, knowing their own rights and liberties will not be governed by way of oppression and so, little by little, all kingdoms will be like to Macaria [a Utopia]" [20, p. 168].

At first, the press was viewed as a good thing by all involved. But, "Gutenberg's invention probably contributed more to destroying Christian concord and inflaming religious warfare than any of the so-called arts of war ever did," and it led to religious and political fundamentalism as well as to modern science [20, p. 176].

Eisenstein repeatedly stresses the difference between Catholic and Protestant behavior, and not just attitudes, towards the science the printing press facilitated as well. She cites many examples of Protestant authorities saying they were opposed to, and of Catholics saying they supported, some new scientific book or other, but the specific policies in the two groups appear very different. On the basis of the evidence she presents, Protestants tended to be much more liberal in the books they permitted to be printed and distributed, while Catholics were much less so in actual practice.

Moreover, the impact of the press on the religious beliefs and practices of ordinary people was markedly different from the impact of science on them. "Protestant's use of the press made religion more accessible to the people, empowering them, while science, for Protestant and Catholic alike, relying on mathematics and arcane terms, remained remote and mysterious to most people—to this very day, perhaps because of choices made at the time" [20, p. 306].

It would be a huge mistake to assume that the subject matter of the early printing presses was primarily religious, philosophical or scientific texts, or other publications of piety and intellect. The "contemplative attitudes associated formerly with spiritual devotion also accompanied the perusal of scandal sheets, 'lewd Ballads,' 'merry bookes of Italic,' and other "corrupted tales in Inke and Paper" [20, p. 104].

Indeed, this is a good place to point that much, perhaps most, of what was originally printed—and that most certainly made the most money—was not the Bible or other religious or educational material, and most emphatically not scientific tomes. It was job printing. Peter Stallybrass observes that the "printed calendars and indulgences that were first issued from the Mainz workshops of Gutenberg and Fust ... warrant at least as much attention as the more celebrated Bible" [51, p. 315]. "The first dated text that survives from Gutenberg's press is not a book but an indulgence" [51, p. 315]. "Gutenberg was already printing his great Bible when he stopped working on it to print 2,000 copies of his thirty-line indulgence in 1454–5. He undertook this work because it was paid for upfront and brought an immediate cash return" [51, p. 316]. By following the money, so to speak, "Gutenberg both kept afloat and subsidized his larger project by printing broadsides" [51, p. 316]. Records show the same was true for all other printers of the time. Even centuries later, Benjamin Franklin said that "the 'little Jobs' took precedence over prestigious folios, because the 'little Jobs' regularly injected cash into the notoriously undercapitalized book trade" [51, p. 324].

Stallybrass also makes another very important point, often overlooked—what did printers actually print for the most part? "Our obsession with literacy rates has tended to obscure the extent to which many printed sheets fulfill their function without being read .... I would argue," he says, "that printing's most revolutionary effect was on manuscript. If we define manuscript in terms of all writing by hand as opposed to the kind of manuscripts that have been the main object of study, we might begin to see that the history of printing is crucially a history of the 'blank'"— that is, of printed forms designed to be filled in by hand. Stallybrass devotes much of his essay to discussing them [51, p. 340].

This interesting though seemingly unimportant comment may be the key to understanding why print cultures spread so quickly in Europe, but not elsewhere, a point we will explore briefly below. Here we note only that in terms of volume and income, most of what was printed by the early presses in Europe were forms, announcements, advertisements, calendars, and the like—things of considerable commercial value without in any direct way being fomenters of revolutionary religious or secular ideas.

As one example of her failure to pay adequate attention to orgware, Eisenstein mentions, but does not discuss in the detail she does many other things, the "rise of the fourth estate" as a powerful new social force [20, p. 110]. The creation of "the press" as a countervailing institution between government and civil society surely is one of the major examples of how the printing press altered power relations as they had been in scribal societies. It was difficult to imagine, much less demand and then achieve, free speech or "freedom of the press" until the press existed as an independent interest group and political force that could exercise and profit from such freedom. Yet she does not discuss this development at all except to mention it in passing.

Eisenstein does, however, stress the fact, often overlooked, that the printing press enhanced visual literacy as much as it did word literacy: "Protestant propaganda exploited printed image no less than printed word—as numerous caricatures and cartoons may suggest. Even religious imagery was defended by some Protestants, and on the very grounds of its compatibility with print culture. Luther himself commented on the inconsistency of iconoclasts who tore pictures off walls while handling the illustrations in Bibles reverently" [20, p. 40]. In another sphere, that of pictures and engravings in scientific texts, "[I]t was not the 'printed word' but the 'printed image' which acted as a 'savior for Western science' in George Sarton's view," Eisenstein states [20, p. 42]. She stresses that it was often the illustrations in the books that made the biggest impact on people's consciousness by making them visually aware of and thus psychologically participative in events far away in places they would never actually visit. "The effect of duplicating images and portraits of rulers—which were eventually framed and hung in peasant hovels throughout Catholic Europe, along with saints and icons—has yet to be assessed by political scientists" [20, p. 108]. As political scientists, we duly note this and suggest this served to strengthen the appeal and bonds of nationalism.

So far, we have focused on the *content* of what was printed as being the major impact of the press. But it would be a serious error to assume that is the most important, let alone only, reason that the printing press served as an agent of social change in Europe. Regardless of what the subject matter was, the printing press had revolutionary impacts on human thinking and acting independent of the material printed.

One point Eisenstein makes frequently in her writing is that "during the millennia that intervened between the invention of writing and the introduction of printing in the West, it never took fewer than ten scribes to feed one clerk. The production, collection, and circulation of books were subject to an economy of scarcity. Recovery and preservation were naturally of paramount concern. Within a century after the installation of printing shops in Western Europe, however, even while old texts reflecting problems of scarcity were becoming more available, a new economy of abundance began to make its presence felt" [20, p. 334]. Within a generation, the vast scribal industry that had flourished for centuries was gone. A few impersonal printing presses took its place: another impact of technology as orgware—because, though they were thrown out of one line of work, now all scribes could look for jobs in the many positions needed in the new, rapidly expanding printing industry.

For all of prior history even the most diligent scholar would never read in a lifetime what almost all serious scholars could master as young students after the printing press. Before, manuscripts were rare and scattered, so that the scholar might spend a lifetime wandering about looking for and pleading to read the few books available. After printing, increasingly, all the books in the world could come into any scholar's own personal library. Scholarship no longer meant spending a lifetime reading and re-reading one or two available texts. It meant collecting, reading, synthesizing and producing new ideas gained from more and more texts. "The era of the glossator and commentator came to an end, and a new 'era of intense cross referencing between one book and another' began" [20, p. 47]. Similarly, "Less reliance on memory work and rote repetition in lecture halls also brought new mental talents into play. Printing enabled natural philosophers to spend more time solving brain teasers, designing ingenious experiments and new instruments, or even chasing butterflies and collecting bugs if they wished" [20, p. 269].

Eisenstein dramatically states that the transitional period between medieval and modern societies was "an elastic period encompassing some 300 years during which Western Europe is seen to have experienced the cultural equivalent of a chemical change of phase" [20, p. 126]. A "phase change" is almost a textbook definition of a transformation—a situation where flowing water "suddenly" and unexpectedly becomes steam, if heated, or ice if chilled; it is the butterfly inexplicably emerging from the cocoon the caterpillar spun. "The shift from script to print also involved a Europe-wide transformation which occurred in a relatively short span of time. In a few decades, printers' workshops were established in urban centers throughout Europe. By 1500, various effects produced by the output of printed materials were already being registered. Compared with the three centuries that stretch from 1250 to 1550 or 1300 to 1600, the age of incunabula is short indeed … . By 1500, one may say with some assurance that the age of scribes had ended and the age of printers had begun" [20, p. 127].

Nonetheless not everyone was equally impacted by the transformation. Then, as now, though many are able to acquire books, many do not, and only a few become serious book readers, with fewer still becoming book-based scholars. From the time of the emergence of writing and the scribal society, manuscripts were typically read out loud—whether in public or private—as though one were reciting from memory and not reading from texts. This continued for a long time after the invention of printing—down to the present day in some cultures. Nonetheless, as we have seen when commenting on reading and women, the trend after the printing press was for silent reading that facilitated privacy, individualism, intrigue, and revolution.

One feature of printing *per se* that made a big impact on thinking and acting—down through Henry Ford's industrial assembly line and beyond—was standardization. Duplicating exactly the same book by hand copying was nearly impossible. Mistakes, omissions, new material crept in almost every time a new copy was made. Of course, not each run of a printed book was identical to others, either. Mistakes were constantly being corrected in later editions, but "the fact remains that Erasmus or Bellarmine could issue errata; Jerome or Alcuin could not. The very act of publishing errata demonstrated a new capacity to locate textual errors with precision and to transmit this information simultaneously to scattered readers. It thus illustrates rather neatly some of the effects of standardization" [20, p. 56].

We saw earlier that with the emergence of literacy from orality, classificatory modes of scholarship were enhanced by writing because now ideas could be more easily decontextualized, studied, compared, and rank-ordered. Eisenstein elucidates this in a section titled, "Some effects produced by reorganizing texts and reference guides: Rationalizing, codifying and cataloguing data [20, p. 71]. She gives as one example the fact that "printed reference works encouraged a repeated recourse to alphabetical order" [20, p. 72] that resulted in a still-thriving data-retrieval system—made redundant first by random "key word" searches and now by "big data" algorithms.

Many of the conventions of printing that we take for granted now arose with the printing press: "regularly numbered pages, punctuation marks, section breaks, running heads, indexes … arabic numbers for pagination … more accurate indexing, annotation, and cross referencing resulted. Most studies of printing have, quite rightly, singled out the regular provision of title pages as the most significant new feature associated with the printed book format" [20, p. 81].

Roger Chartier says that "if one is to find an analogy in the *longue duree* history of writing and reading, one should look at the invention of the codex. By replacing the scroll with the new book form, this revolution, largely forgotten or unacknowledged except by specialists, is the one that led to practices that are still ours today and that were completely impossible with the scroll—for example, leafing through a book, quickly locating a passage, using an index, and writing while reading," all things not easily done with scrolls that the codex form of the book made easier [6, p. 407].

Printing also made a substantial impact by improving preservation. Single handwritten manuscripts were easily lost, stolen, burned, or destroyed by water, mold, bugs, or rats. The only way to preserve a manuscript was to hand copy it, which introduced the probability of errors with every subsequent copy, as we saw before. With the printing press, a single manuscript could be printed in multiple copies, stored in many libraries, and reprinted when necessary.

The role of printing in creating both nations and standardizing their languages should be acknowledged as one of its most important contributions. Again, Eisenstein quotes Steinberg: "Printing 'preserved and codified, sometimes even created' certain vernaculars. Its absence during the sixteenth century among small linguistic groups 'demonstrably led' to the disappearance or exclusion of their vernaculars from the realm of literature … . The preservation of a given literary language often depended on whether or not a few vernacular primers, catechisms or Bibles happened to get printed" [20, p. 92]. "Typography arrested linguistic drift, enriched as well as standardized vernaculars, and paved the way for the more deliberate purification and codification of all major European languages" [20, p. 93].

The printing press was also responsible for another kind of "fixity": Until the advent of printing, the revival of classical thought in ancient Greek and Roman manuscripts sometimes happened locally, but quickly faded. With the printing press, the number of classical texts known multiplied, and their effects became a major feature in the revolution of thought at the time.

The printing press saw the invention of the "author." Previously, one was a scribe (copier), a compiler, or a commentator—not a promulgator of one's own ideas. Initially the term "author" seems to have been given to a person who "writes both his own work and others' but with his own work in principal place … " [20, p. 95]

"The new forms of authorship and literary property rights undermined older concepts of collective authority in a manner that encompassed not only biblical composition but also texts relating to philosophy, science, and law" [20, p. 96].

Printing also allowed certain once-novel ideas to become repeated and amplified endlessly so that "over the course of time, archetypes were converted into stereotypes, the language of giants, as Merton puts it, into the clichés of dwarfs" [20, p. 100].

Repeatedly, Einstein makes clear that the impacts of the printing press on Europe might have been different in other cultural contexts. "The early presses, which were established between 1460 and 1480, were powered by many different forces which had been incubating in the age of scribes. In a different cultural context, the same technology might have been used for different ends (as was the case in China and Korea) or it might have been unwelcome and not been used at all (as was the case in many regions outside Europe where Western missionary presses were the first to be installed) … . Under different circumstances, moreover, it might have been welcomed and put to entirely different uses—monopolized by priests and rulers, for example, and withheld from free-wheeling urban entrepreneurs. Such counterfactual speculation is useful for suggesting the importance of institutional context when considering technological innovation. Yet the fact remains … " [20, pp. 308–309] that the facts remain.

In her 2006 "Afterword," Eisenstein states that when she wrote the first version of her book, commenting on the fact that communication technologies were changing, and changing society in revolutionary ways, that she was referring to Xerox as the big new mutative technology. The only copy of her original manuscript had been on carbon paper. Xerox was going to change all that! 20 years on, in 2006, Xerox was a rapidly obsolescing technology.

That is indeed one of the most interesting things that comes from reading all the sources about the printing press as an instrument of social change: When they do comment on the future impact of the electronic technologies of the time they are writing, their ideas seem quaint and even misguided in light of what we think is happening now. As will the forecasts of this monograph not too far into the futures.

2.4.1 Printing, Power, and Islam

We have seen that the printing press spread like wildfire shortly after its invention in 1450 in Mainz, Germany, and within a short period of time profoundly transformed western Europe, splitting the waning influence of the once truly "Catholic" Church into many often murderously conflicting factions. Nationalism, nation-states, national languages, new occupations, and new ways of governing, learning, and even thinking soon replaced ways millennia old. The story in Islamic societies is quite different. "Print did not begin to become established in the Islamic world until the nineteenth century … " [46, p. 233] Geoffrey Roper puts the issue even more squarely: "Why was book printing not adopted by Muslims for more than 1,000 years after it was invented in China and 250 years after it became widespread in western Europe (in spite of its use by non-Muslims in the Muslim world)?" [47]

Was it because the *ulama* (Muslim legal scholars) were concerned that the products of the printing press would foment religious discord, as they observed it do in Europe? Some researchers maintain that a late fifteenth-century edict was issued in Turkey declaring that "occupying oneself with the science of printing was punishable by death." While the authenticity of that decree is disputed, it has been frequently repeated and seems to capture the official sentiments of the time [8].

Was it because Islamic leaders were naturally suspicious of foreign products generally? If so, why did they embrace western military weapons so eagerly [8]? Not to mention tobacco [47, p. 234].

Roper agrees with Robinson, who says that "the problem was that printing attacked the very heart of Islamic systems for the transmission of knowledge; it attacked what was understood to make knowledge trustworthy, what gave it value, what gave it authority" [46, p. 235]. And, "At the heart of this system of transmission is the very essence of knowledge for the Muslim, the Quran. For Muslims the Quran is the word of God—His very word. It is more central to Islamic theology than the Bible is for Christians or the Torah is for Jews. It is the divine presence. It is the mediator of divine will and grace … . 'Quran' itself means 'recitation,' al-Quran, the recitation, the reading out loud. It is through being read out loud that the Quran is realized and received as divine. Muslims strive to learn as much of it as possible by heart. They recite it constantly through the daily rounds, at prayer times, through the passage of the year, most notably in the month of Ramadan, and through all the stages of life. It is like a sacrament, ever on their lips. For its words are not mere words. 'They are,' in Constance Padwick's magical phrase, 'the twigs of the burning bush aflame with God'" [46, p. 235].

A very important point here is that the Quran is said to derive directly from the lips of the Prophet. Although Muhammad is not the author of the Quran, the orthodox perspective on the text is that it is perfect copy of Allah's book in Heaven. They are the Prophet's very words, transmitted faithfully and fully as personally heard and repeated by his followers. "When, a few years after the Prophet's death, these messages came to be written down, it was only as an aid to memory and oral transmission. And this has been the function of the written Quran ever since" [46, p. 236].

This is completely different from the Christian New Testament. The New Testament was written in Greek by people who some say were divinely inspired, in the case of the Gospels, several hundred years after the death of Jesus. The Epistles of Paul and others were written closer to the time Jesus is said to have lived. But none of the writers whose thoughts are contained in the New Testament were direct auditors or direct transmitters from actual auditors of the exact words of the historical person called Jesus. No one can be sure what Jesus said, but one can be reasonably certain of what the Prophet said. However, given the way in which both the New Testament and the Quran were assembled and compiled over time, and as a consequence of internal conflicts and struggles among the compilers, reasonable doubt can exist about what both Jesus and the Prophet might have meant by the words attributed to them. Moreover, both the Prophet and Jesus (like Socrates and

Homer) were illiterate, dependent on others to document their words in writing. Jesus also spoke Aramaic and not the Greek in which the New Testament is originally written. The Quran is still written and read in the language the Prophet spoke.

As a consequence, "The oral transmission of the Quran has been the backbone of Muslim education. Learning the Quran by heart and then reciting it aloud has been traditionally the first task of young Muslim boys and girls." Moreover, all early Islamic books were "merely an aid to oral publication" [46, p. 236].

To be sure, Islam was not opposed to the written word *per se*. "'Good writing,' declares a tradition of the Prophet, 'makes the truth stand out.' Calligraphy is the highest of the Islamic arts. The beautiful writing of the words of God is the typical adornment of Islamic space. Yet, writing and literacy have always danced attendance on a superior oral tradition in the transmission of knowledge" [46, p. 237].

This applies to all Islamic knowledge, and not just the Quran. "Person to person transmission was at the heart of the transmission of Islamic knowledge. The best way of getting at the truth was to listen to the author himself. Muslim scholars constantly travelled across the Islamic world so that they could receive in person the reliable transmission of knowledge" [46, p. 238]. Very importantly, "No one was to read a book without the help of a scholar" [46, p. 243].

Ziauddin Sardar [49] says the third most frequent term in the Qur'an is *ilm* (knowledge). Knowledge—seeking it, obtaining it, analyzing it, expanding it, sharing it, preserving it, and seeking newer understandings of it—is central to Islam. Originally *ilm* was very broadly conceived, interpreted, and shared, but over the years it came to mean only certain parts of, often secret religious knowledge that few initiates could possess. How did this narrowing and freezing of such a fundamental concept happen?

Sardar reinforces what we have already learned so far—how very important handwritten texts are to Muslims—though we will see that he puts a different interpretation on this from what some others have concluded. He observes, "The first Muslim community, living in Medina, recorded the Qur'an on almost anything they could find: on papyrus, palm fibres, bone tablets, hides, white stones and parchment. The Prophet Muhammad himself had his important decisions documented. Nearly 300 of his documents have come down to us, including political treatises, military enlistments, assignments of officials and state correspondence written on tanned leather. Because he could not read and write himself the Prophet was constantly served by a group of 45 scribes who wrote down his sayings, instructions and activities" [49, p. 91]. After his death, an elaborate system was devised for obtaining and authenticating other teachings that had not been initially written down: "Each saying of the Prophet was traced through a chain of authoritative transmitters right to the lips of the Prophet Muhammad himself" [49, p. 92]. "The methodology of *hadith* collection and criticism, with all its precision and accuracy, combined with the Qur'anic emphasis on *ilm*, became the basis for a host of new scholarly and literary genres," [49, p. 93] leading to the flowering and spread of Islamic culture from the ninth through the thirteenth centuries.

This proliferation of Islamic culture was also "made possible by one of the most revolutionary events in Islamic history … the manufacture of paper" [49, p. 94].

The know-how for papermaking was acquired by Muslims from Chinese captured in Samarkand, but Muslims added numerous features that led to the improvement and mass production of paper, eventually exporting it to Europe in the late thirteenth century. The people who made and sold paper, published and sold books, and served as scribes, often became scholars in their own right. Centers of learning and eventually universities grew up around scholars and their libraries. Reading, writing, widespread research, scholarship, and creativity on every topic imaginable—*ilm*—flourished throughout the breadth of the Muslim world [2].

However, at the same time, some religious scholars (Sardar uses the spelling *ulema*) began to be concerned because wide readership was fostering widespread and differing interpretations of the meaning of what was being read. "The initial response of the *ulema* … was to undermine the concept of *ilm* itself … . *Ilm* was now transformed from meaning 'all knowledge' to meaning only 'religious knowledge'" [49, p. 99]. Eventually very strict rules for determining who could become an *ulema* (by the memorization of the entire Qur'an and of numerous other writings) were put in place. As Sardar explains, "All this had a devastating effect on Muslim culture. From a general and distributive concept, *ilm* became an exclusive and accumulative notion … . Muslim thought ossified and became totally obscurantist. Consequently, Muslim culture lost its dynamism and degenerated, while the Muslim community was transformed from an open to a closed society" [49, p. 100].

Into this stifling environment came the printing press. "Not surprisingly, the arrival of printing produced a hostile response from the *ulema*, who managed to resist the introduction of printing presses in Muslim countries for nearly three centuries. The mechanical reproduction of the word of God or material connected with it, they argued, was irreverent. Furthermore, they insisted that the only way to understand a text and retain its uncertain authority was to hear or read it aloud, phrase by phrase, by or in the presence of someone who has already mastered it, and to repeat and discuss it with such a master. The mass printing of books would lead not to understanding and appreciation of sacred and classical texts but to misrepresentation and misunderstanding" [49, p. 101].

This belief in the primacy of the spoken over the written is not much different, except perhaps in purity, fervor, and insistence, from learning everywhere in oral societies and scribal societies, including Europe before the printing press. As we have seen above, the spoken oath, along with a handshake, or with one hand on a Bible, persisted for years—right down to the present time. Even though my grandmother insisted that I learn to type, she also insisted that I handwrite all of my letters to her. It was impolite, too impersonal, for me to type them. Similarly, though the printing press played a role in the rapid drafting and dissemination of the Constitution of the United States in 1787–1789, the final document itself was handwritten, and not printed. It may be that the depth and persistence in Islam of preference for the oral and handwritten over the mechanically printed was extraordinary, but it was not unique. Robinson himself states "that the widespread printing of books was also not adopted in the Hindu, Chinese and Japanese worlds until the nineteenth century" [46, p. 240]

So why did the acceptance of printing finally happen? Roper and Robinson give somewhat different political reasons. Robinson says, "Muslims came to adopt printing only when they felt Islam itself was at stake and print was a necessary weapon in the defense of the faith" [46, p. 240]. Thus Muslims in India, where they were a minority, were among the first to set the Quran and other basic works into print so that the faithful could keep the faith pure in a hostile environment. In a culture where one is surrounded by everyone reciting the Quran, written copies are not so necessary. When most people around you are heathens, with their religious ideas freely available in cheap publications, it is necessary to see that yours is, too, so that younger generations will not forget the truth. Similar developments happened in Southeast Asia, Indonesia and Africa—wherever foreign imperial powers threatened Islamic culture.

One consequence of the spread of printed Islamic material was a deepening and intensifying of the pan-Islamic sense of the *ummah*—the global community of all believers. "Without the press this pan-Islamic horizon could never have been seriously explored," Robinson states [46]. At the same time, as the Quran and other sources were eventually translated and published in local vernacular and not in the original Arabic, the ultimate authority of the *ulama* was in fact seriously challenged and undermined by the abundance of printed materials, fewer and fewer of which were officially authenticated or whose reading was done in the presence of a proper teacher. Indeed, eventually there was a kind of "protestant Islamic revolution" led by people who freely interpreted the words of the Prophet, translated into their language, according to what those words meant to them presently reading them, and not as the orally transmitted tradition declared them to be and mean.

"By breaking the stranglehold of 1,200 years of oral transmission, by breaking the stranglehold of the madrasa-trained *ulama* on the interpretation of Islamic knowledge, print helped to make possible an era of vigorous religious experiment. Print came to be the main forum in which religious debate was conducted; it was an era of pamphlet wars and of religiously partisan newspapers and magazines … . The result was a rapid fluorescence of sectarianism" [46, p. 246]. In summary, Robinson concludes that "all these changes are results of what we might term the mass production effects of print. They are results of the revolution in access to knowledge that print makes possible" [46, p. 250].

Roper makes a slightly different political argument. He also contends that the initial resistance to printing was by Islamic rulers who resisted printing because "printing challenged the entrenched monopolies of intellectual authority enjoyed by the learned class (*'ulamā'*), and threatened to upset the balance between that authority and the power of the state" [47, p. 25]. Then, paradoxically a few centuries later, "this was indeed one important reason why printing was eventually sponsored, in the eighteenth and nineteenth centuries, by modernizing rulers. They wanted to create a new, broader military and administrative class, versed in modern sciences and knowledge, who could bolster the power of the state against both traditional hierarchies within and new threats from outside. The printing press was seen as an indispensable instrument for achieving this new order" [47, p. 26].

In terms of the focus of this monograph, both arguments vividly demonstrate that changing communication technologies did, or were thought they might, change power relations in societies, which some favored and others opposed. Few regarded the printing press as neutral. Although some considered it demonic, most understood it to be transformative. When the gates were open and books and other printed material poured forth in Islamic countries, "the ready availability of inexpensive copies of a standard authorized version of the Qur'ān transformed the attitude of many Muslims to the sacred text, and the uses to which they put it. Its function ceased to be primarily ritual and liturgical, and it came to be regarded as a direct source—not necessarily mediated by scholarly interpretation and authority—of guidance and wisdom in human affairs." And, "The new accessibility and role of the Qur'ān consequently led some believers to adopt fundamentalist attitudes to Qur'anic doctrine, with considerable consequences in the social and political spheres. Others, in contrast, gradually abandoned traditional scholastic and legal interpretations in favour of their own reconciliations of Qur'anic ethics with modern life and politics. This divergence remains an acute feature of modern Islam, reinforced by outside pressures and new sources of authority in what continues to be above all a book-based system of belief" [47, p. 39].

Cosgel et al. give an economic, game-theoretic explanation for both the resistance and the end of resistance to the printing press in Islam. Noting also the fact that the same rulers who successfully resisted the introduction of the printing press very eagerly embraced the introduction of western military weapons, they argue that the reason the Ottomans resisted the introduction of the printing press was because of the financial importance of Islam in the overall political economy of the empire. To allow the easy spread of new ideas by printing would undermine the authority of existing Islamic institutions and threaten the finances of the state. It was economic and not religious reasons that were primary for Islamic resistance to printing, they insist. The close relationship between Church and state in Europe had already been significantly loosened, Cosgel et al. point out, and there was thus no similar financial incentive for the state to forbid the introduction of new religious or scientific ideas. "The Ottomans eventually sanctioned printing in Arabic script in the eighteenth century after alternative sources of legitimacy emerged," Cosgel et al. point out [9, p. 2].

By the same token the Ottoman rulers welcomed advanced weaponry from the west since it served to consolidate and enhance their ability to rule over and extract revenue from their subjects. Cosgel et al. perform meticulous research and calculations to show that their economic analysis and reasoning is sound [9]. They question the explanations given by Roper, Robinson, and others as incapable of precise quantitative testing; that indeed some of the traditional, cultural, religious, even political reasons given seem vague and perhaps contradictory. Dittmar [16] took a similar quantitative approach in trying to determine if the printing press made a positive economic impact in Europe by showing that, controlling for other variables, the population of European cities that first used printing presses grew while those that did not have presses did not.

Nonetheless whether qualitative or quantitative, political or economic, the results seem to be the same—the printing press was a substantial agent of social change in the areas where it was able to flourish.

2.4.2 Note on Printing in China and Korea

As we have hinted, Gutenberg was not the first person to invent the printing press with movable type. This technology was known and used in China and Korea far earlier. That it did not have the same impact in those countries as it did in Europe is a good example of the fact that the mere existence of a piece of hardware is not in and of itself sufficient to produce social change. Pre-existing orgware may effectively resist it. Moreover, it was not because of cultural or intellectual "backwardness" that the printing press in Korea and China did not serve as the agent of change that its later counterpart did in Europe, as some observers have claimed.

As the title of a book by Thomas Francis Carter makes clear, printing *per se*—namely extensive woodblock printing—may have been invented in China and used in Korea and Japan before moving westward to Europe and elsewhere [5]. However, Kai-wing Chow observes that "in most standard histories of western European printing, the advent of print is fixed at the point when Gutenberg printed a Bible with movable type no later than 1456," ignoring the earlier existence of xylography, or woodblock-printed books [7]. Furthermore, "A recent study of the development of printing in China, Korea, Japan, and Europe has demonstrated that once woodblock printing was in use, printers experimented with movable type, first using wood movable type, then metal types" [7, p. 173]. In Europe, Chow says, woodblock printing was viewed as "art" for aesthetic expression and not as a mode of communication as it was in east Asia [7, pp. 175–180]. Consequently, he observes, "One is amazed at the ignorance about the history of printing in China found even among experts on the history of printing" [7, p. 185]. Chow asserts that the fact that Chinese and Korean writing required the printer to have a large number of complete Chinese ideographs compared to the ease of compilation that European languages, based on a small number of characters in the alphabet enabled, did not discourage Asians from using the printing press, as is sometimes said to be the case. He also quotes scholars who point out how inexpensive woodblock printed books were in China because of "abundance of wood and cheap labor for carving" [7, p. 186].

Another reason Chow gives to explain why the printing press did not come to dominate in China as it did in Europe was a matter of software. China did not need a press *per se* while Europe did. Western paper was made from rags and so was uneven and resistant to ink. Such paper needed a heavy press in order to imprint the ink successfully. Chinese paper, typically made from rice, was smoother and did not need heavy pressure to absorb the ink [7, p. 188]. Western sources often give cultural reasons for China's continued use of wood block printing, not acknowledging that there were good economic and material—software—reasons instead, Chow concluded [6, p. 187].

Similarly, in her introduction to *Printing and Book Culture in Late Imperial China*, Cynthia Brokaw also writes that, "Before the twentieth century, Chinese printing was dominated by xylography" [4, p. 8]. She continues, "To be sure, block printing was not the only technology available to Chinese printers … . Moveable-type printing had been developed in China as early as the eleventh century.

Xylography remained the preferred method, however" [4, p. 8]. And, "As long as carving costs remained low, xylography was the more attractive method for economically-minded publishers" [4, p. 9].

Brokaw goes on to give many reasons why xylography continued to prevail over movable-type printing in China until current times. For example, she points out that a western printer had to spend a great deal of money upfront to set up his business and buy his fonts and the press itself, compared to a Chinese woodblock printer. The westerner then tended to print things that required a long run of a single text or form. To reprint a book later required the time and expense of resetting each page of the entire book. "With woodblock printing … the greatest expenditure in the printing process was the initial carving of the blocks. This, however, might not be too onerous an expense, as block carving did not require long training or even literacy on the part of the carver. And once the blocks were carved, the printer could produce as many or as few copies of the text as he liked." If a new run of the same book was later required, "no new heavy investment in labor was required; he could simply print off the original blocks" [4, p. 9]. Moreover, printing in Chinese ideographs, being based on the meaning of the character and not its pronunciation, could be read by people in many languages other than Chinese. This provided an enormous market for Chinese books, while sale of books in European alphabetic languages were limited to people who could read each language [4, p. 11]. Brokaw elaborates on other such economic—software—reasons for the continued use of block printing in China.

The situation in Korea was slightly different, but with similar consequences. Korea learned woodblock printing from China and excelled in the art and craft so fully that many Korean publications became highly prized in China. Moreover, "In addition to the woodblock tradition, Koryo craftsmen, drawing upon their highly skilled metal-casting techniques, produced the world's first moveable metal type. Exactly when this happened is not known for certain. The first known use of moveable metal type was in 1234 to print twenty-eight copies of *Sanjong kogum yemun (Prescribed Ritual Texts of the Past and Present)*. This was more than two centuries before Gutenberg. Indeed, some historians have speculated that knowledge of Korean moveable metal type may have reached Europe and inspired the development of printing there. The Koreans, however, did not invent a printing press" [49, p. 114].

2.4.3 The Printing Press, Constitutionalism, and Logo Fundamentalism

Certain words—and often words *per se*—are believed to have magical powers in most oral and scribal societies. It turns out that the belief that words are magical is found in modern print-based societies as well and has not diminished even now that words can be spread at the speed of light.

Although few people in "developed" nations may believe that their "curse" or "swear" words actually cast a solemn spell on anyone—"God Damn You" doesn't really mean that for most people—"the seven dirty words you can't say on television" or in a classroom, or in front of "ladies," and the like still have the strong force of law and custom behind them. They are just too powerful. There are also "fighting words" that should never be uttered, but if they are, give leave for the auditor to exterminate the utterer.

The example of religious fundamentalism based on the infallibility of the Bible or other religious texts has been amply illustrated above. But there is economic fundamentalism as well, with Adam Smith's *The Wealth of Nations* being the sacred text (though seldom actually read) for free market neoliberalism, as well as political fundamentalism that is best exemplified in the reverence in which many Americans—not only Tea Party sectarians but also some justices of the US Supreme Court—hold the sacred words of the American Constitution.

Fortuitously, Britain's American colonies in revolt provided the *tabula rasa* upon which was realized the extraordinary notion of "constituting" a new nation by assembling a group of highly privileged men to discuss and then eventually write down a set of basic governing principles for the newly imagined United States. Informed by Greek and Roman classics, and based on cutting edge ideas and technologies of the day—especially Newtonian mechanics, deistic theology, and the hand-powered printing press (steam-powered printing presses did not come into existence until about 30 years after the United States did)—the US Constitution was a breathtaking social invention, brilliantly overcoming a host of design challenges, though by no means all of them, while creating serious future problems as well. It was designed for, and fit for, a vast, overwhelmingly agricultural society with a small, widely scattered rural population of semi-illiterate farmers and plantation owners, many of whom wanted political independence from their mother country, far, far away.

The fundamental principles of "constitutionalism" have been widely copied. Since 1789, there have been very many opportunities for polities to envision and fashion new forms of governance—the governments of the internal American states themselves; the political revolutions in England, France, and elsewhere in Europe in the nineteenth centuries; Russia in 1918; Japan, Germany, and other "Axis" nations after the Second World War; numerous former colonies in South America, Africa, the Middle East, and Asia, also after the Second World War; the collapse of socialist systems in 1990; the attempt to create a European union; and most recently "nation-building" opportunities after the United States has brought down existing tyrannical governments.

In almost every case, people sat down and wrote a constitution, unreflexively imitating the Newtonian mechanistic and rationalistic assumption of the late eighteenth century, and acting as though the only communication technologies available for governance are still the printing press and the spoken word. "Representatives" are still expected physically to assemble somewhere in a central location, debate policies, and "make law" (itself a very modern pretense, compared to the older understanding of "discovering law") by writing down their decisions, which are subsequently to be administered by bureaucratized humans and enforced by officers of the law backed by the threat or use of deadly force. Most nation-states still preserve and expand their "right" and ability to destroy other nation-states.

Internally, disputes are formally resolved in courts of law where people specially trained in the meaning of the words of laws and constitutions verbally battle it out in front of judges who are elevated in every sense of the word. In some places, there are special courts with special judges who have, or have usurped, the exclusive right to determine the meaning of the words in the written law and written constitution.

Certain printed words (and those who wield and interpret them) have thus obtained over time a kind of arcane, magical, holy, superhuman power vastly exceeding that of other printed words. When the power of these words seems to fail, instead of reaching beyond the logo-centric cosmologies and technologies that underlie them, and trying to base social order on newer cosmologies and technologies, most people, rulers and ruled alike, look for stronger words and more powerful, more magical, phrases.

The documents intended to form the basis of the European Union are stubbornly logo-centric. It is no wonder that whenever young people in Europe have a chance to vote on them (which they seldom are allowed to do), they vote them down. Although many young people in Europe seemed to be proud to be "Europeans" and not only citizens of their current nation or locality, and once relished in the common currency, borderless travel, articulated educational and professional standards, and other advantages of what has been achieved so far, they instinctively understand that the cumbersome, word-larded framing documents are largely inadequate for providing a governing basis for "Europe" in a globalized world of the twenty-first century.

Things in the United States are even more glaring in this regard. A stunning kind of logo fundamentalism has captured both church and state. The US Supreme Court is currently controlled by men who believe that the original words of the US Constitution have an essential and unchanging meaning that is not only separate from and superior to what those words might have evolved to mean now (much less how they might now be better interpreted to mean), but also that they have essential meanings separate from what even the Founding Fathers themselves might have intended the words to mean. These judges are not especially concerned with what the Founding Fathers thought the words meant. They believe the words themselves speak clearly, flawlessly, and eternally.

The source of this kind of interpretation might be the fact that some of the most influential members of the court were educated at a time when what was known as "The New Criticism" was popular in departments of English in US universities, a perspective put forward by Margaret Talbot [52].

The New Criticism was popular in the United States and United Kingdom during the 1940s and 1950s and has influenced literary and cultural critics ever since. As Talbot notes, "New Critics treat a work of literature as if it were a self-contained, self-referential object. Rather than basing their interpretations of a text on the reader's response, the author's stated intentions, or parallels between the text and historical contexts (such as author's life), New Critics perform a close reading, concentrating on the relationships within the text that give it its own distinctive character and form" [52].

Walter J. Ong, who we have discussed before as one of the more influential scholars in understanding how the emergence of writing changed human thinking, behavior, values, and institutions uses the New Critics as a "prime example of text-bound thinking" [43, p. 160]. He goes on to argue that "to say that the New Critics … have been text-bound is not to degrade them. For they were in fact dealing with poems that were textual creations. Moreover, given the preceding state of criticism, which had devoted itself in great part to the biography and psychology of the author to the neglect of the text, they have warrant to stress the text … . New Criticism thus appears as a shift from a residually oral (rhetorical, contextual) mentality to a textual (non-contextual) mentality. But the textual mentality was relatively unreflective. For, although texts are autonomous by contrast with oral expression, ultimately no text can stand by itself independent of the extratextual world. Every text builds on pretext" [43, p. 162].

Ong attributes the New Criticism's exclusive focus on the text first to the academic shift from the study of Latin and Greek sources to contemporary vernacular literature (the study of which was never part of academics in previous millennia), and then to the creation of academic departments of English, most importantly as graduate studies, after World War I. Noting there was no such thing as "Old Criticism," this concentrated academic focus for the first time, after the 1930s, made "deep study" of decontextualized texts possible and fashionable. Postmodern scholarship has made this mode of analysis even more fashionable and pervasive, extending it to visual images in cinema and advertising, and not just written texts.

No institutions in the world today are more obsolete than governments. Although logo fundamentalism plagues religions and economic theories alike, both religions and economies have mutated marvelously since they were originally created. Many religions flourish today, each with different attachments to what is felt to be traditional and what is felt to be current. One function of the Holy Ghost in Catholicism is to help keep the Church up-to-date. Similarly, Evangelicals are guided by the Spirit, which is very much alive within them. Other Christians ask "What would Jesus do?", understanding that Jesus is alive with them today, and not speaking from a past that has been dead for two millennia. Even those Christian denominations that insist on following precisely the 2,000- to 3,000-year-old written Word of God rely not on the original words in Hebrew or Greek as they were understood when written, but on various modern English (or other vernacular) versions where the words have contemporary meanings that may not be those of the original words at all.

Although some economists may contend that their views are based on the eighteenth-century ideas of Adam Smith, as subsequently revealed by Milton Friedman and disciples, there is little or no relation between the economic institutions of Smith's (and the Founding Father's) time, and now. Economic institutions are constantly mutating as technology, ideology, and power provoke them.

And yet, most strangely, all constitutionally based governments everywhere still follow the cosmologies and technologies that inspired the Founding Fathers in 1789. In spite of a myriad institutional additions and Supreme Court decisions, the original words of the Constitution still rule in the United States, and the spirit of constitutionalism rules everywhere written constitutions exist, which is almost everywhere.

In the next section we will show how electricity and electronics have mutated power and most of society over the late nineteenth century to the present.

There have been numerous feeble attempts to create "electronic democracy," first via newspaper, radio, and television [13] then via the Internet [14]. But logo fundamentalism still rules the thoughts and behaviors of many academics, lawyers, bureaucrats, and the general public.

What if, instead of words, basic principles of governance were expressed in pictures? If governance is intended primarily to regulate the way people behave, what better way to illustrate those principles than by pictures that clearly depict proper and improper behavior? Linear words do a very inadequate job of explaining the desired and undesired behaviors now. Might not pictures do much better?

However, since behavior is complex and situational, static illustrations alone might not sufficiently do the job. For this, basic principles of behavior could be expressed in the algorithms of detailed computer programs linked to sophisticated three-dimensional dynamic audiovisual displays. The new Bills of Rights would deal, among other things, with making those algorithms transparent to all.

The words "to govern" come from Greek words meaning "to steer." A "governor" is the "steersman" of society. In a constantly mutating society such as ours is now, it makes little sense to be governed by an anchor, rather than by a rudder—if not more accurately by the rudder of a ship tied fast to the dock.

References

1. Bickerton D (2010) Adam's tongue: how humans made language, how language made humans. Hill & Wang, New York
2. Bloom J (2001) Paper before print: the history and impact of paper in the Islamic world. Yale University Press, New Haven
3. Boë LJ et al (2007) The vocal tract of newborn humans and Neanderthals: Acoustic capabilities and consequences for the debate on the origin of language. A reply to Lieberman (2007a). J Phonetics 35(4):564–581
4. Brokaw CJ, Chow K (eds) (2005) Printing and book culture in late Imperial China. University of California Press, Berkeley
5. Carter TF (1955) The invention of printing in china and its spread westward. The Ronald Press, New York
6. Chartier R (2007) The printing revolution: a reappraisal. In: Baron SA et al (eds) Agent of change: print culture studies after Elizabeth L. Eisenstein. University of Massachusetts Press, Amherst
7. Chow KW (2007) Reinventing Gutenberg: Woodblock and movabletype printing in Europe and China. In: Baron SA et al (eds) Agent of change: print culture studies after Elizabeth L. Eisenstein. University of Massachusetts Press, Amherst
8. Coombe RJ (1998) The cultural life of intellectual properties: authorship, appropriation, and the law. Duke University Press, Durham
9. Coşgel MM et al (2012) The political economy of mass printing: Legitimacy and technological change in the Ottoman Empire. J Compar Econ 40(3):357–371
10. D'Anastasio R et al (2013) Micro-biomechanics of the Kebara 2 Hyoid and its implications for speech in Neanderthals. PLoS One 8:12
11. Dator J (1968) Non-verbal, non-numerical models and media in political science. American Behavioral Scientist

12. Dator J (1983) The Honolulu electronic town meeting. In: Page W (ed) The future of politics. Frances Pinter, London
13. Dator J (2006) Will America ever become a democracy? In: Mannermaa M et al (eds) Democracy and futures. Parliament of Finland, Helsinki, pp 61–68
14. Denny JP (1991) Rational thought in oral culture and literate decontexualization. In: Olson DR et al (eds) Literacy and orality: conference: selected papers. Cambridge University Press, Cambridge
15. Diamond S (1971) The rule of law versus the order of custom. In: Wolff RP (ed) The rule of law. Simon & Schuster, New York
16. Dittmar JE (2011) Information technology and economic change: the impact of the printing press. Quart J Econ 126(3):1133–1172
17. Drake C (1993) Fujii Sadakazu. In: Fitzsimmons T et al (eds) The New poetry of Japan—the 70s and 80s. Katydid Books, Santa Fe
18. Eisenstein EL (2012) Divine art, infernal machine: the reception of printing in the West from first impressions to the sense of an ending. University of Pennsylvania Press, Philadelphia
19. Eisenstein EL (1979) The printing press as an agent of change: communications and cultural transformations in early-modern Europe 1. Cambridge University Press, Cambridge
20. Eisenstein EL (2012) The printing revolution in early modern Europe. Cambridge University Press, Cambridge
21. Enos RL (1990) Symbols in the prehistoric Middle East: developmental features preceding written communication. In: Enos RL (ed) Oral and written communication: historical approaches. Sage, Newbury Park
22. Feldman CF (1991) Oral metalanguage. In: Olson DR, Torrance N (eds) Literacy and orality: conference: selected papers. Cambridge University Press, Cambridge
23. Feldtkeller A (2005) Scriptures, forms of practice, and comparative religions. In: Andersen P, Reiter FC (eds) Scriptures, schools, and forms of practice in Daoism: a Berlin symposium. Harrassowitz, Wiesbaden
24. Finlayson C (2009) Neanderthals and modern humans: an ecological and evolutionary perspective. Cambridge University Press, Cambridge
25. Furniss G, Gunner E (2008) Power, marginality and African oral literature. Cambridge University Press, Cambridge
26. Gledhill J (2000) Power and its disguises: anthropological perspectives on politics. Pluto Press, London
27. Goody J (1977) The domestication of the savage mind. Cambridge University Press, Cambridge
28. Goody J (1987) The interface between the written and the oral. Cambridge University Press, Cambridge
29. Goody J (1986) The logic of writing and the organization of society. Cambridge University Press, Cambridge
30. Goody J (2000) The power of the written tradition. Smithsonian Institution Press, Washington, DC
31. Illich I (1991) A plea for research on lay literacy. In: Olson DR, Torrance N (eds) Literacy and orality: conference: selected papers. Cambridge University Press, Cambridge
32. Jack BE (2012) The woman reader. Yale University Press, New Haven
33. Johansson S (2005) Origins of language: constraints on hypotheses. John Benjamins Publishers, Amsterdam
34. LaFleur WR (1986) The karma of words: Buddhism and the literary arts in medieval Japan. University of California Press, Berkeley
35. Le May M (1975) The language capability of Neanderthal man. Am J Phys Anthropol 42(1):9–14
36. Lee KM (1997) The inventor of the Korean alphabet. In: Kim-Renaud, Y.-K. (ed.) The Korean alphabet: its history and structure. University of Hawaii Press, Honolulu.
37. Lewellen TC (2003) Political anthropology: an introduction. Praeger, Westport
38. Lieberman P (1998) Eve spoke: human language and human evolution. W.W. Norton, New York

39. Madden AD et al (2006) Information behaviour in pre-literate societies. In: Cole C, Spink A (eds) New directions in human information behavior. Springer, Dordrecht
40. Maugham WS (1977) Collected short stories. Penguin Books, New York
41. May C, Sell SK (2006) Intellectual property rights: a critical history. Lynne Rienner, Boulder
42. Olson DR (1991) Literacy and objectivity: the rise of modern science. In: Olson DR, Torrance N (eds) Literacy and orality: conference: selected papers. Cambridge University Press, Cambridge
43. Ong WJ (2007) Orality and literacy : the technologizing of the world. Routledge, London
44. P' Bitek O (1968) The song of Lawino. In: Beier U, Moore G (eds) Modern poetry from Africa. Penguin Books, New York
45. Ramsey SR (1997) The invention and use of the Korean alphabet. In: Kim-Renaud YK (ed) The Korean alphabet: its history and structure. University of Hawaii Press, Honolulu
46. Robinson F (1993) Technology and religious change: Islam and the impact of print. Mod Asian Stud 27(1):229–251
47. Roper G (2010) The history of the book in the Muslim world. In: Suarez MF, Woudhuysen HR (eds) The Oxford companion to the book. Oxford University Press, Oxford
48. Rose M (1993) Authors and owners: the invention of copyright. Harvard University Press, Cambridge
49. Sardar Z (2003) Paper, printing, and compact discs: the making and unmaking of Islamic culture. In: Inayatullah S, Boxwell G (eds) Postmodernism and other futures: a Ziauddin Sardar Reader. Pluto Press, London
50. Seth MJ (2006) A concise history of Korea: from the Neolithic period through the nineteenth century. Rowman & Littlefield, Lanham
51. Stallybrass P (2007) Little jobs': broadsides and the printing revolution. In: Baron SA et al (eds) Agent of change: print culture studies after Elizabeth L. Eisenstein. University of Massachusetts Press, Amherst
52. Talbot MM (2005) Supreme confidence: the jurisprudence of Justice Antonin Scalia. The New Yorker
53. Thomas R (1989) Oral tradition and written record in classical Athens. Cambridge University Press, Cambridge

Chapter 3
Communication Technologies and Power Relations, from Electricity to Electronics

3.1 Electronic Communications and Power Relations

From our perspective in the first quarter of the twenty-first century, the pace of development of new communication technologies was quite leisurely during the long interval between the evolution of speech to the invention and impact of the printing press. After each mutative technology—speech, handwriting, the printing press—had been introduced and diffused, things more or less settled down. Appropriate software emerged, and powerful orgware protected both from substantial further change until the next new communication technology (with its own modes of software and hardware) triumphed over them—or, more accurately, put the old technologies "in their place."

Just as our discussion of the evolution of writing focused on the Middle East, and of the effect of the printing press mainly on Europe and then Islamic and northeast Asian areas, from this point on our narrative will concentrate mainly on the United States, with occasional glances elsewhere. In order to grasp the scope and depth of the changes that were about to come, it is worth repeating that the United States—whose written constitution became the cosmological and technological base upon which the constitution of all other polities in the world down to the present time were created—was written in 1789 by and for a geographically vast, very thinly populated, almost entirely agrarian society. Its main communication technologies were speech, handwriting, and printing via the hand-powered printing press. Its driving cosmologies were from the Middle Ages (channeling aspects of ancient Greek and Roman philosophy), Newtonian mechanics, and deism. All of these cosmologies and technologies changed profoundly in the United States over the next 50, and certainly 100, years.

Beginning with the water mill and steam-powered printing press and then the fossil-fueled motorized printing press, the pace of change rapidly picked up. While newssheets, often with advertising, were widespread since the advent of the hand-powered press, the mechanized press brought multi-page weekly and daily newspapers that made them primary forms of mass communication for the next two centuries.

J.A. Dator et al., *Mutative Media: Communication Technologies and Power Relations in the Past, Present, and Futures*, Lecture Notes in Social Networks, DOI 10.1007/978-3-319-07809-0_3,

However, it was a social technology, rather than a physical technology, that set the initial stage for the changes yet to come: the governmentally organized postal service, which had its origins in the American colonial period and helped foment and focus the movement for independence from England via Committees of Correspondence that existed in the separate colonies. The functions of reliable mail delivery were understood to be so vital to the operations of an effective networked government that Benjamin Franklin (previously postmaster in Philadelphia) was named the national Postmaster General by the short-lived US Continental Congress in 1775. The first US Congress, in 1792, created after the adoption of the Constitution in 1787, provided for only three executive departments—War, State, and Treasury—along with the offices of the Attorney General and the Postmaster General, a clear indication of the centrality of good communications for nation-building even though the existing transportation system itself was woefully inadequate—something the Constitution wanted fixed by allowing the US government to build a network of "post offices and post roads" (Article 1, Section 8).

This nexus also reminds us that communication and transportation are in many ways aspects of the same thing. Transportation is often for the purpose of communicating. This became slowly (though still very inadequately) recognized, as it became possible to "tele"-communicate more quickly, cheaply, and effectively—a point we shall emphasize later.

One of the other social technologies related to the post office needs to be mentioned in passing as a form and process that makes the conjunction of transportation as communication crystal clear—the invention of the Pony Express. The preferred riders were young boys, preferably orphans, of which there were many on the American frontier. The Pony Express thrived until after the American Civil War (1866), when the invention of the telegraph in the early 1800s onward and the creation of cross-continental wagon routes and then railroads ended it. The telegraph was a truly counterintuitive electrical device that enabled aural signals to be relayed, over wires, eventually at great distances. However it was not until John Morse invented the software that bears his name—a series of short and longer electronic pulses (so-called "dots and dashes") entered by the finger of a skilled orgware operator at one end and an earphone-listening skilled orgware operator at the other—that the technology took off. In 1838, Morse is said to have made an even-handed prediction of his invention, clearly showing that he understood it would impact the existing balance of power in society: "This mode of instantaneous communication must inevitably become an instrument of immense power, to be wielded for good or for evil, as it shall be properly or improperly directed" [7]. Twenty years later, Charles F. Briggs and Augustus Maverick determined the telegraph to be transformative and wrote enthusiastically:

> Of all the marvelous achievements of modern science the electric telegraph is transcendentally the greatest and most serviceable to mankind .... The whole earth will be belted with the electric current, palpitating with human thoughts and emotions .... How potent a power, then, is the telegraph destined to become in the civilization of the world! This binds together by a vital cord all the nations of the earth. It is impossible that old prejudices and hostilities should longer exist, while such an instrument has been created for an exchange of thought between all the nations of the earth. [7]

The monochromatic photographic camera was invented during the first third of the nineteenth century. Here was a technology that enabled humans to see the world as it had never been so surely seen before: in black and white and not color to be sure, but in stop-action that previously could only be imagined in mind or paintings. Thus (for a famous example) in 1878, the photographer Eadweard Muybridge was able to prove that at certain points when moving, all four feet of a horse left the ground—something in dispute that the camera allowed to be clearly demonstrated.

For the first time, people could repeatedly look at pictures of themselves—or their loved ones—as babies, or children, or other stages of life and death. Such personal pictures were rare. For many years some people might for the first time own a solitary picture of themselves as an infant, taken with great care and expense by a professional photographer. Cheap "candid cameras" that allowed "everyone" to take and keep pictures of themselves arrived much later, most famously the Kodak camera, a development so powerful it came to be the generic name used for all personal cameras for several generations.

Wireless radio—the impossible magic of "voices in the air"—arrived in the last decade of the nineteenth century with the first transatlantic broadcast in 1902. Guglielmo Marconi is considered to be the father of long distance radio transmissions. His early transatlantic network was involved in transmitting information about the Titanic disaster, since two of his radio operators were on board the ill-fated vessel.

Radios surpassed the newspaper in bringing instant news, but could never fully equal print for depth of coverage. But radios brought music, sports, and drama to everyone for the first time in their homes, workplaces, and automobiles. In a stunning revolutionary moment, one did not have to "go" somewhere to be entertained. The world came to them. True, it was voices without pictures (though often with clever sound effects), but that made the medium even more enchanting as it updated the antique modes of communication in oral cultures, such as the telling of stories around the campfire, and powerful, moving speeches by exceptional orators.

The telephone was invented in the 1870s. It was originally conceived of as a better form of the telegraph. Both depended on electricity moving over wires. An improved telegraph was pursued partly by people who wanted to break the telegraph monopoly of the time by basing telegraphy on different principles and technologies. In the process, it was discovered that it was possible to transmit human speech over wires from mouth to ear, and so a fundamentally new technology was born. The telegraph required special talent on the part of its users. The telephone only required one to be able to speak and to hear a common language. It was what Ivan Illich would call a "convivial tool" since it was "user-friendly" [9]. It was not convivial to the extent that no ordinary person could understand how a telephone actually worked without special training and scientific understanding. Although there were craft skills required for hand printing press operators, most ordinary people could figure out how a mechanical press worked by watching it in operation. The radio seemed to operate by magic—no wires, but invisible sounds over the air. Thus the phone was somewhere in between the press and the radio from the perspective of conviviality—its operation (and repair) was not as easy to comprehend as that of a printing press, nor as incomprehensibly mystifying as a radio. More importantly, in use, the telephone was fundamentally interactive and completely intuitive.

The software and orgware of the telephone was also initially comparatively simple. The most difficult part was connecting the person speaking with the person spoken to. That was solved by inventing the local "central" telephone exchange—part physical, part social technologies. People paid to be physically linked to it by wires, and asked "central" physically to connect them to some other person also linked to the exchange. At one early point in the development of this technology this meant that a user would lift a speaking/hearing instrument from a cradle that would send an electrical signal to an operator at the central exchange who would then ask the caller "number please?" On hearing the number, the operator would physically connect the caller to the numbered electrical line of the recipient, sending an electrical signal that rang a bell that prompted the receiver to pick up the instrument from its cradle and say "Hello?" and the conversation would begin—all wonderfully easy from the user's perspectives. So simple, a child—or even a woman—could do it. Indeed, "central" often was a woman, and for a while telephone companies employed thousands of women who connected local callers to local callees, disconnecting them when the conversation was finished.

Calling from one local exchange to another was complicated by the fact that telephone technology in one locality might not be easily compatible with that of another locality, so that any truly long-distance call—cross-country or across the world—required scores of operators being notified beforehand so that they could all plan to connect locality to locality until a person on one side of the planet was physically routed through a myriad of local exchanges to a person on the other side of the planet. This was enormously time consuming—often taking days of planning—and very expensive. Even with the invention of the rotary number dial phone, which destroyed the need for thousands of human operators for local calls, human operators were still necessary for calls outside the local exchange for many years, until a series of other technical and social developments enabled it all to be entirely automatic.

So let's reflect for a moment on the social, ideological, power-related underpinnings of our story so far, using as our example the telegraph and the telephone. W. Bernard Carlson offers "[an] example of how ideas about the relationship between technology and politics shapes technological change" [1, p. 15]. Carlson shows that a major figure in the development of the telephone, Gardiner Hubbard, envisioned the telephone as becoming a technology for democracy. That belief influenced many of the technical choices he and his partner, Alexander Graham Bell, made along the way. "He thought that the telephone could be a direct instrument of democracy for the average middle-class American citizen. His vision of democracy shaped the kind of telephone system he promoted. For him, telecommunications also required the active intervention of the state, and his conviction that technology would have a deterministic social and political effect was instrumental in driving this technological development" [1, p. 15].

Carlson explained how Hiram Sibley had been able to create the Western Union telegraph monopoly by encouraging businesses to use the telegraph primarily to send their business messages, rather than using it to read the latest newspaper reports or for personal messages. He only invested in technologies that aided that business plan. In contrast, "Hubbard believed that the telephone would be used for domestic and social purposes, and thus a telephone network would be more democratic than Western Union's business-oriented telegraph system. In his correspondence and his promotional efforts, Hubbard told of how middle-class and upper-middle-class people would use the telephone to coordinate servants, order groceries, and respond to social invitations … . Hubbard saw the telephone as a device that would allow the middle class to create a space for itself in a chaotic world" [1, p. 43].

Carlson informs our research by concluding: "Technological artifacts are not 'neutral' tools whose design and utilization are determined by economic necessity or efficiency. Indeed, artifacts do have politics, and the telephone came to embody meanings that were central to the middle class" [1, p. 47].

3.2 From Electricity to Electronics

The invention of the vacuum tube prefigured the age of electronics as the successor to the age of electricity. It allowed for vast improvements in radios, long-distance telephones, and many, many other devices. But the tubes were fragile, requiring careful attention by humans to replace when they burned out, and they were very hot, requiring space between them for air circulation cooling. They also required a lot of electricity. And they were relatively big.

All of that changed with the invention of solid-state transistors that were sturdy, reliable, automated, cheap, and progressively smaller and smaller. All of these factors also enabled devices utilizing them to be more mobile instead of fixed to walls or desktops—another revolutionary factor, since communication devices once the size of a large room could be microminiaturized into something so small that it was necessary to make them larger again simply so humans could hold them, see them, hear them, and punch the necessary buttons.

So among the many things that made the current almost fully automated and user-directed mobile network of today possible were numerous developments in hardware, software, and orgware, almost all of which from this point on in our story of communication technologies are crucial also for the invention and operation of all the other advancing technologies, making our story even more difficult to tell in a linear way.

Moreover, the story so far has mainly been about live communication in "real time." A big development, that (as is usually the case) both integrated and spawned many other developments, were devices for recording and replaying sounds (and eventually, images). Many of the same people involved in telephony were also involved in developing what became the phonograph. Although attempts were made initially to find a practical use for this new recording and playback device, such as for stenographic purposes, it was the entertainment value that made the phonograph take off—the ability to play back music at home and elsewhere.

Significantly, the ability to record was initially separate from the ability to play back. At first, one had to buy phonograph records that some company had made for them to play back on their home phonograph. Later, the development of home recorders using wire and then magnetic tape made it possible for ordinary people both to record and to play back their own material. These recordings could be copied to other wires or tapes for others to play back, but that required manual, physical connections for transfer from one recorder to another. It was not until the "analog" signals on tape or wire were transferred to "digital" signals that (with the aid of other technologies) recordings could be shared instantly electronically with many others worldwide—creating a whole new set of pleasures and penalties dealing with the stealing of "intellectual property," which has become a complex phenomenon with diffuse social, political, and technological, impacts. As Coombe notes, "The extension of proprietary rights to cultural forms has created immense new fields of potential economic value, engendered new industries, and raised a host of legal and ethical quandaries" [3], p. 7. However, as Coombe observes, many of the core issues are perennial—representation, ownership, and access to information. She continues, "The 'problems' of rapidity of transmission, deepening anonymity of authorship and readership, the fragmentation of works and their reception—supposedly characteristic of late or postmodernity—were all faced in the transition to modernity" [3, p. 249]. The major impact of IP has much to do the subtle, and sometimes not so subtle, ways in which it influences the conditions of possibility for technological, intellectual, and artistic development and diffusion.

With the emergence of rap and hip-hop in the 1970s and 1980s, issues over copyright came to the cultural fore, and as "sampling" became a staple of the genre, copyright litigation proliferated and led to major changes in the attitudes and practices of artists. As Chuck D. explains, "Copyright laws pretty much led people like Dr. Dre to replay the sounds that were on records, then sample musicians imitating those records" [13]. But, records were not the only recordings stirring the cultural pot.

As far as the telephone is concerned, a major technological contribution made by recording devices was the answering machine. This, too, revolutionized telephony and its impact on behavior. It was no longer necessary directly to be physically present to "answer" an incoming call. Now it could be recorded for playback at a later time—or never at all. Suddenly, it was very difficult to "ignore" other's attempts to reach you by pretending to be out by simply not answering when a phone call came in. The incoming message sat there, with its flashing red light, demanding your attention whether you wanted to access it or not. As the reliability of the recording technology improved, attempts to blame technology for your failure to respond became indefensible.

Microminiaturization, repeating ground stations, and (to some extent) Earth-orbiting satellites made it possible for people to have "mobile phones" that could be carried easily on one's person. No one would ever be alone again, doing things on their own privately. Everyone could always be under surveillance. Everyone's movements and many actions became easily traceable. Some people purposely resisted mobile phones for this reason. Since messages could be waiting on return home, why permit the world to contact you when you are away? How is it possible to do nefarious deeds if you have to carry and answer a mobile phone *cum* tracking device?

And then Apple invented the iPhone, and everything changed. A phone was no longer a phone any more. It was everyone's ears, mouth, eyes, heart, brain, and very life's blood. The invention of the software and orgware of the so-called social media (Facebook, Twitter, Instagram, etc.) made it even easier to monitor everyone else's thoughts and movements.

3.3 Moving Pictures

We need now to return to the black and white camera and trace developments in audiovisual communication technologies, since the invention of that strange but eye-opening device. Still photography in color was an important step, but moving pictures were far, far, far more breathtakingly mutative. Their story starts first with halting but startling results that came from flipping stacks of infinitesimally progressive stop-action photos so that they simulated motion, a development that became an attraction for peepshows at the Penny Arcade, especially when the subject being viewed was dancing the hoochie-coochie.

The revolution occurred when humans were able to replace the stack of individual still pictures made by a stop-action camera with a camera that moved photosensitive film past a lens so that (when projected) the moving pictures produced a continuous stream of images that unfolded as life seems to do—seamlessly before our naked eyes. The movies were an enormous hit—a profound development—even though they were at first entirely silent as well as in lifeless black and white.

Audiences in movie theaters are said to have screamed and ducked as a train seemed to rush towards them from the silvered screen. "Special effects" may have been discovered when someone interrupted the filming of a scene that had a flower vase on one side of the table and resumed filming, only to discover on playback that the vase magically appeared on the other side of the table. Someone had unthinkingly moved the vase while the camera was off. The "effect" was that the vase had spontaneously and instantly jumped across the table, producing laughter and confusion among the viewers. Many other such effects were discovered by accident, and/or enabled by technological development—such as the "zoom" lens, which made it much easier to appear to move closer to a subject than was possible with the fixed focus lens previously.

Recorded sound without accompanying pictures and recorded moving pictures without sound co-existed weirdly for a while as two separate and discrete phenomena—radio and movies. When movies "learned to talk" the consequences were multiplicative and not just additive. With the addition of color to moving pictures with sound, the impact was even greater. Movies were becoming progressively more "lifelike"—while at the same time actually becoming farther and farther away from being like life at all. Editing, special effects, lighting, scripting, mood-directing music, et al., produced something far beyond "life"—something deeper, richer, more involving, more powerful. Movies were more dramatic, better produced, faster paced, more emotional than real life itself. As McLuhan explains, "In England the movie theatre was originally called 'The Bioscope,' because of its visual presentation of the actual movements of the forms of life (from Greek *bios*, way of life)" [15, p. 248]. Close-up shots of an actor's face with a voice-over gave the viewer access to a person's innermost secret thoughts that real life seldom if ever permitted. Time no longer inexorably flowed "forward." In the movies, events could be experienced out of natural sequence—the consequence being shown before the cause. Many causes being shown instead of one. Many different interpretations of the cause being offered instead of one. When asked to talk about the events in their daily lives, more and more people referred not to their direct experiences but to scenes they had "experienced" in the movies. Fiction became larger and more real than life.

This feature became even more prominent with the advent of live, broadcast television, at first also in black and white and eventually in color. Now, instead of people "going" to the movies for a communal experience, the movies came to them, at home or in private. And, as with radio, it provoked a huge increase in interest in sports and in the creation of growing numbers of professional athletes whose exploits both on and off the sports field could now be watched effortlessly from one's couch at home, beer in one hand, snacks in the other. In the United States, professional football was nothing until television channeled impressively controlled real violence directly into the home.

The sparking orgware development here was advertising. Publicly funded radio and television were popular, but being limited in income, were also often limited in programming. With advertising, the sky was no longer the limit. Advertising, especially on television, produced a gigantic positive economic feedback loop between products, consumers, and entertainment. The economy depended on TV and radio to get people to want to buy what they otherwise would not buy. TV and radio depended on advertisers to pay for programs that would attract viewers. The people wanted to be entertained "without paying for it" and were willing to be lured to "shop till they dropped." To ensure the cycle kept spinning, far more money, time, effort, and creativity often was spent on producing a brief advertisement than on producing a full-length television show. The show was meant primarily to keep people watching between advertisements. The advertisement was meant to impel people to buy something. Greater talent and care went into the advertisement than into the entertainment, since advertising had to result in proper action.

Of course "we are being more than entertained" [2]. Each show is full of propaganda, rarely critical and overwhelming supportive, of the ideology of some government, corporation, or other sponsor. Some shows or advertising critical of the supporting ideology only get shown in the dark of early morning while most people are asleep. Others—though fully funded—are not allowed to be shown on mass-oriented television at all. But viewers don't mind. They will ultimately "watch television" regardless of the content of the show. Here, as elsewhere, the medium is the message perhaps more than the message itself is.

The advent of recording devices for television played an even more important role in making television a profound agent of social change than recording did for radio and telephones. It was what made it possible to produce entire virtual realities instead of merely transmitting "real" reality. While a lot of information and values can be conveyed by just pointing a camera at something and absorbing the ambient sounds and pictures, a lot more information, misinformation, and disinformation can be conveyed by editing and supplementing those sounds and pictures.

Since their emergence more than thirty years ago, electronic interactive games have progressed from being played primarily in public spaces with very clunky cartoon-like features to being played at home on mobile devices anywhere batteries are available, displaying environments that are almost "lifelike" in all aspects, including not only the visual effects but also (in the case of athletic games) the crowd noises and the comments by announcers or spectators. The deep complexity—as well as the stunning graphics—of many of these games is riveting.

These games are sometimes called examples of "virtual reality." However it is very important to understand that well before videogames were created, all "reality" already was virtual reality. Society is very much a social invention, and not an objective entity that impresses itself the same way on everyone. What each of us "knows" about the world is known largely because of the way it has been constructed for us by our culture—its myths, beliefs, language, and social structures as well as one's own personal experiences and memories (often false!).

Whatever may be objectively "real" out there will never be fully known to anyone except by the devices and metaphors through which each human community perceives and communicates it. That there is some kind of a "real" reality outside of us seems highly likely, given the power of modern science to measure and control it. As the doubting Bishop Berkeley was challenged, if you don't think that rock there is real, go ahead and kick it. The pain might change your mind—since your mind didn't change the stone.

All cultures tell stories, make up dramas and plays, carve statutes and form other visual images, sing songs, beat drums, blow horns, invent rituals, get drunk and stoned, give explanations for events, and in many other ways embellish the bare facts of every simple "real" sensory experience. Since the stories one culture tells often differ markedly from the ones other cultures tell, people often live in very different realities constructed by their language and culture.

Nonetheless, we recently have become even more extraordinary storytellers because of technologies that have made storytelling more vivid and multisensory than what was possible in the old days when we could only speak, sing, dance, carve, mold, weave, or paint. As we have seen, it was the printing press that made "fiction" possible on a large scale. Before that time, very few merely popular stories were ever written down. Some were, but writing was generally preserved for "serious," "real," and "true" things like laws, religious documents, military plans, economic accounting, and pornography.

With the invention and then widespread use of the printing press, the production and spread of information and disinformation became comparatively cheap and abundant so that not only serious fact and ennobling fiction but also "trashy" novels—be they romances or westerns or mysteries or science fiction—began to flow forth, first as a trickle and then as a flood. With the subsequent invention of the social technology called the public school system, children were taught, often against their will, how to read or write. Some began to read and write not just what they were taught was proper but rather whatever they wanted to read or write. Although that might be law, religious documents, and scientific tomes for some, it was engrossing fiction about made-up people in made-up situations for most.

As we saw, the next development in this speeding train of events was when universities in the United Kingdom and English Departments in the United States solemnly taught fictional literature written in or translated into the English language. Students were typically required to take such courses. That is to say, students were required no longer simply to "pursue truth" as described in ancient religious or cultural texts and in modern scientific research. They were required to study fantasies and to learn how to produce compelling fantasies of their own. This was a perhaps counterintuitive development that contributed to the eroding of the authority of religion and science in defining what was important and real and what was not. The power struggles resulting from this underlie many political controversies everywhere today—between the "two cultures" of science and the humanities and/or between religious orthodoxy and secular humanism.

Over the eighteenth and especially nineteenth centuries, more and more people began to spend more and more of their time in more and more fictional places—in virtual realities—and not in the "real" reality of their five senses or received texts. Then, as we were reminded, in the twentieth century came the radio, and movies, and television, and board games (like "Monopoly"), and electronic games, and eventually in the twenty-first century … well that is another story about to be told here.

Among other lessons, all of this has taught us how to live in many alternative presents that may help us gain perspective and perhaps crucial distance from the single "crackpot realism" that "authoritarian" rulers, priests, teachers, and parents may wish to impose. Instead of daydreaming, we can and do "escape" from the boring real reality of our everyday lives by reading, watching television, playing electronic games. For one consequence, as suggested above, most of us when asked to explain something, will give an example, not from our everyday "real" lives, but from a movie or TV show we have seen. Mediated reality is far more real for most of us than is real reality. If this increasingly is the case, then we may wonder as a Chinese philosopher did many, many centuries ago, "whether I am a man dreaming I am a butterfly, or a butterfly dreaming I am a man." Or, as a not quite so old TV commercial put it, "Is it real or is it Memorex"?

The stage was finally set for what many thought would be the next big step in literacy—away from words to images—visual literacy. No more reading brain-numbing linear texts. With the further development of television we would now communicate primarily with audiovisual images. Marshall McLuhan triumphant!

Alas, it has not happened, yet. We will contemplate what happened to "visual literacy" while we review the development of computers. And yet, we will see that the time when visual literacy replaces print literacy may not be so far off after all.

3.4 Computers

The first computers mechanical, and then electro-mechanical, devices for doing the math on something, such as the trajectory of artillery shells. Certain technologies that were precursors to computers had been used to improve the speed and efficiency of factory weaving machines through a series of automatic instructions delivered by holes in paper templates that activated or prevented the movement of the various spindles, pulleys, wheels, gears, threads, and other parts.

The popular appreciation of the distinction between hardware and software came from the understanding that the operation of interrelated mechanical, electric, and then electronic devices had become so fast and often so counterintuitive that humans could not be solely or even primarily responsible for their operation. Humans could carefully devise routine paths for the machine to follow, but once devised, operationalized, and functioning, the system operated correctly without much if any human intervention. That is what software does; it provides detailed instructions for the automatic operation of hardware.

Although the first software relied entirely on physical forms—paper tape or stacks of cards with holes punched in them—the software soon relied on analog and then digital signals on moving tape, and then spinning disks, and most recently mysteriously hidden in tiny solid state devices too small for the unaided eye to see.

However, computers for a while stayed computers and controllers, very useful for "crunching" ever larger numbers of data, but that was about it until someone discovered how to use them as "word processors"—a phrase, that, when first heard, was startling, making no sense whatsoever. How can you "process" words? And why would you want to?

My first glance at the operation of an early Wang word processor explained to me why. Text no longer lay flat and lifeless on paper. It was suddenly electronically alive and pliable in a way it could never have been before. The "copy and paste" function alone was stupendous for advancing scholarship and skullduggery alike. No need to prepare an outline, or otherwise to think before you write—just hammer away, and correct things later. It became harder and harder to have a "finished version." It was always too easy to add a bit more, change a bit here, delete a phrase there.

New ideas were no longer necessary! You could now cut and paste from one document to another, keeping the same ideas and phrases going forward forever. Examples of that are found throughout this document going back not only to the earliest days of word processors but also even earlier to scanned documents originally written on typewriters. As more and more documents became available electronically, it became easier and easier to copy and paste from the world's store of knowledge, and make it your own—or as though it were your own simply by not citing the source or putting quotation marks around it. Plagiarism became irresistible at the very moment the concept of patentable "intellectual property" was invented. God always tempts us with both the apple and the snake—telling us not to eat of the fruit of the tree of the knowledge of good and evil while making good and evil knowledge dangle tantalizingly before us, just within the reach of our prosthetically augmented arms.

However, the first word processors were stand-alone instruments—little more than typewriters on vitamins. What changed computers was networking. Then they were on steroids.

Most people like to tell the story as though the Internet evolved from an early military network called Arpanet. Maybe that is the case, but there is also another story. It evolved from activities in the US. Office of Emergency Preparedness within the Executive Office of the President from 1968 through 1973 which sought, as a consequence of the development of "packet switching," to create an electronic network among the central and ten regional OEP offices across the United States of such resiliency and redundancy that it could withstand anything that might disable communication among all eleven locations, be it a nuclear exchange, an NEO impact, or a massive electrical impulse, natural or manmade. When the office was terminated in 1973, Murray Turoff, who developed the "computer conferencing" system, EMISARY, for OEP went to the New Jersey Institute of Technology. There, with Starr Roxanne Hiltz and others, and with support from the National Science Foundation, he created the Electronic Information Exchange System (EIES) that went online in 1976. I somehow was invited to join the system.

When I originally came to Hawaii to stay, in 1969, my mainland friends kissed me goodbye, assuming they would never see me again. Jet plane flight between Hawaii and the mainland was new. Communication was slow and expensive. There was no direct satellite TV transmission. We saw our TV shows one week late since they were flown to us from the US mainland on videotapes that were rebroadcast here after they had already been shown on the mainland. Most information floated across the Pacific in books and magazines, providing us with "news" that was anything but new. Although this had changed somewhat by 1976, EIES brought me, and the few others on it (mainly in the United States but some in Europe and perhaps elsewhere), instant global communication that was previously beyond any scholar's experience. I now knew things my departmental colleagues in Hawaii did not know. I was communicating intimately with people I had never seen or even heard of before. One evening a strange set of poems appeared, from a poet named Racter, who turned out to be a computer program that may not have been as autonomously creative as it once was claimed to be.

The Texas Instruments terminal that I used for EIES was connected to a networked computer at NJIT via an acoustic modem (the NSF grant paid the considerable long-distance charges), so I could read what others had written on a small screen, and type in and send my replies. However the terminal had absolutely no memory at all. If I wanted to preserve what was being communicated, I had to "echo" it out on paper via an attached printer, which I did when possible.

When the NSF grant was over, and I was asked to pay for the service myself if I wanted it to continue, I tried to get some kind of support from my university, without success. I needed money for a computer conference? Well, ask for travel money to go to the conference. No? Well ask the computing center for help. Nothing there.

I felt like a junky must feel, suddenly deprived of his daily fix … until some years later when the UH computing center set up a primitive, largely local, email system, and I was among its first users (with most students dropping classes when I required them also to use email for purposes of continuing class discussions, since they found the technology confusing and frightening).

At the same time I also experimented with Stuart Umpleby's PLATO system that operated out of the University of Illinois. It demonstrated the possibility of enticing, immersive, and interactive computer-based learning.

More and more people began to experience the power of instantly networked communications as the failures and foibles of the ARPANET/NSFNET/BITNET/EIES became ordered, orderly, cheaper, more reliable, and easier to use with the adoption of the TCP/IP standard; the rise and fall of various networking systems leading eventually to the World Wide Web; browsers, such as Netscape Navigator and Internet Explorer; search engines such as Gopher, WAIS, Mosaic, Yahoo, Altavista, and Google, along with hypertext that could be "hot linked" from one site to another; and protocols allowing file sharing not only of text but eventually also of sound and video.

Clearly, without email, the Internet, Google, and the jet plane I could never have lived in the most remote spot on the globe, Hawaii, and yet interacted intimately and continuously with people and ideas from all over the world. But it would only be part of the story if the credit card had not been invented as the fifth enabling factor. Indeed, the entire world of production, consumption, commerce, and finance of the present is impossible without the electronic hardware previously discussed; the software of neoliberalism; the fuel of cheap and abundant oil; and the orgware of economists, bankers, financiers, and clerks all working together to destroy the national and local political economies of the twentieth century while creating what was promised to be the global networked society of the twenty-first century. As Alvin Toffler titled it one of his many prescient books, the world was experiencing a *Powershift: Knowledge, Wealth, and Violence at the Edge of the 21st Century* [20].

3.5 The End of Authority?

Theilhard de Chardin's "Noosphere"—the global mind that he anticipated in the 1940s—was emerging electronically and physically, though not spiritually as he envisioned [19]. Electronic communication technologies spread ideas that the controllers of cultures based on printing found threatening and often repulsive. And because electronic communication technologies are interactive while those of print lie fixed on the page, "dangerously" self-empowering ideas began flowing around the globe at the speed of light, with alliances being created among people thousands of miles apart. Ideas your mother, your priest, your teacher, your boss, and your government didn't want you to know were everywhere in the electronic surround. Marriages broke apart and new partnerships formed online. Scientific experiments were conducted, new technologies developed, business plans hatched, and products bought and sold in cyberspace before many of the controllers of print technology were even aware of any of them.

Experts who once were effective gatekeepers to knowledge were bypassed as people went online to ask one another for ideas and information. No one with easy access to the Internet need go to a library unless she needed a safe, quiet, dry place to sleep. People with ailments go online for cures before they consult a live doctor, if they consult one at all. So also with lawyers and scores of other erstwhile "authorities"—most certainly priests and politicians who no longer command the respect nor power they once did as people form their own ideas about god and the purpose of life, and form friendships and loyalties that stretch well beyond their parish, neighborhood, or nation. Indeed, more and more people were using electronic communication technologies to thwart, if they could not yet overthrow, the obsolete political institutions that prevented self-government.

Kevin Kelly, with his "Nine Laws of God," showed that self-organization (rather than hierarchical command and control) is at the base of all viable systems, natural and human-made. He pointed out that being "out of control" is a *good* thing while attempts at top-down control will surely fail ultimately [11]. Organisms are made up of many interacting parts, some vital for survival, some expendable, and some difficult but not impossible to do without. Yet these parts all work and coordinate with each other without there being any god giving organ orders to a pope who gives orders to a cardinal who give orders to a bishop who give orders to a priest, who tell the parishioners what to do—with no feedback to the top allowed. Instead, cells each send numerous messages among themselves continuously, and coordinate themselves with amazing efficiency and effectiveness. If each of the legs of a cockroach did not have important measures of autonomy, the brain would be incapable of telling each leg how to run, jump, or stop quickly enough. On the other hand, the legs do have to coordinate with many other cockroach parts for the beast to scurry and thrive, which cockroaches have done very successfully for a very long time.

Artificial systems—such as religions and nations—also operate best, Kelly showed, if they work from the bottom up rather than the top down. The Internet demonstrates repeatedly how effective self-governance is possible.

Of course along with all of the great and free ideas flowing through the electronic ether, there also are lies, spoofs, spams, and urban legends. Sorting truth from fiction and valid email from spam and malware is a tricky, time-consuming, and costly business. Hacking introduced a completely new reason for concern. And the old political, religious, and economic forces improved their efforts to censor content, charge for access to it, use the technology themselves mainly to monitor, apprehend, and (sometimes literally) to kill what they cannot control and profit from. Politics is often a struggle between freedom and order. And order usually wins.

During the height of the euphoria about the transformative powers of electronic technologies, in writing about the impact of these technologies on the form and practice of law, Ethan Katsch insisted that the word was out—or soon would be—and that law, in form and practice, was about to be transformed once again. Basing his argument on analogies from the role of the printing press as pioneered by the works of Marshall McLuhan and Elisabeth Eisenstein, Katsch convincingly argued that law needed to, and would, find a new basis in electronic images, and that new forms of governance would emerge.

Katsh noted that "during the past five centuries, the law has had an unrecognized ally in working toward its goal of managing the pace of change. This silent partner, which has assisted in fostering a public image of law as an institution that is both predictable and flexible, is the communications medium that has dominated the legal process for the past 500 years, the medium of print … . As the new media [of the late twentieth and twenty-first centuries] begin to take on some of the duties performed by print, one of the consequences will be to upset the balance that the law has worked so diligently to achieve over several centuries" [10, p. 25].

The concept of "law" shifted, Katsch argued, from being the fluid, adaptive oral statements of judges in the old medieval courts, to becoming fixed in printed documents (expressed in written "constitutions" and laws) of the recent modern age, and now to being fluid once again as elusive electronic bits. Everything written has become just a draft that can be cut and pasted into other documents for numerous purposes. In the current "Information Age," nothing is ever final. Everything is fluid, flexible, temporary. "Consequence" becomes more important than "Precedents." If we move beyond the information age, perhaps to a "Dream Society of Icons and Aesthetic Experience," "law" may become as temporary as everything else in the society it seeks to regulate. "Law" might become a fleeting suggestion expressed in audio/visual/olfactory/tactile images in N-dimensional cyberspace [10].

The practice of law also has changed over time as the technologies for communication changed. With electronics there is a movement away from geographically-defined "law offices" and "law libraries" to "virtual communities," perhaps linked to virtual courthouses globally dispersed and then throughout the inner Solar System. Electronic communication technologies are changing the "persona" of law. Once upon a time, intelligence, such as it is, was a human monopoly. With the rise of artificial intelligence, we can expect reliance not only on intelligent legal and judicial software, but also on cyber lawyers, cyber judges, and Bills of Rights of Robots protecting cyber beings accused of committing crimes or adultery.

Indeed, it is not clear why humans need to be involved in routine judicial decision-making at all. Of all social inventions (except mathematics itself), law is especially fit for computerization for all but the most novel aspects of judicial policymaking. For forty years, a major aim of many legislative bodies in the United States has been to eliminate the discretion of judges by mandating determinant sentencing and other limitations on human judgment. It makes sense now to eliminate human error, fatigue, and bias altogether by eliminating humans and relying entirely on judgments rationally made by impartial artificial intelligences. We are doing this in more and more areas of life. How can—why should—judiciaries (or legislatures) be immune?

All current forms of governance are being undermined by current electronic communication technologies. How much longer will the creaky, old (once grand and admirable geographically limited, print-based) structure persist? When will something finally bring it to its arthritic knees, and allow new, more appropriate structures to emerge, based on the best current cosmologies and technologies?

These were the questions that once were on the lips of all who saw electronic technologies as liberating and transformative. But, as we will soon see, the bloom is most decidedly off that rose. Will justification for such optimism rise again?

3.6 Which Medium Gave the Biggest Massage?

What was the most transformative advancement in communication technology in the twentieth century? What is the equivalent of speech, writing, and the printing press? Is it movies and television, as Marshall McLuhan [14, 15] and others once convincingly argued, or is it the Internet in all its still emerging glory, as Dewar and Ang more recently said: "The Internet is more important than the radio, telephone, television or VCR. It is like the printing press" [6]. "If the Internet were to have anywhere near the impact the printing press has had, its importance would beggar that of its more modern parallels … " [6, p. 365f]. Making the typical distinction between one-to-one communication (talking; telephone); one-to-many (books, radio, TV—also can be considered "few-to-many"); few-to-few (CB radios), Dewar and Ang state that, "the Internet is the first true many-to-many communications medium (though we prefer to think of it as an any-to-many medium)" [6, p. 366]. On the other hand, Hansen says that "Within the history of technology, the crucial moment informing this reversal in the image's trajectory is the shift from photography to cinema, from the static to the (mechanically) moving image" [8, p. 261].

Perhaps the conclusion is that still, and then moving, pictures made a bigger impact on the way we think, while the Internet made more impact on the way we act and interact. For a while, Wang's "wicked word processor" arrested the movement from word to image that once seemed irresistible, while the resurgence of electronic games, YouTube, and even Twitter may be heralding the time when the dominance of the brain-damaging, linear, written word in our thinking will end, permitting us once again to think as we naturally are expected to think, in images, metaphors, allusions. These are issues to be contemplated again when we consider for the immediate and then the alternative futures before us.

3.7 Age-Cohort Analysis and Technological/Social Change

It was our intention to use age-cohort analysis as part of our research for this project. However, we were not able to find the kind of information needed for each period of technological and social change that we covered. Although we strongly suspect that there were generational differences in the adoption of each of the new communication technologies, just as there are in the present, we could not document that. We did find some evidence that early adopters of new technologies tend not to be people in roles firmly entrenched in the orgware of the older, still-dominant technologies. "Modernizers" who tried to "transfer" technology from "developed" to "underdeveloped" parts of the world have often said that it was likely to be the misfits and people generally not in power who would be willing to try the technology introduced to them by the outsider. This sometimes then gave the early adaptor or his family and friends power advantages once the new technology began to take hold.

This also accords with the fact demonstrated repeatedly in our research that substantial social change from a new technology does not typically occur when the technology is first invented or developed. It is not until the diffusion and maturity stages of a technology are reached that its social impact is most strongly felt. That impact should also coincide with when the technology is in fact no longer new for most users, but rather is something that has been part of their entire lives. It might have been new and strange for their parents or grandparents, but it was a normal part of their environment since the time they were born.

Age-cohort analysis [4, 18] is probably most useful for a society where social change is substantial and frequent, perhaps even continuous, as it has been increasingly for more and more people over the last several hundred years. Although generational differences associated with aging, social roles, and biological processes generally are probably universal, the kind of generational differences characteristic of rapidly changing modern and postmodern societies may be unique.

Age-cohort analysis is based on the observation that people born and growing up during the same time span, and in the same cultural space, tend to share ideas and beliefs about the world, some of which are different in important ways from the ideas and beliefs held by members of age-cohorts only a few years older or younger than they are. Thus, when an age-cohort with one "worldview" retires and leaves positions of political and economic power, and a new age-cohort with a different "worldview" comes in, the world changes because, holding different beliefs, the actions and policies of the newer cohort differ substantially from those of older cohorts. In these situations, studying the interaction between new technologies and new and old age-cohorts is useful in order to understand important aspects of the past, present, and futures.

Consider the United States in 2014. Many of America's currently oldest citizens were members of the cohort born in the 1910s and 1920s. They grew up during the Great Depression of the 1930s, and fought during the Second World War in the early 1940s, carrying with them forever the dashed hopes of the glittering post-World War I "Flapper Era," followed by profound poverty during the Great Depression, the horrors of World War Two, and then the sweet triumph of complete victory and global American dominance—tempered by the death of so many friends and loved ones. These events were the "galvanizing experiences" that defined the GIs as a cohort (GI is the abbreviation of the term "general issue" that was used to describe ordinary, often drafted military personnel of that war). The GI cohorts had a "can do" attitude towards almost anything, having been teased, tested, tempered—and triumphant. They earned and deserved the label "The Great Generation," living their adult lives during the height of a period when, after a troubling start, America ruled the world with sublime confidence in itself, its values, and its actions.

However, American children generally in all of the following age-cohorts have experienced neither significant widespread economic collapse nor war on a mass-mobilized, global scale. Many of them only know, and expect as a natural right, internal peace and prosperity without their having to struggle for or otherwise earn it. With one exception, each subsequent cohort has had its own defining galvanizing experiences (and of course many individuals and social groups in America have suffered excruciatingly or excelled effortlessly), but the experiences of cohorts *qua* cohorts after the GIs have not been of the wrenching profundity and extent of the Great Depression and World War II.

In addition to galvanizing experiences, childrearing fashions change, too, and influence adult behavior. One of the largest cohorts ever born in the United States—the so-called "Baby Boomers" born between the late 1940s and 1960, who are now beginning to retire from active work in large numbers—were reared by parents who followed the advice of Dr. Benjamin Spock in his enormously popular book of many editions, *The Common Sense Book of Baby and Child Care* [17]. Many of the parents of the Baby Boomers lived for the first time in suburban isolation, trying to rear four or five children without other, older, experienced family members around to guide them. Dr. Spock's book filled the void, telling them to just let their children "do their own thing," freely and without restraint. Trust your children's basic instincts. Drink up, and let them be.

Yet many of the children in the cohort of the 1930s and early 1940s, called the Silents and who were born before the Boomers, had been reared in a completely different way—"scientifically" and according to "the clock." According to *Psychological Care of Infant and Child* by John Broadus Watson, children were expected to eat at specific times (not sooner or later), to move their bowels on command (and not before or after the command), to take naps and go to bed at an exact moment on the clock, and in general to be disciplined by scientific, strict, mechanical, external forces—not by their own whims and internal rhythms and certainly not by the emotions or loving instincts of their mothers. Indeed love had nothing to do with child rearing, and mothers' ways generally were judged inferior to the scientific principles discovered, of course, by men [23].

For another example, over much of American history—beginning with the first president, George Washington—one had to be a war hero to be elected to national office. Generalissimo Dwight D. Eisenhower, an iconic WWII hero and American president, was another prominent example. All American presidents from Eisenhower through George H. W. Bush had served in the US military and had experienced active combat service (except for Ronald Reagan, who imagined he had). However, Bill Clinton, Al Gore, Newt Gingrich, George W. Bush, Barack Hussein Obama, Mitt Romney, and many more all became national leaders without having been in the military at all. Only about a quarter of the members of the US Congress in 2013 had been in the military. The life-warping experience of military life and especially active combat that conditioned almost all males and many females (and certainly almost all prior major political leaders) seems to have come to an end with Bill Clinton. It may be that people who have experienced active, boots-on-the-ground warfare are less likely to want to send others to fight and die in wars than might people for whom war is something abstract and glorified in movies and electronic games.

In the 2008 presidential election, only one of the main candidates for the presidency was a Gen Xer—the cohort born in the 1960s and 1970s. All the rest were Boomers—or older Silents. But the 2008 victor turned out to be a person who broke all the old rules about who could be elected president. Obama was the first Gen X president, born after the military draft had ended and when military service was no longer a widespread possibility and obligation. Obama's Republican opponent, John McCain, was a Boomer Vietnam war veteran who tried to use his experiences as a prisoner of war to get him elected. That was unappealing to young citizens, who massed to vote for hope and change—which then of course never happened as anticipated. Mitt Romney, Obama's Republican opponent in the 2012 presidential race, was also a Boomer who was able successfully to avoid the draft and military service.

It is worth noting the age-cohort of members of the US Supreme Court, since they are the final arbiters of controversy in the American political system. Who they are and what they think impacts every American for generations to come. Of the nine members of the 2014 Supreme Court, almost half—four of the nine—are antique Silents (listed from oldest to youngest in each cohort: Ginsburg, Scalia, Kennedy, and Breyer). Most of the rest—four more—are fading Boomers (Thomas, Alito, Sotomayor, Roberts). Only one of the members of the US Supreme Court might be considered Gen X—but only barely so (Kagan).

These are the people who make official and often final decisions about technologies proposed or developing, and about how people should or should not use them. How might they decide, given their cohort experiences? How representative are they of current much less future generations, whose lives they strongly influence by their decisions?

The age-cohort labels used here come from William Strauss and Neil Howe's *Generations: The History of America's Future, 1584 to 2069* [18]. Strauss and Howe persuasively demonstrated that there have been four successive "generations" of Americans who have cycled through American history from colonial times to the present, and, they forecast, on through the twenty-first century, into the futures.

The four cohort-types found in the past and present, and expected in the future in the United States are labeled:

Idealists
Reactives
Civics
Adaptives

Then the cycle begins again with new Idealists, then, new Reactives, and so on.

As the name implies, the Idealists have some new vision of the future that they strive to articulate, but are not able to achieve in their lifetime. The next generation, Reactives, reject the Idealists' dream, and harken back to the ideals of earlier cohorts as their guide. Then the next cohort, the Civics, accept the Idealists' vision as given, and do their best to see that it becomes reality; they see the world through the lens of the Idealists, and strive to actualize it.

However, the vision is spent and weak by the time the next generation comes along, and yet they have no viable alternative to offer. So these Adaptives simply do the best they can with the old ideals, but are cynical about the possibility of anything new or better for the future, until a generation of new Idealists comes along with a new ideal … and so on forever through American history and futures, say Strauss and Howe.

The authors wrote several more very influential books describing in more detail the differences between the cohorts. They have changed their terminology and some of the details along the way, but their basic formulation has remained. From our perspective, what is most important about their scheme compared to other examples of age-cohort analysis is that theirs intends to be predictive. Their research convinced them that the cohort cycles extend back in American history to 1584 and can be projected to 2069 and beyond. They believe the cycle of cohorts provides general guidelines by which to anticipate the overall contours of the attitudes and behavior of each future cohort.

There has been considerable dispute about this. But for our purposes here, we follow their original formulation as we consider the cohorts from the GIs to the Millennials and beyond in terms of the technologies that shaped each of them and that they then shaped by virtue of the specific manifestation of their generic cohort characteristics.

It is important to remember that age-cohort analysis is a sociological tool, describing overall, average, typical behavior. It thus is an abstraction, generalization, or perhaps a caricature in relation to any specific individual's behavior. It also is more likely to be true of the middle classes than of either the upper or lower classes of American society, and should be more likely descriptive of people born in the "middle" of a cohort than of those born near the beginning or the end of a cohort. Finally, while Strauss and Howe's research is based on cohorts in the United States, it has spurred considerable interest elsewhere in the world, and many people in cultures similar to that of the United States informally report something similar to what Strauss and Howe claim.

The GI's are the last American generation that learned primarily by direct experience of hard manual labor, especially on the farm. They are the last cohort who knew how to skin a moose, churn butter, and prime a pump. All formal learning was by live lectures and sermons, and reading and writing (though only a small portion of them did much reading or writing until the GI bill sent thousands of them to college at federal taxpayer expense who never would have gone otherwise, setting the stage for America as a future information society). Newspapers, radio, black and white still photographs, and black and white silent movies were part of their environment when young—talking movies came later. Color movies and live television were introduced when they were adults and were considered to be entertaining non-essential frills—frosting on a pound cake of reality. For them, the empirical world of their senses was what mattered. Media were something they consumed as they chose. Producing ideas through any medium other than speaking, writing, and manufacturing never occurred to most of them.

The automobile made increased auto-mobility possible for some GIs, but not for all. They were extremely thrifty and hardworking. Being Civics, they believed strongly in the dream of America's Manifest Destiny of the nineteenth century, and were fully confident in the ability of real Americans to do anything they put their minds to. They were cautiously optimistic about the future—while also fully aware of its fragility. They were racially prejudiced if white or passively accepting of racial discrimination if not. For a brief period during WWII, their women flooded the workplace, only to be sent home afterwards where almost everyone agreed they belonged.

The next generation, the Silents, grew up with color movies and live broadcast television, but reading and writing still prevailed. Indeed this was the Golden Age of mass newspapers, magazines, and serious book reading. They were also consumers and not producers of new media. The Silents were very few in number—the smallest cohort in American history—and, as Reactives, tended to identify mainly with the older GIs in most essential ways, having no particular distinctive style or influences of their own—save those resulting from their very strict and by-the-clock "scientific" child-rearing experiences.

Vitamins were invented while the Silents were young and given to them for the first time. Moreover, they are the last American generation to have eaten plenty of balanced, home-cooked food instead of obesity-causing fast foods in their youth. Struggles for and against racial integration were a major feature of their youth, and they remain fundamentally racially prejudiced if vaguely tolerant. There have no doubt that a woman's place is in the home though tolerate the "gals" elsewhere. They are as thrifty as the GIs, but much more cynical about life and the future. Basically, they are so few in number that they don't matter, squashed between the triumphant GIs and the numerous Boomers—but this atypical cohort currently dominates the US Supreme Court, as we have seen, exercising great power well beyond their small numbers.

The Boomers—the largest age-cohort in American history—are Idealists by cohort designation. Hippies, flower children, devotees of drugs, sex, and rock n' roll when young, they were loved but pretty much "let be" by their distracted parents, following the advice of Dr. Spock. Audio and videotape enabled them to record and manipulate reality for themselves the first time. But for the most part, they were passive, vinyl natives. Though still educated by reading and writing, their world was increasingly mediated by audiovisual images. As they aged, their preferred analog-mediated realities faded away as they reluctantly tried to adjust to new digital ones.

Boomers expected to have automobiles and air conditioning as a matter of right. Indeed, they have a strong sense of entitlement to everything, in part because of their large numbers and in part by virtue of being Idealists. Struggles for and against racial equality and women's liberation were dramatic events in their young lives. Being world-class complainers without a clue, they once were groupie peaceniks, but later often fueled the Tea Party. They will soon swell high-tech, assisted-living settlements, though some insist they do not ever intend to die.

Pity the poor Gen-Xers, generically called "Reactives" because they have no dreams of their own as a cohort—a cohort so colorless it doesn't even have a distinctive name, just an X. Television was a given, but computers were new to them, though they struggled to master their use. They were latch-key kids from broken homes who grew up by surviving on their own and so are highly individualistic and self-centered—far more so than any other American cohort, past or future. Being the "echo" of the Silents, they are also relatively few in number, and therefore are often squeezed out by the numerous Boomers who think they will never die, and by the persistent and healthy old Silents who actually may never die because their food and lifestyles were so wholesome. One of the distinctive features of Gen X is that absolutely nothing happened to them as a cohort. Though often bitterly remembering their parents' fights, divorces, and neglect, and experiencing personal tragedies, they are unique as a cohort in reporting no generation-defining galvanizing experiences *per se*.

The Millennials started out the same way—in a safe, orderly, plain vanilla world—but 9/11 ended their calm and placid lives. Millennials are relatively numerous Civics who are the best educated and most thoroughly pampered and group-oriented cohorts in American history. They are typically only children (some have one sibling), went to the best schools, acing the AP classes, were driven to Suzuki violin practice and Mandarin lessons by their "helicopter" parents who protected them from every threat real or imagined. They never "went outside" to play. That was too dangerous. Rather they all played soccer on manicured fields, strictly by the rules, on teams with caring adult coaches and referees and cute little uniforms, while their doting parents cheered them on nervously, praising their every move, no matter how inept. Winning didn't matter. At the end, both sides were taken to share ice cream together.

Millennials can't stand the slightest criticism and expect to be given high grades, awards, promotions, and effusive praise for everything they do. If they don't get the praise they want from their parents and teachers—and they don't, no matter how much praise is heaped on them—then they form little peer groups where they praise each other's crappy work, and then tweet to the world about things no one else in the world cares about, but pretends to, so that their own trivial tweets will be read and praised as "Oh My God! That's totally awesome. Like me, one day, at band camp … ." They were raised to be praised, and as long as everyone plays by the rules and no one gets seriously hurt, they are wonderful, group-oriented, hard workers.

Computers to them are like water to a fish, and not for computing—strictly for communicating. They will not read anything unless forced to do so. They are the first true digital natives, suckled by interactive electronic games and not passive TV, and then weaned on iPhones, iPads, YouTube, Facebook, Twitter, Instagram, Vine, and the rest. The Millennials are eagerly awaiting the next generation of technologies, and their heads are in the cloud searching for them. They have made ADD a virtue in their increasingly artificial worlds, and some have observed, with awe, the shifts, if only in perspective, that technological change can and might engender across generations.

On October 6, 2011, a short video of a one-year old entitled, "A Magazine Is an iPad That Does Not Work," was uploaded to Youtube.com [21]. We have no way to judge the authenticity of what is depicted. With clever editing a video can tell any story the editor wants it to tell. But if taken at face value, it is a compelling story. In the opening sequence, a baby is shown playing with Apple's iPad, which has a highly responsive touchscreen interface that clearly stimulates the inquisitive child. In subsequent vignettes, the eager tot is shown repeatedly playing with various magazines as if they were tablet computers to no avail—hence, the video's droll title. In the closing shot, the child is again shown using the iPad and three lines of text appear: "For my 1-year old daughter, a magazine is an iPad that does not work. It will remain so for her whole life. Steve Jobs has coded a part of her OS" [21]. Although Steve Jobs, the iconic former CEO of Apple, is given credit, it should be clear, if not obvious, that a veritable symphony of *actants*, from mining operations in the Democratic Republic of the Congo to the availability of retail space within American shopping malls, played an integral part in the coding of the baby's OS. As the global footprint of new technologies has grown, generational perspectives on social phenomena has kept pace.

As the most diverse generation in US history, Millennials are largely without prejudice concerning ethnicity, gender, or sexual preference—since that would require them to make a judgment about something which they absolutely cannot do. But the Great Recession royally jolted them. They had made a bargain with adults that if they played by the rules, studied hard, did community service, amassed tons of college tuition and consumer debt as they were told to do, then they would all get great high-paying jobs. When they fulfilled their part of the bargain but the jobs did not materialize while their debts grew, they fell back on what always worked for them as children. As if enacting the will of their Gen-X predecessors, who shared their frustration, Millennials decided to Occupy Wall Street and other public spaces, keeping them neat, tidy, and nonviolent while inventing one of the coolest social communication technologies ever—the Human Microphone [22]. Nonetheless, if things really go bad, they are ripe for a good dictator/parent/referee who promises to make the trains run on time.

Some futurists say that the era of the information society is over and that the next technologically driven era emerging is the Dream Society of icons and aesthetic experience [5]. For most of human history, the production of food and material goods required enormous amounts of human labor and attention. With the scientific-industrial revolution from the eighteenth and nineteenth centuries, these activities became increasingly automated and trivial, requiring fewer and fewer people to produce more and more food and material goods. From the 1960s in the United States and other countries, the production and consumption of information became central, and so an information society emerged. Now, the production and consumption of unique identity and dreams via social media and popular culture products is replacing information in centrality and importance, some say.

Elements of a Dream Society already exist in the behavior of the Millennials, but it may dominate the lives of the next generation, initially labeled the Cybers by Strauss and Howe. Cybers are presently being born or are still in school, and thus are difficult to characterize confidently. The Cybers are generically Adaptives. As such, certain things about them can be anticipated if the theory holds up.

They will tend not to have strong opinions on their own. They will probably identify initially with Millennials, and, later in their lives with the Idealists who will come after them. Their young lives will be lived almost entirely in dynamic virtual realities of their own choosing or creation. Genetically modified and artificially intelligent beings may be their friends and lovers much to the chagrin of their parents and grandparents, who will be prejudiced against the artilects the Cybers embrace.

The major galvanizing experience for them may occur when they are young adults, when cheap and abundant energy runs out and they discover that nothing has been developed to replace it after the lights fitfully blink out. Environmental issues, long neglected and exacerbated, will demand their attention as the oceans rise, potable water disappears, food becomes very scarce, corporations collapse, the machines stop, and Tea-partied governments are absolutely incapable of doing anything about it. If it occurs, this will be a galvanizing experience beyond any in American history—even eclipsing the Civil War in that regard.

Although tragic for the remaining Boomers and Millennials, the Cybers know how to adapt. They have no expectation of social support from government or corporations to begin with, and so will quickly learn to rely (peacefully or violently) only on their friends, neighbors and themselves as the Dream Society vanishes and they wake up to new, unmediated realities.

Of course, that is only one possible future. Industrial/Information societies may continue to dominate, while an extended Dream Society is always possible, but increasingly likely as well is a prolonged period of economic stagnation, energy shortages, environmental challenges, and political stalemate. For this, the Boomers will deserve a lot of the responsibility because there are so many of them demanding to be instantly gratified until death doeth them part. Surviving Gen Xers will be busy taking care of Number One and to hell with everyone else as they have always done, while the surviving Millennials will be tweeting each other on foot-pedal-operated twittering machines. Only the adaptive Cybers will thrive, as many of the values and institutions of their great, great grandparents, the GIs and Silents, become relevant once again, but without the ethnic, gender, sexual prejudices and violence of their time.

But who can predict the futures? We will consider other alternatives later in this report.

For most of human history, the majority of individuals and communities have lived in "one present" and looked forward to "one future," in part defined by one level of technologies. For most of human history, technological change was rare, slow, and the social and environmental consequences of new technologies went almost unnoticed. During most of this time, people lived, thought, and communicated orally/aurally and collectively in small face-to-face groups, not separately and individually. There was no clear experience of—and hence often no concept of—"privacy" or "my individual rights." With the emergence of literacy, some Chinese, Indian, Greek, Roman, and Islamic philosophers began to experience a world of the private, inner self somewhat separate from that of their local oral/aural community.

But the overwhelming majority of humans neither imagined nor experienced privacy or individual moral freedom. Though the seeds for individualism had been sown with the invention of writing, the social utility and impact of what the earlier philosophers experienced and discussed in their tomes was near zero, until they were rediscovered in the late European Middle Ages and early modern era.

This all changed with the scientific-industrial revolution and events leading up to it (the Reformation, Renaissance, and Enlightenment) when people began using technologies that gave them the repeated experience and then the concept of individualism and individual freedom, while the flood of ideas spread by the invention of the printing press and later the social technology and orgware of the universal literacy programs of the modern public school systems gave them the words to explain and justify their experiences and feelings.

Among the first social scientists to chart this development and in a way forecast what would become early twenty-first century beliefs and lifestyles were David Riesman, Nathan Glazer, and Reuel Denney whose best-selling sociology book, *The Lonely Crowd: A Study of the Changing American Character*, anticipated the rise and fall of individualism within American culture over sixty years ago [16].

Throughout most of human history, as we have seen, humans lived their entire lives in small homogeneous groups. The "mores of the tribe" predetermined all required, allowed, and prohibited behavior (and probably thoughts). Anyone socialized into those mores knew without question what was right and wrong, and since they seldom ventured outside of the confines of their small community, the rules worked wondrously well in every situation they encountered.

With the rise of "civilization" and monotheistic or otherwise absolutist religions based on writing, some of these tribal mores became written religious doctrines so that even during the height of the vast Holy Roman Empire during the European Middle Ages, the system of moral rules and enforcement of the Roman Catholic Church, called casuistry, exemplified in many ways, including the confessional, provided most people of the time with a complete set of absolute rules of behavior and of punishment for violation of the rules.

With the eventual collapse of the Church's monopoly and the rise of Protestantism, the Renaissance, and increased modes of physical and social mobility, the old casuistic method became increasingly problematic for all the novel situations people encountered that required new ways of determining and enforcing moral and ethical behavior.

Protestantism was in part a revolt against casuistry and its perceived abuses, but Protestants, no less than Roman Catholics, believed in absolute right and wrong. However, instead of trying to create a huge matrix that included all possible behaviors on one side, all possible situations on another, and all possible remedies in the resulting cells, as casuistry did in effect, Protestants, in the terminology of Riesman et al. created and implanted a "gyroscope" inside each believer that enabled each mobile human to "look inward" in order to determine for himself or herself what was right and wrong in every situation encountered. Riesman et al. said that early modern humans—the kinds that established and led the United States for the first

125 years or so—were "inner-directed" individualists. But with the decline of an agricultural society composed of many small, closely knit, and isolated communities not only in the United States but in all "developed" nations, and with waves of people from all over the world flooding in to cities with repeatedly clashing cultures and values, even the gyroscope could no longer cope. Gradually, and with much uncertainty, criticism, and anguish, people began to become "other-directed," guided by a kind of "radar" bouncing off of all of the myriad new people in new situations one meets. Most people, especially young people, were no longer inner-directed individuals with absolute standards of right and wrong fit for every circumstance, but other-directed members of ever-changing groups with ever-changing notions of right and wrong. They exhibited what came later to be called "situational ethics"—ethics determined by one group of people in one situation that might not be appropriate for themselves or another group of people in another situation.

By identifying this behavior Riesman et al. were among the first to recognize that not only was the United States not predominantly an agricultural society any longer but also that it was swiftly morphing into a post-industrial, service—later designated "information"—society where what was important was not what one's culture, church, family, or god said was right or wrong, but what one's peers said when one's peers were also in rapid flux throughout one's life.

One of the most influential developments encouraging the spread of the idea of and demand for privacy in the United States was an essay written by Samuel Warren and Louis Brandeis in *Harvard Law Review* in 1890 titled, "The Right to Privacy." They specifically based the notion of such a right on recent technological developments such as "Instantaneous photographs and newspaper enterprises [that] have invaded the sacred precincts of private and domestic life; and numerous mechanical devices [that] threaten to make good the predictions that 'what is whispered in the closet shall be proclaimed from the housetops.'" [12, p. 35]

Later, as a Supreme Court justice, Brandeis wrote a dissent to the 5-4 *Olmstead v US* wiretapping case in 1928, arguing that Olmstead had the right to be left alone in the privacy of his home that the wiretap violated. In the past, Brandeis noted, government tortured people, or physically broke into their homes and stole information. That has been forbidden by the US Constitution. Now, however, "subtler and more far-reaching means of invading privacy have become available to the Government, by means far more effective than stretching upon the rack, to obtain disclosure in court of what is whispered in the closet." Even more presciently, Brandeis anticipated that "ways may someday be developed by which the Government, without removing papers from secret drawers, can reproduce them in court, and by which it will be enabled to expose to a jury the most intimate occurrences of the home" [12, p. 36].

Indeed, as Brandeis anticipated, through the third quarter of the twentieth century, societies were increasingly redefined by successive waves of individualizing technologies, spreading worldwide. Highlighted by the individualizing influences of the automobile and the telephone especially, each new technology seemed to free (or alienate) the individual from the traditions of the geographically defined, oral/aural community, eventually creating new humans each with what seemed to be their own unique sense of self and their future—their unique set of personal values and beliefs—leading to the opportunities and disasters characteristic of modern times.

From the mid-1950s, however, new technologies began to emerge that at first continued to individualize, but soon tended once again to collectivize. Because they often operated at a global level and frequently in conflict with values and institutions based on earlier local, collectivizing technologies, they were often initially mistakenly interpreted as intensifying the long-run individualizing trend.

The first of these technologies that initially seemed to act as continuing the experience of individualization but soon led to a new collective consciousness and behavioral preference was television (creating what Marshall McLuhan correctly labeled "the global village"). The second was the personal computer when global social networking began and the monopoly of established local expert authority ended. And the third are the currently expanding social media and their emerging hive mind, perhaps enhanced and at least not deterred by their desires for collective security and comfort. Preferences for group work, decision-making, and behavior expressed by the Millennial age-cohort seem both to exhibit and reinforce this trend. "This has led," Jill Lepore observed, "in our own time, to the paradox of an American culture obsessed, at once, with being seen and with being hidden, a world in which the only thing more cherished than privacy is publicity. In this world, we chronicle our lives on Facebook while demanding the latest and best form of privacy protection" [12, p. 36].

This stupefying ambivalence may be facilitated by something else unique that also began to occur during early modernity and continues to accelerate today: technological and social change became so rapid that individuals and communities were caught for the first time in a whirlpool of technologies, values, and institutions, some of which were obsolete and vanishing, some were old and fading, some were current and thriving, others were new and emerging, and others so vividly imagined in fiction and fantasy that they seemed real, but in fact have not yet been achieved.

Thus, at the present time, older age-cohorts still live by vanishing and fading technologies, values, and institutions; middle-aged cohorts by fading and thriving technologies, values, and institutions; while younger cohorts embrace emerging and imagined technologies, with new cohorts and new technologies still to be born. Nonetheless, each cohort, individual, and the community as a whole are also at the same time possessed in some measure by the technologies, values, and institutions of all four sequences.

Something like this may have been experienced by people caught in earlier periods of technological/social/environmental upheaval and change. But as a potential "new normal," it may be unique to human experience for each age-cohort to live in its own substantially different world while at the same time having to cope with beliefs, behaviors, and institutions comfortable to other cohorts. Intergenerational communication and easy understanding becomes even more difficult. Cultural chaos reigns. Age-cohort analysis thus becomes an even more vital additional tool for anticipating the futures.

If we adopt once again the conventional designation of agricultural, industrial, and information societies, and consider the values, technologies, and metaphors from each level that still exists in the present, our situation might be described as follows:

3.7.1 Agricultural era Metaphors, Institutions, and Values Still Persist in the United States

With the printing press as the iconic technology and the Bible as the iconic text, many Americans still say that God is their king, with Heaven and Earth as His kingdom while they are His loyal (or disloyal) subjects with no rights or wills of their own. Alternatively, going back to even earlier nomadic societies, they may say God is their shepherd and that they are His ignorant and willful sheep in need of (kindly) protection and (sacrificial) salvation.

Another very clear example of how the rhythms of long-dead agricultural societies still control us today is found in the structures, processes, and holidays of American educational institutions. Classes from kindergarten through graduate school typically are held in classrooms in buildings on campuses to which one must physically go. Lectures begin in the fall, after the crops are in and winter beginning, and end in the late spring and summer when all hands are needed in the fields to bring in the crops. Air conditioning apparently has not yet been invented. Classes are not held on weekends in order to keep the Sabbath holy. Classes are not held at night in order that everyone can go to bed early and get up with the chickens. Administrators are called principals, provosts, chancellors, and other medieval terms, while faculty members and students have no effective role in hiring or firing them. Faculty and students dress like medieval monks trying to keep out the cold with their thick and flowing robes on graduation day, the most formal ceremonial academic event of the school year, when Latin is spoken and parchment displayed. All of this makes no sense at all in our current world and yet so far even MOOCs seem unable fundamentally to change the agricultural images and practices of our schools, even though no cohorts who could recognize one end of a cow from the other are either going to school or working there.

Even though we are all touched by globalization, we still are urged to retain local loyalties, prize glorified small town communities, and root for the Home Team.

3.7.2 Industrial Metaphors, Institutions, and Values Linger

Transportation technologies defined and dominated the industrial era, producing first the railroad, then the automobile, then the airplane, thus creating both the city with its suburbs and the nation as two iconic institutions.

The automobile, providing auto-mobility, was the dominant icon. Reinforced by the landline telephone, nothing provoked the sense of individualism, freedom, personal identity, and social irresponsibility more than the automobile. Its allure and power is still extraordinary. Everywhere it goes, the automobile transforms obedient, community-focused peasants and workers into reckless pleasure-seeking teenagers of all ages.

Commuting, "rush hour" traffic jams, horrendous deaths and injuries, environmental pollution, and oil wars are its side effects, in spite of which the attraction of personal identity through sports car/SUV auto-mobility is far too strong to allow telework to end commuting, or for other forms of transport, especially bicycles and walking, to end pollution and oil wars until the oil runs out.

Suburbs continue to sprawl with highways, grotesque McMansions, and strip malls eating up farmland everywhere. The examples are American, but the process now is global.

3.7.3 Information Metaphors, Institutions, and Values Shape Lives

Just as individualizing transportation technologies shaped industrial societies, so also do collectivizing communication technologies define information societies. First movies and then television were the initial icons, followed by personal computers and the Internet, and now social media.

The focus of life is no longer production to satisfy human needs, but endless consumption in order to fulfill the mania of perpetual economic growth that ruling economic ideologies require; the end of the human expert/authority and the rise of personal and peer fantasies; and the dominance of entertainment, and especially of professional sports, and of virtuality over "reality" in general.

Space for living has moved from the local community, to the nation, to the global in effect, though old local and national institutions massively restrain and restrict globalization.

Cohorts defined primarily by one of the three modes of technology struggle to co-exist with cohorts and environments defined by the other two. Agricultural, industrial, and information institutions, values, and cohorts uneasily co-exist, with none able to supplant the others. What's next?

References

1. Carlson WB (2001) The telephone as political instrument: Gardiner Hubbard and the formation of the middle class in America. In: Hughes TP et al (eds) Technologies of power: essays in honor of Thomas Parke Hughes and Agatha Chipley Hughes. MIT, Cambridge, pp 1875–1880
2. Cirino R (1977) We're being more than entertained. Lighthouse, New York

3. Coombe RJ (1998) The cultural life of intellectual properties: authorship, appropriation, and the law. Duke University Press, Durham
4. Dator J (2008) Next generations: reactives to civics to adaptives. Educ Technol Change J http://etcjournal.com/2008/10/01/jim-dator/. Accessed Oct 2010
5. Dator J, Seo Y (2008) Korea as the wave of a future: the emerging dream society of icons and aesthetic experience. In: Hoare J et al (eds) Korea: the past and the present: selected papers from the British Association for Korean studies. Global Oriental, Folkestone
6. Dewar J, Ang PH (2007) The cultural consequences of printing and the Internet. In: Baron SA et al (eds) Agent of change: print culture studies after Elizabeth L. Eisenstein. University of Massachusetts Press, Amherst
7. Elon University School of Communications (2014). Imagining the Internet: A history and forecast. 1830s-1860s Telegraph. http://www.elon.edu/e-web/predictions/150/1830.xhtml Accessed 20 Jan 2012
8. Hansen MBN (2000) Embodying technesis: technology beyond writing. University of Michigan Press, Ann Arbor
9. Illich I (2009) Tools for conviviality. Marion Boyars, London
10. Katsh ME (1989) The electronic media and the transformation of law. Oxford University Press, New York
11. Kelly K (1994) Out of control. Perseus Books, Reading, MA
12. Lepore J (2013) The Prism. http://www.newyorker.com/reporting/2013/06/24/130624fa_fact_lepore. Accessed 25 Jun 2013
13. McLeod K (2004) How copyright law changed hip hop. http://www.alternet.org/story/18830/how_copyright_law_changed_hip_hop Accessed 17 Mar 2014
14. McLuhan M (1962) The Gutenberg galaxy: the making of typographic man. University of Toronto Press, Toronto
15. McLuhan M (1964) Understanding media: the extensions of man. New American Library, New York
16. Riesman D et al (1950) The lonely crowd: a study of the changing American character. Yale University Press, New Haven, CT
17. Spock B (1946) The Common Sense Book of Baby and Child Care. Duell, Sloan and Pearce, New York
18. Strauss W (1991) Generations: the history of America's future, 1584 to 2069. Quill, New York
19. Teilhard de Chardin P (2004) The future of man. Image Books/Doubleday, New York
20. Toffler A (1991) Powershift: knowledge, wealth, and violence at the edge of the 21st century. Bantam Books, New York
21. UserExperienceWorks (2011) A magazine is an iPad that does not work. http://www.youtube.com/watch?feature=player_embedded&v=aXV-yaFmQNk. Accessed 12 Jan 2012
22. Wanenchak S (2011) Mic checking the man: the evolving human microphone. http://thesocietypages.org/cyborgology/2011/11/17/mic-checking-the-man-the-evolving-human-microphone/. Accessed 20 Nov 2012
23. Watson JB (1928) Psychological care of infant and child hardcover. W. W Norton, New York

Chapter 4
Communication Technology in the Extended Present and Futures

4.1 What's Next?

If you do not know what the above image is, then you are either behind the times or well ahead of the time these words were written. Indeed, this image is a bit behind the times. Given how quickly technologies change and society is changed by technology, you should not be surprised or feel bad. Quick Response (or QR) codes were invented in the mid-1990s by a firm working with Toyota to track auto parts through the manufacturing supply chain. By the late 2000s, QR codes became popular with advertisers seeking to exploit the rapid growth of the smartphone market,

J.A. Dator et al., *Mutative Media: Communication Technologies and Power Relations in the Past, Present, and Futures*, Lecture Notes in Social Networks,
DOI 10.1007/978-3-319-07809-0_4, © Springer International Publishing Switzerland 2015

but due to some challenges, primarily issues with scanning and broken links, QR codes have fallen from grace with the tech community, although they can still be seen and found in many places and remain popular with artists and museums. The rise of QR codes would have been impossible without the advent of smartphones, which would have been impossible without the rise of wireless Internet access, which would have been impossible without the rise of high-capacity processors, and so on and so on, as we have shown. Ultimately, no technology emerges in a vacuum, and all technologies reflect the world in which they emerge, which is to say that they are deeply and intimately entwined with social and political phenomena.

Unless you have a smartphone and the connectivity available in 2014, you may be unable to scan the above image. If you cannot scan the above image, you will not be able to watch the YouTube video described below that introduces this section. We chose to create a technological barrier or bridge to demonstrate and problematize not only the "digital divide" but also the structural ways by which media mutate and are mutated. Although we wanted to highlight the barriers technology can create, there are often workarounds and hacks for various technological obstacles, and so as to level the playing field one *might* also be able to view the video using the following link: http://bit.ly/IAygOl.

With the invention, development, and diffusion of the Internet, humankind launched itself into an unprecedented era of dynamic, interactive communicating—simply put, we have been mutated once again. As with other communication technologies, the Web as medium *massages* its users, and the basis for its efficacy as a system is built on the backs of politically charged protocols that provide limits as much as possibilities. Ultimately, the Internet's mutative mediation is a result of the ability for the *many* to communicate directly with the *many* or *any* for the first time in known history, which has led to the development of new kinds of software and orgware. There are many examples of this emergent phenomena, with Eric Whitacre's virtual choir perhaps being one of the best. The 'choir' was composed by blending electronically the singing of 2,000+ solo singers from around the world who each individually sent in videos of their part in the musical ensemble. This 'choir' exemplifies the Web's mutative capacity.

Marveling at the plight of a choir member from rural Alaska, Whitacre reflects, "Humans beings will go to any lengths necessary to find and connect with each other. It doesn't matter the technology. [...] People seem to be experiencing an *actual* connection. It wasn't a virtual choir ... there are people now online ... they're friends ... they've never met ... myself ... I feel this virtual *esprit de corps* with all of them. I feel a closeness to this choir ... almost like a family" [46]. Whitacre's virtual choir gives voice, literally, to the communicative proclivity of humans, including those who seem closed off from the rest of the world. Noting the intimacy engendered by the Web's many-to-many and/or many-to-any interface, Whitacre alludes to the diffuse challenges and opportunities of (relatively) new media, which seems to differ markedly from its predecessors.

As we have discussed, humans have had the capacity to engage in one-to-one, one-to-few, and few-to-few communication since the dawn of orality, which enabled and perhaps was enabled by new software and orgware. As Ong observes, "Primary orality fosters personality structures that in certain ways are more communal and externalized, and less introspective than those common among literates. Oral communication unites people in groups" [30, p. 67]. From there, we expanded to one-to-many communication with the invention of writing, printing, telegraph, telephone, radio, and film/television, which also engendered and was engendered by new software and orgware. The Internet, as Whitacre's remarks denote, does both, while many-to-many communication has only been made possible in the era of networked communication. The capabilities of social media in the first part of the twenty-first century take advantage of this ability for many-to-many communication, and this shift has had profound social impacts on the power structures in society. We have seen the hopes for an Arab Spring, which some ordained a "Facebook" [39] and/or "Twitter" [19] revolution, and the Occupy movement, both of which utilized the galvanizing capabilities of social media to spur and inspire social movements. Whether or not these events would have happened without the existence of the Internet-based communication technologies cannot be proven one way or the other. There have been numerous revolutions and social movements in the past when such communication technologies did not exist. With that said, it *is* clear that these events relied heavily upon the speed and public visibility afforded by social media and the Internet as a new means to achieve their ends. When Egypt attempted to shut down the Internet at the height of the Tahrir Square protests, the potentially mutative power of these technologies became readily apparent.

As we will argue, this era of many-to-many communication may be now on the brink of yet another transformation. The coming transformation has to do with machine-based algorithmic learning and communication as well as biologically engineered communication technologies, including, and perhaps especially, nanotechnology [8, 12]. Both of these burgeoning fields are extraordinarily mutative in that the technologies being created, within their very source code, contain the structural ability for futures' mutation beyond their original development and diffusion. All communication technologies, as we have shown, typically begin with one intention and then mutate to fill other previously unintended and unimagined roles in society. But until recently this mutative capacity typically has been deeply interdependent upon human agency. A cell phone might be mutated to become an IED (Improvised Explosive Device) or mutated to become a networked learning device. But with the advent of machine learning and bioengineering we may see the mutations and transformations of communication technologies occurring from within the technology itself without the necessity for human agency to unleash, or even guide, these mutative potentialities. Humans may, in many ways, no longer be primarily in the driver's seat. As a result we may see the technologies themselves taking on a much more profound role in the shaping of society in the futures beyond the capacity of human agency, which has always been shaped by the tools that make and remake us as humans. The "we" in McLuhan's off-quoted phrase who shape technology, only to be reshaped by the technology themselves, may no longer just be old *Homo sapiens, sapiens*, but also many new forms of intelligence as well.

4.1.1 Life in "Real Time": Temporality and Visibility in the Internet Age

In our analysis of technological change throughout history and into the futures, the critical importance of temporality has become clearer. We have observed, along with many scholars before us, that often a new communication technology will not emerge unless it enables communication that is faster, with more storage capacity, greater dispersion and accessibility, or a combination of those than what was previously thought possible [33]. Among these, the increase in speed has particular ramifications for human social interaction.

The communication achieved with a letter sent via a national postal service is very different from that achieved with an email or text, for example. Both the style of communication and the information communicated will be deeply affected by the medium used to communicate. As Mary Ann Doane argues in *Information, Crisis, Catastrophe*, "The noeme of photography is the … 'that-has-been' … the principle gesture of photography would be that of embalming … The temporal dimension of television, on the other hand, would seem to be that of an insistent 'present-ness'—a 'this is going on.'" [10, p. 250] This present-ness is a thirsty engine always demanding the new, with the consequence being a very short collective memory span. Writing in the 1990s, Doane did not foresee the Internet and the speed of 'real time' information, a virtual deluge of information that accosts any consumer of media today. Nor did she apparently note that television also constantly re-animates and then re-embalms the past via endless reruns of old movies and television shows.

Our ability to access media resources from the past is greater than it ever has been. Where once one had to go to a library to access limited available resources, today anyone with a smartphone, iPad or other networked device has access to vast amounts of written literature, radio, as well as past and present visual media. There is a kind of "nowness" to the past that is unique and important to note. The present now extends 150 years—if not 150,000 years—into the past, and through science fiction and futures forecasts, into the futures. This access has had important ramifications in the area of education. The discourse of 'twenty-first century' learning addresses the role of the teacher as shifting from 'pedagogical master who conveyed expert knowledge' to 'facilitator of information who helps learners organize and communicate the information' that is literally at their fingertips—the clichéd shift from the "sage on the stage" to the "guide by your side."

This sense of 'real time' interaction and access to the source of information is meant to engender a feeling of control in the consumer of information. We are made to feel that we are directing the search as we comb the Web for the latest—or oldest—news and information. But if we look at the protocol with which we search, we find that we are actually only able to expand our choices "within a commodity driven economy while leaving intact the restricted, corporate-produced definition of choice" [10, p. 263]. In other words, the software, hardware, and orgware matter deeply. By equating the real with the now, we may lose certain critical connections and fail to see important interrelationships. In reference to the events of September

11, Doane argues that our addiction to real time effectively transforms "a political act into something with the proportions of a monumental natural disaster (or a grandiose battle between an abstractly defined good and evil), at the expense of any more nuanced attempt at historical explication" [10, p. 262]. At a time when converging environmental, social, economic, and political pressures are challenging humankind, our ability to focus and muster the patience needed to understand complexity may be a critical capacity. But at the same time, our access to diverse information is important for expanding our capacity of understanding these complex issues.

Also, perhaps, as McLuhan suggested, electronic communication technologies are reviving certain dominant features of primitive orality. Oral speech is overwhelmingly about events of the now on the one hand and the repeated ritualized mythic exaggerated remembering of certain heroic people and acts in the past on the other. Our ability to stop time and analyze ideas, and to go back to sources giving different interpretations of mythologized past events was only enabled first by writing, and then deeply ingrained through the orgware of educational and legal practices enabled by the hardware of the printing press.

With the rise of first the Internet and then social media there has also been a shift in our sense and acceptance of public visibility. We now create multiple digital personas, some of which are wildly different from our real-world one. We allow deeply personal information about ourselves and our loved ones to be openly and widely disseminated with little thought to where that information goes or how it is used. There has also recently been more discussion around our 'digital identities' and what happens to all this information about us when we die. This phenomenon is exacerbated by the sense of gossipy private intimacy provoked by social media. Some claim to have been haunted by "ghosts of Facebook," or users who have died but who through the interface remain "alive" to their network of friends. The orgware surrounding this mutation seems to be struggling to catch up with the media that stalk the living [49].

Being seen and known online found great purchase in one of the first massive social media websites, MySpace, which allowed community members to post images of themselves, a profile, songs they like, and so on in an effort to connect to others with similar interests in an online 'community.' [5] Although MySpace eventually faded and gave way to Facebook, Twitter, LinkedIn, Pinterest and others, the idea is much the same. You create an identity, shape it, tend it and share it as widely as you choose. A friend of mine recently questioned her 15-year old niece about her 2,000+ 'friends' on Facebook only to find that many of them were entirely new connections, not people she had ever met or even 'friends of friends.' The willingness to accept virtual strangers into our worlds heralds a new understanding of the shifting personal boundaries we are willing to tolerate in a networked world.

As we saw with the creation and rise of 'the press'—the Fourth Estate—as a social force, with the wide dissemination of the printing press, we are now seeing the rise of 'the people' as a social force within today's networked world. Although the idea of "the people" has been around for a long time, the shattering of national and cultural boundaries that define "the people" now, and the speed and visibility with which "the people" can coalesce is *mutating*. The Arab Spring and the Occupy movements are two meta-examples of this trend, which we will discuss in more detail later. But we can also see this notion of increased speed, dissemination and visibility of 'people power' in such simple daily examples as the online petition and the nature of viral videos. The Kony2012/Kony2014 campaign to oust the Lord's Resistance Army leader Joseph Kony garnered some 3.7 million supporters worldwide who have actively pledged to help the campaign and has close to 100 million views on YouTube. Many of these are people who had never heard of Kony before the campaign.

Another critical concept that has found renewed energy in the Internet age is the idea of Open-source and DIY (Do It Yourself) technology, also known as "maker-culture." This movement builds upon the notion we discussed earlier of "convivial technologies." Our current investment in the paradigms of the industrial era have psychologically divided us into the categories of 'producer' and 'consumer.' But as Alvin Toffler forecast in his 1980 book *The Third Wave*, this trend is new to recent history and is now reverting back to the notion of what Toffler calls the 'prosumer.' Toffler explains that, "until the industrial revolution, the vast bulk of all the food, goods, and services produced by the human race was consumed by the producers themselves, their families or a tiny elite" [44, p. 37]. As a result of this split, "a market had to be formed or expanded to connect the two; new political and social conflicts sprang up; new sexual roles were defined" [44, p. 45]. The current shift towards a hi-tech DIY 'maker-culture,' which is paralleled by its low-tech handmaiden, the homesteading movement, which seeks to re-skill people in the arts of homemaking such as canning, cooking, sewing, and the like, has the potential to spur new social roles, conflicts, and markets in the future. Current discourse around the 'sharing economy' where people opt freely to share or rent products to others rather than purchasing them may be one outcome of this 'prosumer' shift that has potentially important consequences for the futures.

In the world of high technology, for a long time, computers and the Internet remained a mystical force understood by only a select group of 'coders' and 'hackers' who had spent enough time enveloping themselves in the knowledge needed to build and rebuild the hardware and software of computers. Breaking down this notion of inaccessibility is the idea of 'open-source,' which values free sharing of information, software codes, and the like, combined with the accessibility of hardware components such as the Arduino board, which is an inexpensive single board microcomputer that can fairly easily be purchased pre-assembled or in do-it-yourself kits for individuals to use in whatever capacity they need. A *Popsci* article featured 12-year old Quin Entyre, who teaches how to make many different kinds of things with the inexpensive Arduino boards and free software [26].

Although a lot of the 'maker culture' is associated with kitchy gadgets, the broader trend of open-source and do-it-yourself technology has potentially important implications for the future as digital natives such as Quin find tinkering with technology to be as simple as making a sandwich and increasingly regard the virtually free or affordable access to this hardware and software as a right.

Increased speed and visibility is changing the way we communicate with one another interpersonally and in professional settings. Where we once wrote a letter, we now send an email or a text. In many cases, emails and texts have replaced phone calls as the preferred mode of communication. It's normal to see people walking down the street side-by-side texting simultaneously, in some cases texting each other. Text message shorthand and Internet acronyms have exploded to the point where there are numerous websites aiming to catalog and define them all [40]. As subsequent digital generations become more versed and comfortable in this mode of communication, we are already beginning to see a decrease in conventional spelling ability and a greater reliance on both shorthand and visual modes of communication such as 'emoticons' (cute, cartoon like images that are meant to convey an emotion) and less cohesive storytelling or communication techniques. Spellcheck effectively ended having to know how to spell several decades ago. One of us remembers very vividly when an advanced graduate student haughtily justified turning in homework with bad spelling because her spellcheck program was malfunctioning. It never occurred to her that we would expect her to check it herself. Demands for and the possibility of standardized spelling of one's native language is little over 100–200 years old anyway, and may be in the process of becoming personalized again—or nonexistent if the dominance of the written word fades away.

For many in the working world, the ubiquitous nature of email has engendered an 'always on' culture where work follows you home, on vacation, in the gym, virtually any time day or night. The tireless barrage of emails has some executives deciding to opt for 'email sabbaticals,' where any email received during a specified period of time is summarily deleted with a kind automated note explaining the situation. But despite these small pushbacks, the 'always on' culture is something most people have come to accept as normal, expected and desirable. And while it has created a situation for some that thankfully involves more flexible work hours and the ability to work at home, the blurring of work-life/personal-life lines will undoubtedly change the way we view our vocations in the future. We can already see a shift away from the idea that one should have *a* career for the whole of his or her working life towards a notion of multiple careers, even multiple, simultaneous careers in a lifetime. Although there are admittedly many factors (economic, political, etc.) driving this shift, it is partially a result of the multitasking nature of work-life in the Internet age and the realization that if you are always on, you had best enjoy what it is that you do.

As the printing era brought into existence the figure of the 'author,' so also with the Internet age we see the rise of the 'blogger' as a pervasive purveyor of content and knowledge. The critical shift between these two roles has to do with the conveyance of authority, and this has broader implications for society. Whereas Elizabeth Eisenstein showed that the author began as a collector of the thoughts of others, as well as his or her own, and only later became primarily a creator of original content (though often based upon the previous work of others as source references), the blogger is seen once again as a relayer or regurgitater of content. Many blogs simply rehash previously published information with little to no changes or additions by the blogger. There is almost always a very particular slant or bias attributed to the blog based on the blogger's personal beliefs or cultural biases, but the speed and regularity with which blogs can be published allows for incredibly fast dissemination of information, as one news story is rehashed and republished by numerous blogs almost instantaneously. What this process sometimes lacks is credibility and fact-checking. When a tragic shooting spree occurred at the Newtown, Connecticut, elementary school, the media hastily released the name of the suspected shooter and identified what they thought was his Facebook page. This bit of misinformation led to death threats for Ryan Lanza, who was unfortunate enough to have a similar name to the real shooter Adam Lanza [1]. As a result of this miscommunication, the user-generated news site Reddit would not allow its members to try to identify the man who went on a shooting rampage at the Washington Navy Yard in 2013 in order to prevent a similar misidentification [23].

This trend to publish breaking news 'first' or rapidly share news without journalistic diligence has produced in the public consuming information a sense of what we might call 'virtual reality.' This is the idea that what we are reading or seeing is probably in some sense true but in some sense doctored or skewed by bias. This is seen in written media such as blogs, where the reader commentary often calls into question the legitimacy of the blogger, as well as in our consumption of visual imagery where we often either accept the validity of an image only to find out later that it was egregiously doctored or we learn to question the validity of most images we see so that none is really accepted on face value. During Superstorm Sandy in October of 2012, an image of the Statue of Liberty being engulfed by massive waves went viral on the Internet and was republished on numerous serious news sites before being exposed as a Photoshopped stitch of two unrelated images [3]. This sort of erroneous news and image making clearly happened in the past with other previous forms of media. Airbrushing out defamed leaders by Soviet media during the Cold War in part contributed to the development of "Kremlinology"—scrutinizing published group photographs of Soviet leaders to see who was in and who was out of power when other means were unavailable. It is the speed and volume of dissemination in the era of networked communication that is making it both more ubiquitous and more difficult to find and correct. The result is a widespread and growing distrust of media in general as a mirror for the 'real' on the one hand and a contradictory growing acceptance of the 'reality' of the 'virtual,' on the other.

4.1.2 Access and Points of Control

One of the greatest issues to consider as we talk about the futures of the Internet and social networking is the issue of access. We've addressed this a bit in our discussions of the physical hardware of the net and the orgware that has developed around both the Internet and social networking in recent decades. Returning to some of Deleuze's theories of the control society, it is critical to think about the noise of data, the virtual soup of information from which we now sup, and then we must consider the control points where protocols and filters are placed to either sift through, sort, prioritize, or censor certain information. There are two million cell phones in North Korea, but it's illegal to make an international call. Iran induced what newsmakers coined an 'Internet coma' just before the 2013 elections, with all high-speed, filter-free Internet service brought to a standstill. Agencies of the US government secretly and illegally surveil the messages and websites of its citizens with impunity. So the reality of a free and interconnected network is intricately bound by the constraints of the governance and economic structures and ideologies and the physical limitations within which it survives. We see that networked communication does not change the reality of oppressive nation-states or oppressive power regimes. Even in developed and democratic states, there are numerous control points that are carefully created and managed by corporations such as Google, Apple, and Amazon that have become ubiquitous household names and products. The immense power of corporate actants, specifically Google, which controls 65 % of the global Internet search market [37], raises some critical concerns, particularly with regard to the ways in which the global economy has embraced new media. Outlining the techno-economic flows of life in an age of *info-normativity*, Sweeney argues, "Capital, as it were, is produced from one's personal circumstances—from uploading a picture of one's dog to adding a dentist appointment to one's calendar; Google has found a way to monetize the mundane monotony of everyday life—the ultimate game of power from which one cannot be distracted" [38].

Since this process of filtering and managing the noise of ceaseless data is not without politics, we must consider again the physicality of the Internet. When Senator Ted Stevens of Alaska described the Internet as a series of 'tubes' in 2006, he was ridiculed across the media and throughout the halls of Capitol Hill. But as Blum and others have shown, the Internet *is*, almost above everything else, a series of tubes covering the globe. The construction, location, management, ownership, and upkeep of these tubes is, and will continue to be, an arena fraught with politics and one in which inordinate amounts of control over access to increasing vital information will be wielded. As political theorist Alexander Galloway has argued, "The net … is founded on control, not freedom" [7, p. 7]. Perhaps one of the seminal issues for the futures of the Internet is this issue of access and control over information and physical resources, and this is not a new struggle. As we have seen throughout our historical survey of communication technologies, the S-curve invariably tends towards exertion of power over the technology until a new technology arises from the fringes to take the place of the old.

4.1.3 Ubiquitous Society: Surveillance Society

For some time, some people, especially in Japan, Korea, and northern Europe, have observed that as communication technologies have gotten smaller and smaller and smarter and smarter, so also are they being embedded in everything in the environment, including the human body. This is resulting in the emergence of what is sometimes called a "Ubiquitous Society" wherein smart, interactive technologies surround, surveil, assist, and guide us to do the right thing while perhaps making it impossible for us to do the wrong thing.

Currently, these technologies make sure there is gas in the car, air in the tires, and the door is closed. Or that our health is good as our urine and stools are sampled unobtrusively as we use the toilet. However, Marcel Bullinga suggests what the governance of a U-Society might soon be like:

> Making rules and enforcing them are important government tasks. Right now, laws are written down on paper and enforced by individuals. In the future, all rules and laws will be incorporated into expert systems and chips embedded in cars, appliances, doors, and buildings—that is, our physical environment. No longer will police officers and other government personnel be the only law enforcement. Our physical environment will enforce the law as well … . Future governments will no longer supply paper laws but will instead supply open-standards software with the appropriate regulatory information and protocols to all citizens' intelligent cars, appliances, buildings, and machines. Intelligent devices will become self-aware to the extent that they will 'know' what laws or regulations apply and how to act upon them. They will make decisions and self-enforce them [6].

4.1.4 From Al Capone to Al Gore to Al Gorithm

Some people find the "intelligent government" described by Bullinga to be completely frightening and utterly undesirable. But it appears that many Americans would welcome it if it gives them a sense of greater security from terrorists. Tea Party and other Libertarian protestations to the contrary notwithstanding, widespread enthusiasm for expanded opportunities for effective participation in governance; movements for electronic direct democracy; and other activities aimed at establishing processes for self-governance seem to have ended with the attacks of September 11, 2001, for many Americans. Instead, the initial passage and repeated expansion and reauthorizations of the PATRIOT Act; the creation and rapid growth of the Department of Homeland Security; general acceptance of the operations of TSA agents at airports; tolerance for surveillance by drones, hidden cameras, and the warrantless capture and review of both regular and electronic mail, of website visits, of bank accounts, and of travel records; support for the prosecution and punishment of "whistle blowers" who have released information about these and other clandestine governmental activities; and even the killing of American citizens who are declared "terrorists"—all made quick and easy by electronic technologies but without due process of law—suggest that most Americans embrace and many positively seek restrictions on rather than expansions of behavior by electronic technologies in ways that at one time would have been deemed intolerable. Public opinion polls confirm this acceptance. America's new national anthem might be the old song by *The Police*:

> Everybreath you take
> And every move you make
> Every bond you break, every step you take
> I'll be watching you
>
> Every single day
> And every word you say
> Every game you play, every night you stay
> I'll be watching you.

Oh can't you see
You belong to me?
How my poor heart aches
With every step you take.

Every move you make
And every vow you break
Every smile you fake, every claim you stake
I'll be watching you. [41]

Yes, governance is a process of balancing freedom and order. Sometimes the scales tip too far towards order, and demands for freedom explode. As of this moment of writing, the Internet and social media are being seen by many people as threats to freedom, privacy, and self-governance and not as its harbingers of freedom and democracy, as these same technologies were viewed only a decade or so ago.

The dream of the "Ubiquitous Society" was first being imagined by Mark Weiser and John Seely Brown, both top scientists at the Xerox Palo Alto Research Center (PARC) in the late 1980s. They foretold of a time when computing technologies would be so ubiquitous that they would literally be woven into the fabric of everyday life and cease to be noticed. In 1993, Weiser wrote that "the challenge is to create a new kind of relationship of people to computers, one in which the computer would have to take the lead in becoming vastly better at getting out of the way so people could just go about their lives" [45, p. 2]. As we've shown with our age-cohort discussion of technology, it was only a matter of years before those digital immigrants gave way to today's digital natives such that my 18-month-old knows how to operate an iPad and computers are woven into our phones, our alarm clocks, our cameras and our cars, without us even paying much notice.

From this notion of a ubiquitous networked society has arisen the idea of an Internet of Things. Based primarily on the hardware of the RFID chip (radio-frequency identification device), the Internet of Things imagines a world where every object has its own unique identifier that allows it to be coded, tracked, and monitored in a vast storehouse of data and information linked to the Internet. This is where the oft-cited notion of 'smart-objects' comes into play, the idea being that if our objects could communicate with us, our world would run more smoothly. These are the visions of the wired-up kitchen making breakfast on command with your refrigerator telling the grocery store what you need to purchase, or every can of Coke being tagged to tell its maker where it went, who bought it, and how quickly it was consumed. The Internet of Things is quickly becoming reality. Cisco's CEO John Chambers recently estimated a $14 trillion market opportunity in the Internet of Things. Their company posted a blog estimating that in 2013 approximately 80 objects connected to the Internet per second with 1,000 per second expected in 2014 [31]. In this emerging reality, "participation is often unnoticeable and membership mandated; effective refusal is impossible. Users become more vulnerable to commercial enticements and marketing approaches" [29, p. 4].

To counter all the excitement and hype over the emerging Internet of Things, authors Christian Nold and Rob van Kranenberg argue instead for an Internet of People. "We are talking about a network of relationships between people. In our vision, people are not just in the loop but it's main locus and scale reference" [29, p. 17]. Citing the software of the barcode and various orgware like the shipping container as immensely important but primarily invisible forces that have brought us to this point in history where an interconnected world is possible, Nold and van Kranenberg also highlight the challenges we face today in a world where issues like climate change and food, energy, and water shortages are becoming equally ubiquitous barriers to a positive future. They see the rise of units of local production organized globally by an Internet of People being a better way to build resiliency for the uncertain future—islands of things being produced and shared across localized units rather than an Internet of Things controlled from the top down by multinational corporate entities. Addressing issues of power, they contend that "the point about technical protocols in that they seem so 'objective,' as if they were natural or 'always there.' This is not the case. Interested parties have always made them. The story of the current RFID standard called 'epc Global' is the story of two standard bodies EAN (European Article Number) and UCC (Uniform Code Council) merging in 2005 to become GS1, an international not-for-profit association with member organizations in over 100 countries" [29, p. 29].

In both of these competing visions of the Internet's future, power is felt in very concrete terms. With the ubiquitous nature of computing becoming so commonplace, some scholars are raising a flag to call attention to some of these ramifications of power and control with what is now being termed the Surveillance Society. But the question remains, has the nature of surveillance changed or merely the tools with which those in power exercise monitoring and control? With recent events, such as Edward Snowden's leak of the National Security Administration's (NSA) vast data-collection program in the United States, it has become increasingly clear that our modern notion of privacy is a thing of the past. As we discussed in relation to age-cohort analysis, we live in an era where people are perfectly comfortable publishing aspects of their life in overt detail to virtual strangers and yet balk anytime Facebook changes their privacy policy. In truth, as we showed before, we must acknowledge that privacy as a notion is a relatively modern phenomenon and may indeed be obsolete now.

David von Drehle observed in *Time* magazine in August 2013, "Almost overnight, and with too little reflection, the US and other developed nations have stacked the deck in favor of the watchers" [11]. With RFID chips in more products all the time, cameras everywhere, more GPS-tracked camera- and video-ready smartphones on the street than there are people, and protocols built into the Internet to track almost every move made, there are fewer and fewer places one can escape notice. And yet, if you ask anyone who grew up in a small town environment, they will likely express having felt there the same sense of pervasive observation and scrutiny without the high tech modes of modern surveillance.

To flip this notion of surveillance and look at it from another angle, Thomas Elsaesser reminds us in his essay "Early Film History and Multi-Media: An Archaeology of Possible Futures," that "with multi-media, another age old dream seems to be coming true … to be is to be perceived" [13, p. 23]. An old magnificent

Calvin and Hobbes cartoon has the characters sledding downhill, exulting in the fact that they are being televised. "We won't be just old Calvin and Hobbes any more," says Calvin. "We'll be 'Calvin and Hobbes—*as seen on TV*'!"

Our identities are now broadcast online to be perceived by anyone with access, and we willingly allow intimate details of our thoughts, our families, and our experiences to be viewed and commented on constantly. As von Drehle also argues, "the same tools that strengthen [the surveillance state] strengthen those who protest against it … Big Brother might be watching, but he is also being watched" [11]. Perhaps the critical question for the futures then is: Upon what freedoms and which controls does this balance hinge? And just as critically, have these same interplays of power always existed despite the prevailing technology? Are we confusing the medium with the message?

4.1.5 Networked Resistance and Control in the Twenty-First Century

The tension between open-source freedom of information on the Internet and the typically state- and corporate-backed forces struggling to contain and control the flow of information has formed the basis of a critical struggle in the beginning part of the twenty-first century. There are countless examples of this struggle playing out almost every day, but for the purposes of our research, we'll focus on just a few key areas. No assessment of social media in the early twenty-first century would be complete without a discussion of the Arab Spring and the Occupy Movement. Beyond those two recent meta-narratives, we will also highlight earlier examples of resistance and control to help us frame and understand the greater battle that is currently being waged over the future of the Internet and to demonstrate the ways in which this battle mirrors others that we have seen throughout the history of communication technologies.

4.2 The Arab Spring, Occupy, and Others: Social Media and Revolution

Hailed in the mainstream media as the "Twitter revolution," the Arab Spring is loosely defined as the revolutionary wave of demonstrations, protests, riots, and civil wars that swept the Arab world beginning in December of 2010. In some cases, Tunisia and Egypt for example, leaders were forced from power. In other areas it resulted in a series of protests, such as those seen in Morocco, Algeria, and Iraq. In all these cases, social media played a visible role in the insurgency and protest. A big open question remains, did social media bring these movements into being or would they have occurred without it?

Of course, the use of early social media for fostering social change in this region of the world is nothing new. "Clandestinely smuggled audio cassette tapes of Ayatollah Khomeini speaking about the revolution played a key role in the movement's mass mobilization, and led Abolhassan Sadegh, an official with the Ministry of National Guidance, to note that 'tape cassettes are stronger than fighter planes.' Ayatollah Khomeini's speeches, circulated through such covert methods, emphasized the power of unarmed resistance and non-cooperation. In one speech, he said, 'The clenched fists of freedom fighters can crush the tanks and guns of the oppressors.'" [51, pp. 190–192] Annabelle Sreberny and Ali Mohammadi also discuss the vital role that smuggled and clandestinely sold and shared audio cassettes of Ayatollah Khomeini's sermons while in exile played in the overthrow of the Shah of Iran in the 1960s and 1970s. For Iranians to hear Khomeini's actual voice repeatedly exhorting peaceful revolution sparked a critical feeling of solidarity that might not have been achieved without that access to a then-cutting edge media technology [36]. So, what social media were to the Arab Spring, in many ways tape recordings were to the Iranian revolution some 40 years earlier.

Moreover, Egypt was not the first place where more recent social media were used for political purpose. In South Korea, online media emerged a decade earlier as a significant arbiter of political power and an alternative to existing, more conservative news media. Chang Woo-Young explains: "The 2002 presidential election was a pivotal event for the online media as they were transformed into the epicenter of political reform led by citizens mobilized online" [48]. This online political activism transformed into off-line social mobilizing and has since sparked a renewed passion for politics in Korea in a way that may not have happened without the opening afforded by online media channels.

The influence of social media probably would not have been so great had not the Korean government itself developed the Korean Information Infrastructure project, aggressively designing, testing, and building high-speed Internet infrastructure applications throughout the country. "The Korean government worked to stimulate demand for Internet services. In 2000, the Ten Million People Internet Education project was launched with the goal to teach ten million Koreans how to use the Internet by the end of 2002. The program was considered a success, with 4.1 million people trained in 2000 alone" [18]. Korea was among the first nations to lure more than 75 % of its citizens to use the Internet by the early 2000s. Moreover since the faster the Internet connection the more likely are people to use it to create and send their own content [18, p. 12], Koreans were primed technically to use social media for the purpose of political organizing well before the rest of the world. Several non-political events, including mass rallies fanned by social media in support of the Korean team during the 2002 World Cup, as well as several anti-American rallies earlier, prepared people motivationally—they saw that flash mobs could affect social change.

The beneficiary of all this turned out to be a relatively unknown youngish and idealistic politician named Roh Moo-Hyun, who ran unsuccessfully for a National Assembly seat from Pusan in 2000. Inspired by his idealism, some people formed an online fan club eventually called Nosamo. By the spring of 2001 it had become a national organization, growing exponentially [18, p. 24]. Nonetheless, Roh's initial steps towards becoming a formal candidate for the presidency were not very successful. In response, Nosamo began a grassroots "piggy bank" fundraising drive that proved spectacularly successful, and Roh's political fortunes rose rapidly. On the other hand, his main competitor, from the conservative Grand National Party, did not use the Internet: "It was a digital versus analogue campaign" [18, p. 27].

On election day, Roh was initially behind in the balloting, according to exit polls. Nasamo sent out millions of emails and text messages, some with the plea, "Don't treat today just as a day off to spend shopping or at home" [18, p. 27]. Importantly, online supporters contacted those offline so that by the end of election day, Roh had "come out of nowhere" to win by nearly 49 % of the three-way vote.

This remains one of the earliest and most successful examples of using social media for political purposes. Unfortunately, the story does not have a happy ending, because Roh's term ended in enormous controversy, and he committed suicide in 2009, leaving a suicide note on his personal computer.

Similarly, Patrick Meier, author of *IRevolution*, points out that in North Africa and the Middle East, "[T]he use of ICT's (Information Communication Technologies) have not resulted in a successful Arab Spring for most countries. From Sudan to Bahrain and Syria to Libya, protests have been brutally repressed and thousands of protesters killed. So does more widespread access to ICT's really empower resistance movements at the expense of the coercive control of repressive regimes, or vice versa?" [25, p. 8] In the case of the Arab Spring it seems that the historical tensions we have seen between the use of a technology for purposes of resisting the state and the state control over that technology repeat themselves yet again. So perhaps the more important question is whether social media enables a different kind of organizing and communication to disrupt the balance of power in a way not seen in previous technologies.

Richard A. Lindsey, author of "What the Arab Spring Tells Us About the Future of Social Media in Revolutionary Movements," argues for a different perspective. He points out that any revolution consists of a series of phases: the latent or incipient phase, where information is spread and supporters rallied; the guerilla warfare phase; and finally the war of movement. So although social media may have powerful effects during the incipient phase, "There comes a point in any insurgency where it must move beyond the reach of social media, and tangible gains must be made on the ground" [21].

Information has always been used as a weapon in war, but it can be argued that the accessibility, speed, and reach of social networking via the Internet is taking that efficacy of information as weapon to a new level. Dennis Murphy and James White propose in "Propaganda: Can a Word Decide a War?" that although "the historical use of information as power was primarily limited to nation-states, today a blogger can impact an election, an Internet posting can recruit a terrorist … all with little capital investment and certainly without the baggage of bureaucratic rules, national values, or oversight" [28, p. 23].

The shift in power afforded by social media's ability to connect the many to the many for the first time in history does potentially offer a different amplification of effects, but similar ends have been achieved before with previous technological means. When a message can instantaneously reach millions of people beyond borders there is a certain degree of individual empowerment that has not existed in the past. That said, social media has some serious limitations. Malcolm Gladwell points out social media's reliance on "weak links" as one of its major limitations. Weak links are the links you have with a "friend" you follow on Facebook but have no personal contact with. You may pay attention to the things they do and say, but you are not likely to follow them into a dangerous or risky situation. In other words, weak links don't typically manifest in the type of high-risk activism that is required during an insurgency. For that sort of involvement, personal relationships are still invaluable and while these relationships may become reinforced by social media, they are not typically created solely through social media. Lindsey argues, "Social media can only facilitate, not create, the leadership that is necessary for insurgencies to survive and succeed. Ground-level, person-to-person organizing and mobilization, with some level of personal investment being necessary, is still the key contributor to the successful mobilization of insurgent populations" [21].

The promise and limits of social media were made even clearer during the Occupy protests that swept the globe beginning in September of 2011 in New York City's Zuccotti Park. As we discussed in our analysis of the Millennial age-cohort, the Occupy movement was a reaction to the rabid disenchantment of a generation that felt its future had been stolen by forces of corporate greed and the financial fallout of 2008. Beginning on September 17, 2011, approximately 1,000 protesters marched up and down Wall Street with the slogan "We are the 99 %" to protest the amassing wealth of Wall Street bankers and multinational corporations and rapidly growing economic inequality in America. A few hundred people then camped out in Zuccotti Park and refused to leave, calling themselves the Occupy movement. Initially, the mainstream media didn't cover the protests at all, but Twitter, YouTube, and Facebook were on fire with information about Occupy. In just under a month from that first protest, similar protests under the Occupy banner had taken place or were still ongoing in over 95 cities across 82 countries.

Remnants of the Occupy movement remain as of the time of this writing in several countries, but the steam really only lasted for a short time. It seems the movement was strong on the incipient phase, targeting a general unease among people worldwide affected by a global economic downturn and tired of seeing the rich get richer while a greater majority of people were suffering job losses, foreclosures, and bleak economic futures. In this way social media played a huge role in spreading the Occupy movement as quickly and widely as it did. With the mainstream media largely out of the picture until Occupy had grown simply too large to ignore, the Internet and social media were the media of choice. But once the initial euphoria of protest had abated, the weakness of social media became readily apparent. Gladwell's argument fits well here when he notes, "Facebook activism succeeds not by motivating people to make real sacrifice but by motivating them to do the things that people do when they are not motivated enough to make a real sacrifice" [16]. And while camping in a park or marching in a protest may be seen by some as a real sacrifice, it pales in comparison to the real work of overthrowing seated power, economic or political.

What we see with the Korean, Arab Spring, Occupy, and other instances where social media is credited with carrying forth revolution, is the return of our oft-cited adage "structure matters." You might create the will for action towards change, but formal cultural, economic, and political structures may eventually thwart sustained change.

Moreover, as Patrick Meier puts it, "Technology (and lack of access) can also be used to repress." To this end, if so called "liberation technologies" do exist, then "technologies of repression" must inevitably exist as well [25, p. 10]. These expressions of power seem to echo Tehranian's matrix that we discussed in Chap. 1, and the idea that power in relation to technology is seldom in unidirectional. The social, governance, economic, and physical structures within and among which revolution occurs matter as much as the tools used to foment that revolution. In other words, the software and orgware are as influential, if not more so, than the hardware itself. Power, repression, control, freedom, and revolution have all existed throughout the history of changing communication technologies; the difference is really one of degree rather than kind.

4.2.1 Amorphous Resistance: Anonymous

Commenting on the novel challenges of our historical moment, MacKinnon observes, "The struggle for freedom in the Internet age is shaping up to be very different from the ideological struggles of the twentieth century. Today's struggle is not a clear-cut contest of democracy versus dictatorship, communism versus capitalism, or one ideology over another … Today's battles over freedom and control are raging simultaneously across democracies *and* dictatorships; across economic, ideological, and cultural lines" [22, p. 5].

Forms of resistance against state- and corporate-sponsored control of the Internet and efforts to keep information free and access open often take shape amorphously, seemingly without leadership, like a vision of the hive mind that gathers and disperses whenever and wherever it is needed. Anonymous is the prototypical symbol of this twenty-first century form of resistance. A loosely associated network of "hacktivists," Anonymous appears to be nowhere but everywhere it wants to be. There is no person or people credited with leadership, and the structure of the organization is primarily decentralized and anarchic. In 2012, *Time* magazine called Anonymous one of the "100 most influential people in the world" for their involvement in such varied activist maneuvers against the FBI, CIA, Vatican, the Syrian government, and various banking firms. Wearing Guy Fawkes masks whenever seen in public, Anonymous is seen by some as the stuff of legends. Members of Anonymous have themselves likened their virtual online activist tactics to physical real-world direct action civil disobedience. Distributed denial of service (DDoS) is a favored tactic of Anonymous whereby a website is flooded with traffic from thousands of independent servers in order to shut down the website to legitimate business for a period of time. When 16 alleged Anonymous activists were arrested for their role in the DDoS attack on PayPal, they faced up to 10 years in prison and $250,000 in fines. In response, some activists pushed to establish DDoS as a legitimate form of civil protest, likening the practice to a sit-in or other non-violent physical civil action that uses human bodies to send a political message by simply occupying space. An online petition related to the case stated, "Distributed denial-of-service (DDoS) is not any form of hacking in any way. It is the equivalent of repeatedly hitting the refresh button on a webpage. It is, in that way, no different than any 'occupy' protest" [42].

In reaction to the death of Aaron Swartz, 26 year-old champion of a free and open-source Internet, Anonymous threatened in January of 2013 to expose mass amounts of sensitive, US government secrets. When Swartz committed suicide, he was facing 50+ years in prison and a $4 million fine for releasing academic articles from the pay-for-view JSTOR database so that people could download this academic information for free [14].

4.2.2 *The Myth of the "Wireless" World*

In 2006, traveling through the Gobi Desert in Mongolia, we were a day away from the nearest town, miles and miles of empty flat desert stretching in every direction around us. Suddenly our jeep crossed over a narrow ditch. It was about a foot wide, a few feet deep, and stretched in a straight line as far as the eye could see across the desert floor. I turned to our Mongolian guide and asked what in the world that ditch was for? With a straight face, she replied, "It's to lay cable for high-speed Internet access" [50]. A Chinese company won the contract to bring high-speed Internet to the farthest reaches of a country with the lowest population density in the world. Hence, broadband cable would be laid across the expanse of the Gobi Desert.

One of the greatest technological myths circulating in the general public today is the idea that the Internet, and all it has to offer is available everywhere "wirelessly." Ask the average young person on an American street where their Internet access comes from and they will explain that they are "wireless" and most likely that they use the "Cloud" to store some or all of their data online. There is a patent illusion of increasing portability and freedom around the Internet, and yet the physical reality is far from this mythic vision. In fact, the Internet is still, and foreseeably will remain, deeply dependent upon hardware that requires physical space for connectivity, data storage, information transfer and general operations. The wireless access point is always connected to a nearby wired access point, which is connected to underground cables, which feed into the larger grid, which is primarily state-controlled and managed. In New York City, for example, there is an entire building dedicated solely to hardware infrastructure that is required to keep the city's primarily "wireless" Internet services up and running. Numerous cables, mostly going to and coming from New York City, have been deployed to shave milliseconds off of trading time for investors [32].

In Andrew Blum's recent book *Tubes: A journey to the Center of the Internet*, he explains, "For all the talk of the placelessness of our digital age, the Internet is as fixed in real, physical places as any railroad or telephone system ever was. In basest terms, it is made of pulses of light. Those pulses might seem miraculous, but they're not magic. They are produced by powerful lasers contained in steel boxes housed mainly in unmarked buildings. The lasers exist. The boxes exist. The buildings exist" [4, p. 9]. The mythical sense of it as a cosmic conglomeration of ethereal connections colliding in space has served to elevate the public perception of the Internet as something that transcends borders, boundaries, and ultimately state control. What we have seen in reality is in stark opposition to this mythos. In Hawaii, for example, the business tax climate has created a situation where several underwater broadband Internet cables have been laid to bypass the islands as they make their way from California to Japan [47]. The choice to link the "wireless" Internet to a decidedly wired infrastructure is both economic and political in that it ties the control of information to both nation-states and businesses involved in the installation, management, and maintenance of the hardware.

For our purposes, a revised understanding of the hardware associated with the Internet is critical to understanding the power relations that operate through, within, and without the "Net." If the tubes and wires required to run New York City's Internet connections are housed in an unmarked building, there are drastically different critical implications for security and control over that building. We need to ask ourselves: who is served by the vision of a wireless world? What is lost when we forget about the physical realities, energy implications, spatial dynamics, and governance requirements of all the hardware and orgware related to the operation of the Internet today and in the futures?

We often do not consider the material with which our tools are constructed, but these physical realities have an important effect on society. This is true for the previous technologies we have analyzed as well as current and future technologies. For just one example, nearly four billion trees a year are cut down for paper [24]. Today, cell phones, laptops and much of the ubiquitous hardware relies upon rare earth minerals for their construction. These rare earth minerals come from just a few places in the world. Coltan is one of those rare earth minerals in almost all devices, and it comes from the Democratic Republic of the Congo (DRC), which has been embroiled in intense conflict and where millions of people have been killed over the last 20 years. The DRC has 64 % of the world's coltan supply, and this has not gone unnoticed by its neighbors. According to a 2001 United Nations report on the Illegal Exploitation of Natural Resources in the Congo, "The consequences of illegal exploitation have been twofold: (a) massive availability of financial resources for the Rwandan Patriotic Army, and the individual enrichment of top Ugandan military commanders and civilians; (b) the emergence of illegal networks headed by either top military officers or businessmen" [15]. And of course there are many multinational corporations involved in the trade of this "conflict mineral."

Another equally distressing by-product of the networked era, and the rise of the mobile Internet specifically, is "E-waste." This is the physical waste that results from producing all the nifty gadgets and electronics that we love to use and increasingly seem not to be able to live without. Coltan and other rare earth minerals along with nasty toxic substances like lead, cadmium, beryllium, and brominated flame retardants go into the production of our consumer electronics. Millions of pounds of E-waste are literally trucked and shipped from the developed world to the developing world, where it is picked over and recycled into second-hand products in an informal economy that has devastating implications on the health of those involved with handling the toxic parts and pieces in an unsupervised and unregulated environment. Surveying a large mountain of electronic trash in Accra, Ghana, political ecologist Paul Robbins noted that a massive pile of brand new radios from China was among the discarded trash, evidence of the bizarre rationalities of neoliberal economics. He revels in the way that "Oceans of organic and inorganic material are drawn from the earth and flow into an enormous feeding machine that re-forms them into myriad configurations … "devours" energy in their transportation across the globe, and then summarily dumps them here, unused, in this deadly metabolic intestine of labor" [35, p. 3].

So, while considering the potentially liberating aspects of networking and connections, virtual or otherwise, that are made possible by the Internet, we must simultaneously consider the potentially violent and repressive aspects of the Net's hardware and orgware as they exist in the physical world. The myth of a wireless world with information stored seamlessly in the "cloud" has led to misconceptions about the physicality of a networked world. Like the technologies before it, the Internet is very much a physical product of the world in which it was created, and there are real and important implications that arise from the material aspects of networked communication structures. As the hardware of the Internet era continues to become more and more ubiquitous, we will be forced to address these physical realities that may lead to consumer behaviors that favor less toxic materials, recycling of hardware, and innovative breakthroughs in hardware construction materials and methods.

4.2.3 *Control: Crock Pots and Child Porn*

> Control is short-term and of rapid rates of turnover, but also continuous and without limit … Deleuze [9].

State-sponsored control of the Internet is obvious in some nations. But the control exercised in democratic nations such as the United States is not always as public or obvious. As Deleuze argues, this type of control is continuous and limitless, it never ceases, and its boundaries are ever expanding. As citizens, we are constantly being normalized to the levels of control so that when new limits are introduced, what once would have felt intolerable no longer feels so extreme.

For Michele Catalano, the notion that "Big Brother" is watching became a reality when six agents from the joint terrorism task force came to her house. Catalano had been googling for pressure cookers, her husband had googled about backpacks.

That and previous searches her husband had done at work, including a CNN piece about how bomb-making instructions are available online, which led to a search out of sheer curiosity for said instructions, led the task force operating in a post-Boston marathon bomber world to believe that there might be a lead worth following. The agents mentioned to Catalano's husband that they conduct searches like this about 100 times a week, with 99 of them turning out to be nothing. In Catalano's case, an employee at her husband's former workplace who was cleaning out her husband's old computer found searches for backpacks and pressure cookers and reported this to the police. And in today's world, the local law enforcement can be deputized and granted federal powers to search without a warrant [2]. So while today it takes human agency to sort through the data and determine whether an investigation is necessary, what will our world look like in the future when AI and Big Data are working together to sort through the information noise, making determinations and decisions without the necessity of any human agency? It's a possible future that is really just around the corner—or may be here already.

What many call the "Deep Web" or "Darknet" is a mysterious place not part of the main World Wide Web. Recent media attention on sites such as Silk Road, an online black market, and Tor, a free software that enables online anonymity to its users, have brought parts of the Deep Web to the surface and into the public eye. In July 2013, the FBI was able to compromise some half of the Tor operated sites by embedding a 0-day Javascript attack on "freedom hosting," the largest hosting provider for .onion sites on the Tor network. This sounds like the stuff of a high-tech spy novel, but underscores the rapid pace of evolution in the struggle between control and freedom on the Internet. Prosecuting the operator of "freedom hosting," Eric Eoin Marques, under charges of hosting child pornography, only strengthens the FBI's case in the public eye. This is why many in the hacking community are left wondering how the FBI was able to track a person using Tor, given all the ways that Tor users are anonymized [34].

4.2.4 Impacts of Electronic Technologies on Thinking and Being

In our research so far we have presented what we feel is compelling evidence that in the past, new levels of communication technology profoundly altered the way humans thought and perceived themselves, their world, and their place in the world. We documented the change apparently wrought by the emergence of speech and language, of handwriting, and of the printing press with all the accompanying hardware, software, and orgware.

What can we say about the impact of electric and electronic communication technologies in this regard? We probably cannot say much with confidence, because we are very much in the middle of whatever changes and continuities there might be. Moreover, the evidence of what is changing, and not changing and why, is decidedly mixed. Arguments warning about the negative impacts of the radio, television, email, blogs, social media, electronic games, and the rest are voluminous. We are being made lazy, stupid, irrational, immoral, violent, and short-sighted—we are losing our fundamental human properties that can only be acquired and transmitted by reading and writing well-crafted texts, many people have insisted for decades.

At the same time, other people have argued persuasively the contrary—that while our interactions via electric and electronic media have indeed changed us, they have made us more inquisitive, more intelligent, more informed, expanded our modes of being rational, perhaps altered what we consider to be moral, immoral, or indifferent, and enabled us to defer gratification for the attainment of greater prizes later obtained by considerable hard work, diligence, and reasoning. Our knowledge of the world has increased, our circles of friends and confidants greatly expanded, our concern about injustice and environmental imbalance deepened as we have come to understand that humans may not be the crown of creation nor Earth the center of the universe.

This is just the current phase of the old argument about all technologies. Some think the newer communication technologies are neutral—it depends on how they are used. Some believe they are inherently demonic and should never—or very sparingly—be used. Others say that are marvelously transforming, that we are becoming as gods! We conclude that the newer communication technologies are indeed mutative; they are not neutral, they are not demonic, they are not positively transformative, but they are once again redefining what it means to be humans living on a planet mutating faster than ever because of other aspects of human technologies and their use.

We also need to point out once again that one impact by communication technologies comes from what is communicated. Most critics and friends focus on that, and we have given some examples. But the more important impact we contend is that communication technologies change the ways we think and interrelate with other humans and the environment broadly.

On April 13, 2012, Evgeny Morozov posted the following on tumblr:

> The telephone changes the structure of the brain.
>
> Spotted on p.65 of "Crowds; a moving-picture of democracy" (Doubleday, Page & Co. 1913) by Gerald Stanley Lee: 'We are not only inventing new machines, but our new machines have turned upon us and are creating new men. The telephone changes the structure of the brain. Men live in wider distances, and think in larger figures, and become eligible to nobler and wider motives.' [27]

Actually, Gerald Stanley Lee had much more to say than Morozov quoted that is directly of interest to our study here. For example, writing about the United States in 1913, on the eve of the First World War, Lee said this:

> The modern imagination takes, speaking roughly, three characteristic forms:
>
> Imagination about the unseen or intangible—the spiritual—as especially typified in electricity, in the wireless telegraph, the aeroplane: a new and extraordinary sense of the invisible and the unproved as an energy to be used and reckoned with. Imagination about the future—a new and extraordinary sense of what is going to happen next in the world. Imagination about people. We are not only inventing new machines, but our new machines have turned upon us and are creating new men. The telephone changes the structure of the brain. Men live in wider distances, and think in larger figures, and become eligible to nobler

> and wider narratives. Imagination about the unseen is going to give us in an incredible degree the mastery of the spirit over matter. Imagination about the future is going to make the next few hundred years an organic part of every man's life today. [20, p. 65]

These are extraordinarily prescient remarks. But does—did—the telephone change the structure of the brain? Do humans who interact with the "intangible"—electricity, wireless telegraph, the airplane—think differently from those who do not. Especially, do they think differently from all of those humans in the past for whom electricity, instant distance communication, and rapid air transportation did not exist?

If we agree that literate people think differently from preliterate ones, and that people who learn by reading many different texts made possible by the printing press came to think differently about themselves and the world from people who learned by repeatedly pouring over a very small number of handwritten texts, or, more typically, learned by hearing those texts read aloud rather than reading them directly themselves, then it is tempting—if not unreasonable—to conclude that learning via radio, television, the Internet, electronic games, and many-to-many social media will produce, if it has not already produced, people who think differently from people who did not and could not do so.

One hundred years after Gerald Stanley Lee wrote his book, Clive Thompson published *Smarter Than You Think: How Technology Is Changing Our Minds for the Better*. In it he said: "Every new tool shapes the way we think, as well as what we think about. … With every innovation, cultural prophets bickered over whether we were facing a technological apocalypse or a utopia. The one thing that both apocalyptics and utopians understand and agree upon is that every new technology pushes us toward new forms of behavior while nudging us away from older, familiar ones. … What are the central biases of today's digital tools? There are many, but I see three big ones that have a huge impact on our cognition. First, they allow for prodigious external memory … . Second, today's tools make it easier for us to find connections—between ideas, pictures, people, bits of news—that were previously invisible. Third, they encourage a superfluity of communication and publishing [43, pp. 20–25].

Are these the main things our "digital tools" do to us? And are these things "good"? Are our minds being changed for the better? The well-known conservative social critic George Will is quoted by Steven Johnson as declaring, "Ours is an age besotted with graphic entertainments. And in an increasingly infantilized society, whose moral philosophy is reducible to a celebration of 'choice,' adults are decreasingly distinguishable from children in their absorption in entertainments and the kinds of entertainments they are absorbed in—video games, computer games, hand-held games, movies on their computers and so on. This is progress: more sophisticated delivery of stupidity" [17, p. xii].

Johnson cleverly inverts this widely shared complaint and asks the reader to imagine what we would say about writing if videogames had somehow evolved before writing so that children had "been playing games for centuries—and then these page-bound texts come along and suddenly they're all the rage"? He suggests the new "frenzy of reading" would be greeted by conservatives like Wills staunchly defending traditional learning by moving images versus the horror of learning by static text somewhat along these lines:

Reading books chronically under-stimulates the senses. Unlike the longstanding tradition of game play—which engages the child in a vivid, three-dimensional world filled with moving images and musical soundscapes, navigated and controlled with complex muscular movements—books are simply a barren string of words on the page. Only a small portion of the brain devoted to processing written language is activated during reading, while games engage the full range of the sensory and motor cortices.

Books are also tragically isolating. Although games have for many years engaged the young in complex social relationships with their peers, building and exploring worlds together, books force the child to sequester him or herself in a quiet space, shut off from interaction with other children. These new 'libraries' that have arisen in recent years to facilitate reading activities are a frightening sight: dozens of young children, normally so vivacious and socially interactive, sitting alone in cubicles, reading silently, oblivious to their peers.

Many children enjoy reading books, of course, and no doubt some of the flights of fancy conveyed by reading have their escapist merits. But for a sizable percentage of the population, books are downright discriminatory. The reading craze of recent years cruelly taunts the ten million Americans who suffer from dyslexia—a condition that didn't even exist as a condition until printed text came along to stigmatize its sufferers.

Perhaps the most dangerous property of these books is the fact that they follow a fixed linear path. You can't control their narratives in any fashion—you simply sit back and have the story dictated to you. For those of us raised on interactive narratives, this property may seem astonishing. Why would anyone want to embark on an adventure utterly choreographed by another person?

But today's generation embarks on such adventures millions of times a day. This risks instilling a general passivity in our children, making them feel as though they're powerless to change their circumstances. Reading is not an active participatory process. It's a submissive one. The book readers of the younger generation are learning to 'follow the plot' instead of learning to lead [17, pp. 19–20]

Yes, reading rots the brain. Electricity enlivens and enlightens it.

References

1. Ackerman S (2012) Internet identifies, threatens wrong man as Newtown shooter. Wired.com. http://www.wired.com/dangerroom/2012/12/newtown-shooter-facebook/. Accessed 24 Jan 2013
2. Adelmann B (2013) Backpacks, pressure cookers, and the truth. http://www.thenewamerican.com/usnews/crime/item/16182-backpacks-pressure-cookers-and-the-truth. Accessed 12 Jan 2014
3. Anghel R (2012) Fake superstorm sandy photos hit the web. http://news.softpedia.com/news/Fake-Superstorm-Sandy-Photos-Hit-the-Web-303252.shtml. Accessed Jun 6 2013

4. Blum A (2013) Tubes: a journey to the center of the Internet. HarperCollins, New York
5. Boyd D (2006) Friendster lost steam. Is MySpace just a fad? http://www.danah.org/papers/FriendsterMySpaceEssay.html. Accessed 15 Mar 2014
6. Bullinga M (2004) Intelligent government: invisible, automatic. Everywhere, The Futurist
7. Chun WHK, Keenan T (2006) New media, old media: a history and theory reader. Routledge, New York
8. Cordeiro J (2013) Radical abundance: how a revolution in nanotechnology will change civilization. Foresight 15(5):420–421
9. Deleuze G (1995) Postscript on control societies. Negotiations: 1972-1990. Columbia University Press, New York (M Joughin trans.)
10. Doane MA (1990) Information, crisis, catastrophe. In: Mellencamp P (ed) Logics of television: essays in cultural criticism. Indiana University Press, Bloomington
11. von Drehle D (2013) The Surveillance Society, http://nation.time.com/2013/08/01/the-surveillance-society/. Accessed 17 Aug 2013
12. Drexler KE (1986) Engines of creation the coming era of nanotechnology. Russell Whitaker, London
13. Elsaesser T (2006) Early film history and multi-media: and archaeology of possible futures. In: Chun WHK, Keenan T (eds) New media, old media: a history and theory reader. Routledge, New York
14. Ferenstein G (2013) Anonymous threatens massive WikiLeaks-style exposure, announced on hacked Gov site, http://techcrunch.com/2013/01/26/anonymous-threatens-massive-wikileaks-style-exposure-announced-on-hacked-gov-site/. Accessed 30 Jan 2013
15. Friends of the Congo (2014) Coltan. http://www.friendsofthecongo.org/resource-center/coltan.html. Accessed 18 Feb 2014
16. Gladwell M (2010) Small change. http://www.newyorker.com/reporting/2010/10/04/101004fa_fact_gladwell?printable=true&currentPage=all. Accessed 29 Jan 2014
17. Johnson S (2006) Everything bad is good for you: how today's popular culture is actually making us smarter. Riverhead Books, New York
18. Joyce M (2007) The citizen journalism web site "OhmyNews" and the 2002 South Korean Presidential Election. Berkman Center for Internet and Society, Harvard University, Cambridge
19. Kassim S (2012) Twitter revolution: how the Arab spring was helped by social media. http://www.policymic.com/articles/10642/twitter-revolution-how-the-arab-spring-was-helped-by-social-media. Accessed 12 Dec 2013
20. Lee GS (1913) Crowds: a moving picture of democracy. Doubleday, Page, New York
21. Lindsey RA (2013) What the Arab spring tells us about the future of social media in revolutionary movements. Small Wars J. http://smallwarsjournal.com/jrnl/art/what-the-arab-spring-tells-us-about-the-future-of-social-media-in-revolutionary-movements. Accessed 22 Feb 2014
22. MacKinnon R (2012) If not Orwell, then Huxley: the battle for control of the Internet. http://www.theatlantic.com/technology/archive/2012/02/if-not-orwell-then-huxley-the-battle-for-control-of-the-internet/252792/. Accessed 13 Mar 2013
23. Mai-Duc C (2013) Reddit halts amateur sleuths from speculation on Navy Yard shooter. http://articles.latimes.com/2013/sep/17/nation/la-na-nn-reddit-navy-yard-shooter-20130917. Accessed 8 Oct 2013
24. Martin S (2011) Paper chase. http://www.ecology.com/2011/09/10/paper-chase/. Accessed 10 Oct 2012
25. Meier P (2014) Calling all UAV pilots: want to support humanitarian efforts? iRevolution: from innovation to revolution. http://irevolution.net/author/fletcherlicious/. Accessed 18 Mar 2014
26. Moran S (2013) A 12-year-old's quest to remake education, One Arduino at a time. Popsci.com. http://www.popsci.com/technology/article/2013-08/short-circuit. Accessed 10 Oct 2013
27. Morozov E (2012) The Nicholas Carr of 1913: "The telephone changes the structure of the brain," http://evgenymorozov.tumblr.com/post/21062887897/the-nicholas-carr-of-1913-the-telephone-changes-the. Accessed 28 Feb 2014

28. Murphy DM, White JF (2007) Propaganda: can a word decide a war? DTIC Document
29. Nold C, Kranenburg RV (2011) Situated technologies pamphlets 8: the Internet of people for a post-oil world. Architectural League of New York, New York
30. Ong WJ (2007) Orality and literacy: the technologizing of the world. Routledge, London
31. Oursler A (2013) Cisco's "Internet of things" has mind-blowing potential. http://investorplace.com/2013/08/cisco-internet-of-things/. Accessed 20 Sep 2013
32. Philips M (2012) Stock trading is about to get 5.2 milliseconds faster. http://www.businessweek.com/articles/2012-03-29/trading-at-the-speed-of-light. Accessed 1 Apr 2013
33. Poe M (2011) A history of communications: media and society from the evolution of speech to the Internet. Cambridge University Press, Cambridge
34. Prakash S (2013) Almost half of Tor sites compromised by FBI. http://www.ehackingnews.com/2013/08/almost-half-of-tor-sites-compromised-by.html. Accessed 9 Sep 2013
35. Robbins P (2004) Political ecology: a critical introduction. Blackwell, Malden
36. Sreberny A (1994) Small media, big revolution: communication, culture, and the Iranian revolution. University of Minnesota Press, Minneapolis
37. Sullivan D (2013) Google still world's most popular search engine by far, but share of unique searchers dips slightly. http://searchengineland.com/google-worlds-most-popular-search-engine-148089. Accessed 25 Feb 2014
38. Sweeney JA (2011) Search on: fictionalizing the sensational micropolitics of Google's Parisian love. CTheory.net.
39. Talbot D (2011) Inside Egypt's "Facebook revolution." http://www.technologyreview.com/view/423884/inside-egypts-facebook-revolution/. Accessed 7 Apr 2012
40. Tecca J (2012) 92 Teen text terms decoded for confused parents. http://techland.time.com/2012/05/03/92-teen-text-terms-decoded-for-confused-parents/. Accessed 8 May 2012
41. Police T (1983) Every breath you take. A&M, Santa Monica
42. Thompson C (2013) Hacktivism: civil disobedience or cyber crime? http://www.propublica.org/article/hacktivism-civil-disobedience-or-cyber-crime. Accessed 20 Feb 2013
43. Thompson C (2013) Smarter than you think: how technology is changing our minds for the better. The Penguin Press, New York
44. Toffler A (1989) The third wave. Bantam Books, New York
45. Weiser M (1993) Some computer science issues in ubiquitous computing. Comm ACM 36(7):75–84
46. Whitacre E (2011) A virtual choir 2,000 voices strong. http://www.ted.com/talks/eric_whitacre_a_virtual_choir_2_000_voices_strong.html. Accessed 7 Jan 2012
47. Wilt DP et al (2013) Hawaii broadband initiative broadband demand projections for Hawaii over the coming decades. http://www.ptc.org/ptc13/images/papers/upload/PTC13_Wilt_Dan_TS7_PPS.pdf. Accessed 8 Jan 2014
48. Woo-Young C (2005) Online civic participation, and political empowerment: online media and public opinion formation in Korea. Media Cult Soc 27(6):925–935
49. Wortham J (2010) As older users join Facebook, network grapples with death. http://www.nytimes.com/2010/07/18/technology/18death.html. Accessed 8 Aug 2012
50. Yee A (2008) Mongolia. http://www.hiluxury.com/mongolia/. Accessed 19 Mar 2014
51. Zunes S (2009) The Iranian revolution, 1977-1979. http://www.nonviolent-conflict.org/index.php/movements-and-campaigns/movements-and-campaigns-summaries?sobi2Task=sobi2Details&sobi2Id=23. Accessed 9 Feb 2014

Chapter 5
Alternative Futures at the Mānoa School

5.1 Introduction

In 1970, the state of Hawaii organized a landmark project to garner public input on possibilities for the futures, called Hawaii 2000—a year-long, cross-island endeavor that utilized then-cutting edge communication technologies and a range of tools for engaging various stakeholders. As Chaplin explains, "A Commission on the Year 2000 for Hawaii, involving not only academics and professionals, but also the young for whom the twenty-first century will exist, could help us focus on where we want to go and how to get there" [5, pp. 3–4]. As Dator et al. recount:

> There were presentations of the idea before a joint session of the Hawaii State Legislature, a year-long formal public lecture series on various future-oriented themes, scores of radio and television programs and newspaper articles and features, various high school and university futures courses, and hundreds of talks about the process and the future in general by members of the Advisory Committee with professional, civic, business, educational and public interest groups on every island. [11]

As one of the first and largest public foresight exercises ever undertaken, Hawaii 2000 did much to elevate awareness of Futures Studies at a global scale and led to the founding of the Hawaii Research Center for Futures Studies (HRCFS) by the Hawaii State Legislature, where it remains housed within the Department of Political Science at the University of Hawaii at Mānoa (UHM). Under the guidance of the author, Dr. Jim Dator, who has served as Director of HRCFS since its inception, Futures Studies at UHM unofficially became known as the "Mānoa School," which references a particular mode of futures inquiry as much as it does the valley where the university is located. Futures Studies at the "Mānoa School" was based on the foundational idea that there is no such thing as *the* future that can be "studied." Rather, among the empirical bases of futures studies were the numerous images of the future that come in a variety of forms, fears, and fantasies. From census data to science fiction, there were many things that one might use to imagine and analyze possibilities for the futures, and it is one of the major tasks of futurists to study, examine, and try to understand how differing images of the futures lead to

J.A. Dator et al., *Mutative Media: Communication Technologies and Power Relations in the Past, Present, and Futures*, Lecture Notes in Social Networks,
DOI 10.1007/978-3-319-07809-0_5, © Springer International Publishing Switzerland 2015

different actions and inactions in the present that help shape the future as the present-yet-to-come. Although there are many ways to approach thinking critically about the futures, Dator's "Laws of the Futures" codified the Mānoa School approach, and outlined as well as contextualized the key tenets of the field. In light of our research, we have updated them accordingly:

1. *"The future" cannot be predicted because "the future" does not exist.*

   Futures studies do not—or should not—pretend to predict "the future." It studies ideas, data, stories, art, etc., about the future—what can be called "images of the future"—which each individual (and group) has (often holding several conflicting images at one time). These images often serve as the basis for actions in the present. Individual and group images of the futures are often highly volatile, changing according to mutating events or perceptions. Aspects of some images may persist. Others may change over one's life. Different groups often have very differing images of the futures. Men's images may differ from women's. Western images may differ from non-Western images, and so on.

   (a) *"The future" cannot be predicted, but alternative futures can, and should be, forecasted.*

   Thus, one of the main tasks of futures studies is to identify and examine the major alternative futures that exist at any given time and place. To "predict" means "accurately to say what will happen before it happens." We once lived in world where it was possible to "predict" significant parts of the future. No longer. To "forecast" means "to say what might happen in a logical, coherent, theoretically based way that does not pretend to be accurate but does intend to be useful. The Mānoa school does not attempt to predict the future, but it does attempt to develop and forecast alternative futures that are useful to decision makers.

   (b) *"The future" cannot be "predicted," but after alternative futures have been considered, then "preferred futures" can and should be envisioned, invented, implemented, continuously evaluated, revised, and re-envisioned.*

   Thus a major task of futures studies is to facilitate individuals and groups in formulating, implementing, and re-envisioning their preferred futures. Consequently, futurists must critically contemplate the implications of their work and carefully consider the ethical ramifications of receiving compensation for assisting organizations in imagining and ultimately creating the futures.

   (c) *To be useful, futures studies need to precede, and then be linked to, strategic planning, and thence to administration.*

   The identification of the major alternative futures and the envisioning and creation of preferred futures then guides subsequent strategic planning activities, which in turn determine day-to-day decision-making by an organization's administrators. However, the process of alternative futures forecasting and preferred futures envisioning is continuously ongoing and changing. The purpose of any futures exercise is to create a guiding vision, not a "final solution" or a limiting blueprint. It is proper, especially in environments of rapid technological and hence social and environmental change, for visions of preferred futures to change as new opportunities and problems present themselves.

2. *Any useful idea about the futures should appear to be ridiculous.*

   (a) Because new technologies permit new behaviors and values, challenging old beliefs and values that are based on prior technologies, much that will be characteristic of the futures is initially seen as novel and challenging. It typically seems at first obscene, impossible, stupid, "science fiction," ridiculous. Eventually it may become familiar and then utterly normal and "obvious." However, it is unfortunately the case that not all ridiculous ideas are useful—many are indeed ridiculous. Determining beforehand the difference between the two is what makes futures an art as much as a science.
   (b) Thus, what is popularly, or even sometimes professionally, considered to be "the most likely future" is often one of the least likely actual futures.
   (c) If futurists expect to be useful, they should expect to be ridiculed and for their ideas often to be rejected. Some of their ideas may deserve ridicule and rejection, but even their useful ideas about the futures may also be rejected because they run counter to the "crackpot realism" of the present.
   (d) Thus, decision-makers, and the general public, if they wish to consider useful information about the future, should expect it to be unconventional and often shocking, offensive, and seemingly ridiculous. Futurists, however, have the additional burden of making the initially ridiculous idea plausible and actionable by marshaling appropriate evidence and weaving together alternative scenarios of its possible developments.

3. *Futures are not history in reverse.*
   Just as there is no singular perspective and/or narrative that can adequately capture all of the complexities of the past (*history*), the same is true of the future (hence, *futures*). Furthermore, history is too often "his story," which is to say that seeking out marginalized voices from the futures is just as important as discovering silenced voices from our collective past.

   (a) Alternative scenarios are tools for exploring differing possibilities and potentialities—some radical, some not—from a variety of subject positions, enabling and engendering further engagement and speculation from divergent perspectives, especially those that are systematically repressed, muted, and/or ignored in the past and present.
   (b) Pluralizing the future(s) is simultaneously and intentionally a means of decolonizing the future(s). While challenging the normative political structures, systems, and institutions of the present, futures studies does not inherently promote any particular ideology, agenda, and/or telos. However it does strive to enable greater participation in discourses about what the futures can and might be thus bringing with it a commitment to egalitarian, participative, and non-killing values, behaviors, and structures.

As Dator's (updated) "Laws of the Future" denote, futures studies, at least from the Mānoa School perspective, is a profoundly political enterprise—one that confronts the forces driving the future down familiar as well as perhaps unwelcome paths. This dynamic is not partial only to the Mānoa School. Indeed, the origin of contemporary futures studies owes much to the apocalyptic tensions of the Cold War that led many people to think that perhaps there would be no future at all. As well as whether the ideas, institutions, technologies, and cultures that led to the Cold War were the best that humanity could so. Surely, many said, if we open dialog about preferred futures to everyone in the world, and not keep it the preserve only of certain groups in certain cultures, we might be able to create a better future than we had obtained from the past.

Futures studies, then, is as much about critiquing and perhaps disenabling certain images of the future from coming to pass as it is about imagining, crafting, and enabling preferred futures. For many, extending the imbalanced power relations of the present is desirable, for others undesirable indeed. For many, if not most, people the future they see before them is merely an extension of the present—what Dator calls "continued growth," or the "official" view of the future of all modern governments, educational systems, and organizations [10, p. 8]. Although a future filled with continued economic growth might seem like a good thing to many, the question of who will foot the bill, in the future as well as the present, becomes critical, especially as the costs of growth are often externalized and paid for by the biosphere, indigenous peoples, and all our children and grandchildren, even of those who reap the purported rewards of living all-too-modern lives.

Through years of empirical research, Dator determined that all of the billions of images of the future that exist are actually specific manifestations of one of four generic alternative futures: *Grow (Continued Growth), Collapse, Discipline,* and *Transformation*. This insight forms the basis of the Mānoa School Scenario Modeling Method. As Dator explains, "Each of our four generic forms differ from each other fundamentally in cosmology, epistemology, and often deontology, and are not variations on a common set of themes" [10, p. 7]. Arguing that all "images of the future" can and might be sorted using four generic archetypes, Dator's framework emerged near the dawn of futures studies as an academic and applied discipline when he "along with many other early futurists were trying to make sense of the many often conflicting images of the future" [10, p. 5].

Offering a mechanism for contextualizing various images of the future, Dator contends that "Each generic form has a myriad of specific variations reflective of their common basis," which is to say that the archetypes are just that: frameworks or containers into which content for specific scenarios will vary according to the theoretical, methodological, and data choices that are part of the process by which one theorizes social trends, identifies drivers of change and continuity, analyzes trends, pinpoints emerging issues, and ultimately models critical intersections of change and stability within each scenario life-world [10, p. 7].

Although the process of modeling, and ultimately crafting, scenarios is highly qualitative, which is to say an art, it also very much relies on data from a range of sources, historical as well as current, including economic, demographic, resource, cultural, and other facts and figures. This is what separates futures studies from mere fantasy, creativity, and science fiction. Creativity and imagination are needed, but so is good historical and contemporary knowledge about crucial elements of society. By combining facts with creative imagination that result in stories with varying degrees of possibility, plausibility, and probability, futurists create a means by which to evaluate policy to guide actions in the here and now for moving with some confidence into uncertain futures. Furthermore, specific scenarios vary according to the client and/or project. Knowing the history and present situation of whatever "X" is being considered is integral to modeling effective and useful scenarios that are meant to help individuals, communities, and institutions prepare effectively for continuity and change.

With the above as a basis, the four generic archetypical images of the futures used by the Mānoa School are:

Grow (or *Continued Growth*)—This archetype is based on the idea that present trends and emerging issues will continue in a kind of business-as-usual format. This is the dominant image of the future in almost every public discourse today. Most people assume that the future will be a continuation or extrapolation of what they think they know and experience today as is evidenced by the fact that many of us go about our daily routines without any thought for the morrow. But, in reality, when we look to the past and all the extraordinary things that that have happened and not happened in just the last 50–100 years, we can see that there have been truly mutative changes as well as desirable and undesirable continuities in the way many of us live. Although continued growth typically implies increased economic development, it also very much includes the diffuse challenges enlivened by increasing growth. Getting people to envision a future beyond continued growth can often be one of the most important and difficult aspects of being a futurist, since all institutions of modern society (especially education, governance, and of course the economy) are aimed at promoting growth, usually economic growth.

Collapse (or *New Beginnings*)—This archetype is now typically based on the conviction that economic, environmental, government, and social systems as we know them are unsustainable and will collapse—perhaps are collapsing—necessitating new ways of life, some of which might not be "new" at all. Although dystopian and backward-looking images of the future have been popular at various historical moments, collapse scenarios are not inherently negative, bad, or stressful. This form focuses as much on what happens after the storm, so to speak, as on the storm itself. As easy as it is to imagine various ways in which humanity might go extinct, it seems hard for some people to imagine ways in which humans might in fact thrive following catastrophe and crisis, even though history certainly offers many examples. Indeed, many people and organizations argue that collapse of current systems could allow us to return to earlier, better, purer ways of life, ridding us of "demonic technologies" that have distorted our lives and allowing us to return to life on a human, and not a mechanical, scale. Collapse provides a wonderful opportunity for "new beginnings."

Discipline (or *Sustainable*)—One version of this archetype is based on the idea that we can and might avoid environmental, social, economic or cultural collapse by restraining our behaviors so that we become sustainable in all these areas. However, although sustainable futures are inherently disciplined, not all disciplined scenarios are sustainable. Other versions of a disciplined image of the futures say that even if continued growth can be made sustainable in terms of resources and the environment, continued economic growth by its very nature destroys certain fundamental natural, human, cultural, religious, ideological, or other values that should instead be the basis of a good life. To fulfill our human destiny we must cease endless, destructive "growth," and live our lives according to these fundamental, superior values, some people say. Discipline may imply authoritarianism, but by no means necessarily so. A discipline society can also be designed so that educational, institutional, structural, and similar systems encourage people to live cooperative, peaceful, content, and meaningful lives that are contrary to the values and behaviors permitted or required by similar systems in a society that demands continuous economic growth.

Transformation—This archetype is based on the idea that a technological and/or spiritual revolution will enable novel behaviors producing values and institutions so profoundly different that the world as we know it now and have known it previously will seem unrecognizable. In transformational images of the future, humanity experiences a total metamorphosis so that old-fashioned *Homo sapiens* may no longer be at the center of it, or perhaps even survive in its present form. From messianic religious traditions to those beckoning the advent of the technological Singularity, transformational scenarios have much to do with transcending old borders and limits of the human, society, and the interstices between the two. Just as the butterfly is unpredictable from the caterpillar who weaves the cocoon around itself, so the contours of a transformational future are unpredictable from the technological and social forces driving transformational processes.

5.2 The Seven Driving Forces Matrix

In order to craft and shape the content for the alternative futures scenarios of some "X" (institution, idea, process, etc.) under consideration—here our X is the futures of communication technologies and power relations—it is necessary first to have a theory of social change and continuity guiding the research process. The theory we used is that of technological change, as previously described. That theory first directed our attention to the past.

When were the first communication technologies created? What kinds of people were involved? What were the social, environmental, biological, and technological conditions of the time that led communication technologies to assume the form and trajectory they did? What subsequently changed and why at various stages between "then" and "now"? What kinds of people are involved now? What are the social, environmental, biological, and technological conditions now, compared to then? And where are communication technologies tending? What are the "trends" from the past and present driving them into the futures? What are the forces of resistance in the present to those trends? And what are those luring it forward?

Table 5.1 Seven driving forces matrix

Futures Forces	*Grow*	*Collapse*	*Discipline*	*Transform*
Population	Increasing	Declining	Controlled	Post-human
Energy	Sufficient	Scarce	Limited	Abundant
Economy	**Dominant**	Survival	Regulated	Trivial
Environment	Conquered	**Overshot**	Sustainable	Artificial
Culture	Dynamic	Stable	**Focused**	Complex
Technology	Accelerating	Limited	Restricted	**Transformative**
Governance	Corporate	Local	Strict	Direct

For this latter, we engaged in a kind of horizon scanning we called "emerging issues analysis"—tiny bits of evidence that might or might not begin to bud as trends and blossom into full-blown problem/opportunities in the futures. We looked not only within the field of communication technologies themselves but also into the broader social, environmental, and technological milieu within which future communication technologies might be embedded. In simple terms, a trend is something that is ongoing, alive in public awareness and discourse, and certain to have some impact on the futures. Many trends are drawn from quantitative data, such as census reports and economic indices. Although trends provide vital content for scenarios, the four generic futures method starts out with a pre-set range of "drivers" that shape past, present, and futures. The seven driving forces matrix (Table 5.1) specifies the fundamental *qualitative* differences for each of seven driving forces and for each of the four generic images. These qualitative differences are then spelled out in qualitative and quantitative detail during our development of each specific description of each alternative future.

We call this "deductive forecasting." By using the four generic futures on the one hand, and by specifying appropriately different values in each future for each historical and future driving force—augmented by appropriate emerging issues, on the other—we are able to describe four very different images of the futures based on a combination of data, reasoning, and imagination.

Commenting on the power and sway that this "extended present" has on our sense as to what is possible, probable, and preferable in the future(s), Sardar notes, "This future is stable, with discernible trends, and can be known. Most reliable forecasts concentrate on this period. It is the domain of the predictive future" [30]. At the Mānoa School, the extended present is where one starts, but, as stated, the four futures scenario modeling method necessitates the integration of emerging issues as well. As Curry and Schultz explain, "Mānoa scenario building assumes that you build the scenarios first as general images of possible futures, and then ask how the [emerging] topic or issue will exist or play out in that environment" [8, p. 48]. As the basis for our general images, the seven driving forces matrix is the foundation from which we modeled our scenarios here, augmented by a variety of emerging issues, especially the author's "Unholy Trinity, Plus One," which refers to the end of cheap and abundant energy, multiple environmental challenges, global economic and fiscal collapse, and the inability of governments to govern [9].

5.3 The Unholy Trinity, Plus One

Public consciousness concerning environmental, energy, and economic issues have waxed and waned as oil prices rise and drop, the world lurches from one economic crisis to another, and debates over climate change and sea-level rise paralyze policy makers and demoralize citizens.

Given the convergence of economic, environmental, and energy challenges now and, as many expect, in the futures, the author has labeled these three forces an "Unholy Trinity," which, as he suggests, have the power of tsunamis. As Dator's metaphor suggests, the potency of these three forces lies not in their individual impact but rather in the synergies between them. As the author explains, "I find very few people have linked the three together. Indeed, most people seem to assume that solutions to each one of the tsunamis lie in the other two without realizing that all three tsunamis are perilously interconnected" [9, p. 34].

Although Dator's Unholy Trinity centers on the force of the three aforementioned tsunamis, there is another aspect, which he calls "Plus One," that is just as, if not the most, important. As Dator explains, "It is government. Or rather, the lack of government—the lack of any kind of formal, communal system that can help us solve any of these three challenges" [9, p. 39]. Although Dator focuses primarily on the American context, it is not difficult to see the global applicability of his argument, especially with regard to ongoing environmental and economic challenges. Dator and Miller updated the Mānoa School method to reflect the Unholy Trinity, Plus One in all four futures, and not in just one or two of them, as had been the case before [12]. Dator and Miller call for the inclusion of this "new normal," which speaks to increasing awareness of the challenges of the Anthropocene to account for the immense impact of humanity upon the planet's complex adaptive systems.

In line with Dator and Miller's diagnosis, Sardar [29] observes that we have entered *postnormal* times, which is to say that the "new" normal denotes a seismic shift in both actual and perceptual social, economic, political, and environmental conditions. Similarly, Beck [2] and Giddens [15] previously observed increasing societal uncertainty, which brings with it a mistrust of present as well as of past solutions. For Beck, Risk Societies "begin where nature ends" [2, p. 10] and suggests that the world has become "a laboratory where there is absolutely nobody in charge" [2, p. 9]. Similarly, Giddens conceives of Risk Societies as places where "we increasingly live on a high technological frontier which absolutely no one completely understands and which generates a diversity of possible futures" [15, p. 3]. Offering a succinct and incisive synopsis, Dator and Miller contend:

> Humans are changing the world faster than we are understanding it. While what our scientists know about the world is extraordinarily impressive, and while new discoveries are announced every day, there is still much we do not know. Indeed, there may be much we do not even know about. We don't know we don't know because we don't know we don't know it. We are discovering our ignorance and errors as fast as we are gaining new understanding, and yet we go on changing the world. [12]

In crafting the scenarios and scanning for emerging issues, we were mindful to account for the author's "new normal," which simultaneously provides limits and enlivens possibilities for what might lie ahead.

5.4 Emerging Issues Analysis

As we showed earlier, analyses of technology and trend life-cycles typically utilize six phases: invention, development, diffusion, maturity, obsolescence, and death. Although we believe that most, if not all, technologies continue to follow this pattern, accelerating rates of change have quickened the pace by which technologies move through this pattern. This has led some to contend that it is no longer applicable and does not account for systemic complexity. In the Mānoa School, our emerging issue analysis (EIA) utilizes this basic patterning and leverages a perspective first identified by Graham Molitor in his landmark article, "How to Anticipate Public-Policy Changes" [25]. As Molitor contends, one ought to be on the lookout for "catalytic events" or, as we call them, emerging issues, in order to anticipate and forecast possible, probable, and plausible effects. Their identification is as much an art as it is a (social) science.

5.4.1 The Life Cycle of an Emerging Issue

As we have shown, everything that exists now at one time did not exist. Everything that is a big problem now—that everyone knows about, is concerned about, has an opinion about, hears discussed on Twitter, blogs, talk shows on TV and the radio as well as over the backyard fence, is the subject of speeches in the legislature—all those problems at one time did not exist. This thing that everyone knows about may be a technology, a social institution, a religious belief, a political ideology, a disease, an astronomical event—anything!

However, at one time it did not exist. No one had ever heard of it, or worried about it, or perhaps even imagined it. But now, "everyone" does. Everything at some point in time "emerged"—peaked up into view, although almost no one saw it when it did. But someone did, and said so on her blog, but no one paid any attention—she was known to be unreliable, a bit flaky, always worried about things that bothered no one else.

Then, a few companions also noticed it, and began to talk about it on their blogs. But who were they? Outcasts, druggies, criminals, misfits, malcontents, street people, college professors, and/or artists.

Yes, finally a college professor noticed it, and mentioned it in class, where no one else could hear. The students had long since known to discount anything that professor said. "Loony toons" they opined.

Then a few of the professor's loony companions took it up, and began to talk about it over coffee and on their blogs. And then someone wrote an article about it, but no respectable journal would publish it, so they posted it online, where it was roundly dismissed. Except that someone in Finland read about it and said he had seen the same thing in Bosnia when he was there recently.

So, more and more people began to notice it, and talk about it, and write about it. Respectable journals of highbrow opinion began to publish articles about it. Then it was mentioned, in passing, on "All Things Considered"—public radio that hardly anyone listens to. But it did appear in a back page of *The New York Times*. And then a public access TV show in San Francisco did a show on it. And that was picked up by a local TV station in the Bay area, and later by the *San Francisco Chronicle*. Meanwhile, academia had begun to focus in on it, and it was being discussed by many scholars. Conventions were being held, and it was often debated online.

Finally, it hit the major TV stations and newspapers. Oprah had some children of perverts who had taken it to extremes tell embarrassing stories about their mothers who had done it. The blogosphere was full of it. Finally, people were demanding somebody do something about this. There ought to be a law. It ought to be outlawed. It was disgusting. But others said no, that it was divine, and began to worship it, and demand religious protection. It became the talk of the town, the rage of the continent. Something everyone had an opinion about.

But, eventually, the furor passed. People got used to it. Young people grew up with it all around them, and treated it as perfectly natural and ordinary; certainly no big thing. And eventually it just sort of died out. No one noticed it any more. In fact, there wasn't much to notice. And then, years and years later, someone wrote a Ph.D. dissertation about it, and that was that. It was as dead as a doornail—whatever a "doornail" is. So there you have it—the life cycle of everything: from nothing to something tiny, to something growing rapidly, to something very prominent, to something accepted and barely noticed, to something declining, to something dead and buried. And sometimes staying buried, but sometimes, years later somehow rising from the dead as something new, unnoticed, controversial, and ... well, on and on it goes.

Trend analysis focuses on things when they are already well under way—long after they initially emerged, but before they have become utterly commonplace. Trend analysis focuses on things that already have a history of development that can be quantitatively traced and forecasted. Emerging issues analysis, in contrast, focuses on things just as they are emerging—as close to their very first notice as possible, certainly before they become a well-established "trend," and never as a commonplace "problem." Too few to quantify.

Trend analysis can use facts and figures, since the thing has been noted, documented, tracked. Emerging issues analysis has no such clear facts and figures. Instead, it tries to see things that are barely visible. Its sources are crazy people, marginal people, off-beat publications and websites, in the recesses of the mind of some scientist or engineer, the concern of some artist or poet, or unpublished novelist. Or at least, after it has emerged a bit, in obscure academic publications or blogs, talked about over too many drinks at one's local pub, or after hours of food and sleep-deprived meditation.

Another way to locate emerging issues in the earliest and subsequent period of emergence, is look for emerging patterns—for something that is for the first time being discussed in lots of different websites, blogs, journals, or academic circles. Patterns are often more important than isolated items, but they are also a bit farther up the life cycle of growth of an issue.

Although it is easy, if not typical, for those looking for emerging issues to focus on either challenges or opportunities, one ought to conceptualize and forecast both positive and negative aspects for every emerging issue. Just ask the newspaper industry. Or Myspace. Or (sometime soon) Facebook. Every emerging issue tells a complex story, and it is the task of the futurist to make the possible seem plausible by starting with evidence in the present. As part of the Mānoa School method, S-curve life-cycles are helpful for telling these stories.

Before long, biochemical processes may replace electronics and lead to brain-to-brain and source-to-brain transfer. Behavioral control may then move not only from humans to the environment, but also from the environment to the brain and central nervous systems. Scientists and engineers may finally break through the limited interface of our biological input-output mechanisms. So far we can't make screens smaller than we can see or buttons too small to push. If we can go beyond the input-output mechanism of eyes, mouths, ears, and fingers, and go directly from brain-to-brain, or source-to-brain, we can do away with all "media" and have direct mind-to-mind communication, either via electronic-like implants or direct mind transfer—"mental telepathy."

However, even if we develop the hardware for that, we still will need the software for it. Developing the software may take much longer. But this kind of high-tech dream and post-dream society may not be realized as quickly as some of us have imagined, or may not be achieved at all. On the one hand attachment to written words may be stronger than we thought. On the other hand, looming and neglected environmental, energy, and economic challenges may make continued high tech societies impossible.

We may effectively run out of oil before we can develop a viable alternative. Long-deferred environmental challenges loom. Global population growth continues catastrophically at the same time that population is declining, or about to decline rapidly, in many parts of the world. All economies are unsustainable to the extent that they are based on endless debt and endless growth in a finite planet. These problems are global and yet we have no way to address them globally. Our obsolete nation-state system is powerless in many ways, and so the future of humanity on Earth is uncertain. It is entirely possible a way of life called "development" that we have only known for a few hundred years is coming to an end.

We may need to become farmers and hunters with their means of communication and conflict resolution once again.

5.5 Some Horizon Scan Hits, Circa 2012–2014

5.5.1 Synthetic Biology and Biotechnology

As the NEST High-Level Expert Group reports, "Synthetic biology is the engineering of biology: the synthesis of complex, biologically based (or inspired) systems, which display functions that do not exist in nature. This engineering perspective may be applied at all levels of the hierarchy of biological structures—from individual molecules to whole cells, tissues and organisms. In essence, synthetic biology will enable the design of 'biological systems' in a rational and systematic way" [27, p. 5].

Humans have always tinkered with biology and genetics since the dawn of agriculture. Plant and animal breeding incorporates genetic selection for certain traits. We select potential mates based on (mis?)understandings of desirable characteristics. But the deep enmeshing of biology and engineering in the field of synthetic biology and the speed with which new technologies in this field are being developed is a significant shift for the future. With the potential ability to program genetic makeup and specifically embed selected genetic traits in living beings, synthetic biology is calling into question what it is that defines us as both humans and individuals in the future. It is also asking us seriously to reconsider our vision of what is 'natural.' Now that we are on the verge of being able to create life, what will be in bounds of play and what will be considered 'unethical' in a future where the next generations have never known a world without these abilities? May we one day walk through Brautigan's imagined "cybernetic forest filled with pines and electronics where deer stroll peacefully past computers as if they were flowers with spinning blossoms."[3]

In 2010, Craig Venter, a privately funded billionaire scientist, created the first synthetic cell from scratch, which he named "synthia" [23]. The July 2010 issue of *Science* magazine published Venter's work, which explained that "The only DNA in the cells is the designed synthetic DNA sequence, including "watermark" sequences and other designed gene deletions and polymorphisms, and mutations acquired during the building process. The new cells have expected phenotypic properties and are capable of continuous self-replication" [14]. Despite being simple bacteria, this was a significant turning point in the creation of artificial life—the J. Craig Venter Institute had engineered a synthetic life form capable of self-replication.

As of 2013, Venter's lab has turned part of its focus towards recreating life forms found in space. In this vision, a probe sent into space would be equipped to send genetic information back to Earth, which would then be coded to re-create the extraterrestrial life forms encountered. Testing the technology in the Mojave Desert, the team expects to have this technology on the 2020 mission to Mars.

Biohacking has simultaneously emerged as a counter valence to the corporate owned and patented neoliberal approach to biotechnology. Inhabited by biotechnology enthusiasts, self-taught and academically trained scientists and activists, the biohacking movement aims to put science back in the hands of the average citizen. Biohacking spaces are set up in communities and open to the public so that anyone can learn how to participate in biotechnology and synthetic biology. This radical reimagining of power structures has its genesis in the Critical Art Ensemble and the first biohacking space in New York City, Genspace. In their book *Digital Resistance,* Critical Art Ensemble attempts to "reveal the ideological infrastructure of the technology and its representation, and to demonstrate that even the smallest Utopian possibility contained in the rhetoric would probably not be generally realized by most of the world's population" [7, p. 46]. This is a direct challenge to the metanarrative of benevolent technology as the arbiter of progress. The "biohacking" project seeks to subvert efforts to control and concentrate biotechnology in the hands of corporations by making the technology and the knowledge accessible to as many people as possible while also raising the specter of harmful possibilities.

Affectionately known as DIY-science—and not affiliated with any academic institution or corporation—biohacking labs are popping up all around the world. The grand vision of the biohacking movement is perhaps best articulated by Genspace founder Ellen Jorgensen when she imagines a world in the not too distant future where personal biotech has become as ubiquitous and normal as personal computing is today [19].

In October 2013, a group calling themselves Grindhouse Wetware became the first group of biohackers to successfully implant an interactive electronic device in a human body [21]. The biosensor they implanted is called Circadia, and it tracks body temperature, sending that information to a smartphone. Admittedly somewhat of a gimmick rather than immensely useful science, this nonetheless marks a movement towards do-it-yourself body modification through biotechnology.

Perhaps the most critical question with the emerging biotechnologies is, who will own the rights to newly formed life and perhaps more philosophically, does ownership as a concept make sense for the futures when it comes to the engineering of life? With the dominant trend clearly moving towards corporate control over engineered genes and patented biological technologies, we may see a shift towards "ownership" over certain aspects of our bodies and our health. If a corporation had a hand in your genetic makeup, might they be able to own the rights to your lifelong health care and a portion of your productivity? On the flipside, how might resistance to neoliberal worldviews through avenues like DIY-science challenge these dominant trends and create subcultures of intense body modification—effectively self-made cyborg citizens? The values of individuality and the sense that we as humans are somehow separated from other living beings may start to fade as we literally see parts of our bodies altered, replaced, or augmented by synthetic biological technologies. Very importantly, who gets to decide these questions? Can we responsibly leave them to a U. S. Supreme Court composed largely of Silents, who will justify their beliefs by reference to words in a document written for the challenges of a pre-industrial society over 200 years ago?

5.5.2 Artificial Intelligence and Machine Learning

Similar to the trends in synthetic biology, the emerging technologies related to artificial intelligence and machine or algorithmic learning portend radical mutative shifts in the futures. We may soon have the ability to upload parts of our mental capacity. If techno-optimists such as Ray Kurzweil are correct, the capacity to upload our brain to a larger neural network may be possible within just a few decades [17]. At the California Institute for Technology, researchers have already taken the first steps towards creating an artificial brain by building an artificial neural network out of DNA that operates in many of the same ways that a human brain can [33].

The ability to expand our mental capacity brings with it a whole host of ethical and political considerations, such as who has access to that information, how and where is it stored and protected, can it be edited or augmented, and who owns it when you die. These are not new concerns, as we've seen with copyright and other related issues since the dawn of printing. But the speed and veracity with which these changes may occur is critical. Can our social, cultural, and psychological systems keep up with such rapid and drastic change, and if so how will they be affected or altered? Perhaps the concept of ownership and intellectual property will have to be re-evaluated altogether. But the reality is that these concepts are so deeply tied to the neoliberal economic system that a change in those values may necessitate or perhaps precipitate wider economic and political changes on a global scale.

There is also the pressing issue of rights. Many images of the futures in science fiction depict artificial intelligent beings, or artilects, as either slaves to the human race or demonic dominators of humanity. Think back to the movies *Terminator, AI, IRobot,* and others. What if in reality, artilects merely want to co-exist with human life forms peaceably but with legally protected rights and social responsibilities? What happens when the first human falls in love with and wishes to marry an artilect? What happens when someone chooses to bio-engineer a hybrid child? [24] These ideas may seem ridiculous from the normative standpoint of the present, but should technology continue on the current pace and trajectory, they may truly not be far off. The flipside is of course whether environmental crises, energy constraints, economic fallouts, and other converging crises of the twenty-first century will stall or effectively halt our capacity to continue innovating in this direction.

The convergence of these trends in synthetic biology and artificial intelligence all call into question what it means to be "human." When a "natural" body can be gradually replaced over time by either new mechanical or synthetic biological parts, we will have to consider at what point a person loses a physical sense of individual self? How does that physical loss affect a mental sense of self? The merging of humans and machines requires a radical rethinking of our place in the flow of life and our position as self-appointed dominators of other life forms.

5.5.3 Nanotechnology

In 1986, K. Eric Drexler, an engineer at MIT, published a book entitled *Engines of Creation: The Coming Era of Nanotechnology*. Widely overused in common discourse to describe any processes that occur at the atomic or nano scale, the concept of nanotechnology as Drexler sees it has two distinct features. The first is that it involves manufacturing that uses nano scale machinery. The second is that the products are built with atomic precision. Drexler has coined this process "atomically precise manufacturing" or APM, and he, along with others, believe that investment in such manufacturing processes will transform the cost, range, and performance of products in revolutionary ways [13].

From visions of ultra-light structures, to molecular scale precise nano-medicine, to laptops exponentially more powerful than what we have today, Cordeiro argues that the advent of APM would enable what he calls a "radical abundance," which is also the title of his new book [6]. In the face of mounting resource shortages and environmental crises, the promise of APM has the potential to have radical impacts on the futures. For communication technologies, the potential of APM to increase drastically the speed of information transfer while simultaneously decreasing manufacturing costs for physical infrastructure is a critical potentiality. A lingering question is whether we will be able to achieve Drexler's vision for nanotechnology while there is still available energy and resources on the planet to do so.

5.5.4 3-D Printing Technology

3-D printing is at the heart of the DIY "maker-culture" that has proliferated in the twenty-first century. Using simple software and hardware that is getting progressively cheaper and more flexible, anyone with a 3-D printer and some printing substance—most commonly an extruded plastic—can independently manufacture a variety of 3-D objects based on his or her own original designs.

Although the earliest results of 3-D printing were seen as novelty, this technology is rapidly evolving and has the potential to explode into a myriad of uses in the very near futures. Having grown in just two decades from a novelty to a $2.7-billion-dollar industry, some applications now being explored include 3-D printing of human tissue and organs using human cells as the printing matrix. At Organovo in San Diego, for example, human tissue is being printed in a lab for use in research and medical treatments [22]. The world's first 3-D printed gun was created in May 2013, and only a few months later it was deposited in London's Victoria and Albert Museum [32].

Forecasts for the futures of 3-D printing range from the ability to print clothes and food at home to the ability to scan almost any object and reproduce it in 3-D. This capacity to micro-manufacture exactly what one needs for oneself when it is needed would actualize Alvin Toffler's notion of the "prosumer" and reverse the separation of producer and consumer that has defined the current neoliberal capitalist production system with profound consequences. As Toffler explains, "From this divorce of producer and consumer came many of the pressures toward standardization, specialization, synchronization and centralization characteristic of industrial societies" [31, p. 177]. Should 3-D printing explode the way some predict it will, we may see these trends reverse and lead to a movement towards diversification, decentralization, and highly individually motivated "presumption," creating massive changes in the ways that our economic and political structures are currently organized.

5.5.5 Teleportation

One of the more radical possibilities for the futures of communication technologies is the potential for teleportation. Although "beam me up Scotty" is still in the realm of science fiction, "beam up my tricorder" soon may not be. Two studies published in *Nature* in 2013 demonstrated that the chance of successful teleportation is increasing. Quantum teleportation, the movement of photons, was first achieved in 1997, and since then scientists have been able to teleport atoms but nothing larger. The new studies show the potential of using infrared light and microwave photons to teleport matter, thus overcoming some of the limitations of the previous methods [4]. These new technologies are only proof of experiments testing basic principles and still need much more development as of this writing.

For communication technologies, radical potentials lie in quantum computing or quantum information transfer. This technology, should it be realized, would enable super-fast computing and secure information transfer using the principles of quantum entanglement. As Professor Nicolas Gisin of the Group of Applied Physics at the University of Geneva in Switzerland explained, "Applications of quantum technologies are still in their infancy. Hence, it is likely that we are not yet aware of most future applications." But he also noted, "These future applications of quantum technology would probably look like magic to people who are around today" [34].

5.5.6 *Infectious Media, Literally*

In early 2012, a small number of teenage girls at LeRoy High School in New York began to develop uncontrollable tics, spasms, seizures, and stuttering. Overall, 19 girls and one adult displayed symptoms similar to Tourette's syndrome, and no one seems to know why, although a variety of causes have been identified, including an infection, environmental factors, mass hysteria, and Lyme disease. Although some thought the afflicted might be faking it, others picked up on the role of social media in the mysterious outbreak. Apparently, the girls who first experienced this behavior were watching videos of persons suffering from Tourette's syndrome on YouTube and mimicking what they saw.

As Dr. David Lichter, a neurology professor at the University of Buffalo, commented to a local news station, "I think you do have the potential for people going online and witnessing other student's behavior, then I think this medium has the potential to spread it beyond the immediate environment." Noting the affective means of transfer between media and the afflicted, Lichter continues, "It is some kind of unconscious mimicry that is going on in individuals who are stressed and suggestible and vulnerable" [1].

5.5.7 *Microwave Missiles*

In October 2012, Boeing, which is one of the largest defense contractors for the U. S. government, successfully tested its microwave missile prototype. As a non-lethal means of attack, the Counter-electronics High-powered Advanced Missile Project (CHAMP) may usher in a new era of military weaponry—one that is solely focused on disabling enemy communication technologies [26]. Whereas one would have had to detonate a nuclear bomb, which would produce an electromagnetic pulse, to achieve the same effect, CHAMP can take out specific targets, which is to say that it is much more precise and far less destructive. As noted by a Boeing employee, "During the test, the CHAMP missile navigated a pre-programmed flight plan and emitted bursts of high-powered energy, effectively knocking out the target's data and electronic subsystems" [18].

5.5.8 Pigeons and Pencils

Not all emerging issues point towards a high-tech future. Futurist Anthony Judge wrote an eloquent piece entitled, "Circumventing Invasive Internet Surveillance with Carrier Pigeons" [20]. Referencing the use of carrier pigeons during World Wars I and II in light of pressing concerns about privacy in the Internet age, Judge posits the return of the carrier pigeon as a decidedly low-tech form of communication outside of the dominant system. As recently as 1982, security contractor Lockheed Martin used carrier pigeons as "the most cost effective means of transferring copies of graphic design projects to workers 30 miles away over twisting mountain roads." And in 1987, pigeons were trained in search-and-rescue operations. UK experiments with carrier pigeons in 2010 showed that pigeons carrying USB keys were able to transport data faster than a video file upload. Considering that Revive & Restore, a group headed by Steward Brand, founder of futures group The Long Now, are working vigorously to de-extinct the passenger pigeon using advances in genomic technologies, Judge's vision may one day be possible.

There are also the outlier trends of slow living that point to futures where high speed technologies are consciously shunned in favor of slower more traditional means of communication. Professor Sirkka Heinonen from the Finland Futures Research Center (FFRC) sees the idea of "slow" as an emerging trend for the potential futures. This embraces a holistic approach to life and a long-term perspective that values interpersonal connections and connections to space, place, and time. In this vein, Heinonen shows how slow cities such as Shiodome and Kakegawa in Japan and Kristiinankaupunki in Finland consciously choose to create structures that encourage slow living and local community [16]. This trend seems to be growing, as there are now Internet fasting camps in Japan [28, 35] and America's first Internet addiction treatment center recently opened at Bradford Regional Medical Center in Pennsylvania [36].

References

1. Admin WKBW (2012) Social networking to blame for spreading LeRoy illness? http://www.wkbw.com/news/Social-Networking-to-Blame-for-Spreading-LeRoy-Illness-138821059.html. Accessed 1 May 2012
2. Beck U (1992) Risk society: towards a new modernity. Sage, New York
3. Brautigan R (1968) All watched over by machines of loving grace. The Pill versus the Springfield Mine disaster. Houghton Mifflin, Boston

4. Buchler B (2013) Teleportation just got easier—but not for you, unfortunately. http://phys.org/news/2013-08-teleportation-easierbut.html. Accessed 10 Oct 2013
5. Chaplin G, Paige GD (1973). Hawaii 2000: continuing experiment in anticipatory democracy. University Press of Hawaii for the Governor's Conference on the Year 2000, Honolulu
6. Cordeiro J (2013) Radical abundance: how a revolution in nanotechnology will change civilization. Foresight 15(5):420–421
7. Critical Art Ensemble (2001) Digital resistance: explorations in tactical media. Autonomedia, New York
8. Curry A, Schultz W (2009) Roads less travelled: different methods, different futures. J Futures Stud 13(4):35–60
9. Dator J (2009) The unholy trinity, plus one. J Futures Stud 13(3):33–48
10. Dator J (2009) Alternative futures at the Manoa School. J Futures Stud 14(2):1–18
11. Dator J et al (1999) Hawaii 2000: past, present and future. Social Science Research Institute, University of Hawaii at Manoa, Honolulu
12. Dator J, Miller M (2014) "New beginnings" within a new normal for the four futures. Foresight, forthcoming
13. Drexler KE (1986) Engines of creation the coming era of nanotechnology. Published for the WWW by Russell WhitakerFourth. Estate, London
14. Gibson DG et al (2010) Creation of a Bacterial Cell Controlled by a Chemically Synthesized Genome. Science 329(5987):52–56
15. Giddens A (1994) Living in a post-traditional society. In: Beck U et al (eds) Reflexive modernization: politics, tradition and aesthetics in the modern social order. Stanford University Press, Stanford, pp 56–109
16. Heinonen S (2013) Innovations in slow living futures. 21st WFSF world conference, Bucharest, Romania
17. Hodgkinson M (2009) By 2040 you will be able to upload your brain.... http://www.independent.co.uk/news/science/by-2040-you-will-be-able-to-upload-your-brain-1792555.html. Accessed 27 Mar 2012
18. Jackson R (2012) CHAMP—lights out. http://www.boeing.com/Features/2012/10/bds_champ_10_22_12.html. Accessed 11 Nov 2012
19. Jorgensen, E (2012) Biohacking—you can do it, too. http://www.ted.com/talks/ellen_jorgensen_biohacking_you_can_do_it_too. Accessed 8 Jan 2014
20. Judge T (2013) Circumventing invasive internet surveillance with carrier pigeons: rewilding the endangered world wide web of avian migration pathways. http://www.laetusinpraesens.org/musings/pigeon.php. Accessed 7 Jul 2013
21. Lallanilla M (2013) "Biohacker" implants chip in arm. http://www.livescience.com/40892-biohacker-tim-cannon-cyborg.html. Accessed 10 Nov 2013
22. Leckart S (2013) How 3-D printing body parts will revolutionize medicine. http://www.popsci.com/science/article/2013-07/how-3-d-printing-body-parts-will-revolutionize-medicine. Accessed 8 Aug 2013
23. Macrae F (2010) Scientist accused of playing God after creating artificial life by making designer microbe from scratch—but could it wipe out humanity? http://www.dailymail.co.uk/sciencetech/article-1279988/Artificial-life-created-Craig-Venter--wipe-humanity.html. Accessed 5 Feb 2012
24. McNally P, Inayatullah S (1988) The rights of robots: technology, law and culture in the 21st Century. Futures 20(2):119–136
25. Molitor GTT (1977) How to anticipate public-policy changes. SAM Adv Manage J 42:4–13
26. Peralta E (2012) Boeing successfully tests electronics-frying, microwave missile. http://www.npr.org/blogs/thetwo-way/2012/10/24/163554934/boeing-successfully-tests-electronics-frying-microwave-missile. Accessed 11 Nov 2012
27. Report of a NEST High-Level Expert Group (2005) Synthetic biology: applying engineering to biology. European Commission
28. Samakow J (2013) Japan Internet "fasting camps" aim to treat screen-addicted kids. http://www.huffingtonpost.com/2013/08/28/japan-internet-fasting-camp_n_3824697.html. Accessed 9 Sept 2013

29. Sardar Z (2010) Welcome to postnormal times. Futures 42(5):435–444
30. Sardar Z (2013) Future: all that matters. Hodder & Stoughton, London
31. Toffler A (1989) The third wave. Bantam Books, New York
32. Wetherbe J (2013) Guns made by 3-D printer are acquired for London museum's collection. http://articles.latimes.com/2013/sep/17/entertainment/la-et-cm-3d-printer-guns-art-museum-20130917. Accessed 18 Sept 2013
33. Woo M (2013) First artificial brain created from DNA. http://machineslikeus.com/news/first-artificial-brain-created-dna. Accessed 7 Jan 2014
34. Crystal quantum memories for quantum communication (2013) http://phys.org/news/2013-09-crystal-quantum-memories.html. Accessed 10 Oct 2013
35. Huffington Post (2013) http://www.huffingtonpost.com/2013/08/28/japan-internet-fasting-camp_n_3824697.html??view=print&comm_ref=false. Accessed 9 Sept 2013
36. Nation's first inpatient treatment center for Internet addiction launches in PA (2013) http://philadelphia.cbslocal.com/2013/09/09/nations-first-inpatient-treatment-center-for-internet-addiction-launches-in-pa/. Accessed 10 Oct 2013

Chapter 6
Gaming Futures

6.1 Introduction

Ours is an age of games. Whether you look at the exponential growth of mobile gaming or the resilience of classic board games, you do not have to look hard to find a variety of platforms, interfaces, and gaming media being used around the world by children of all ages. By the end of 2014, the global mobile gaming industry is expected to surpass $11.4 billion dollars in sales, and some think this number might quadruple the following year [5]. To say that gaming is big business would be a gross understatement, and it is clearly no longer just child's play.

Of course, governments, NGOs, and numerous educational organizations have used games and simulations for decades for research and teaching purposes, often by crowd-sourcing questions and answers, and exploring possibilities for the futures. However, in 2011, researchers working on unlocking the secrets of a particular protein created a gaming platform and opened up their research to the public [4]. Within a few months, the gamers did what professionals working years in a laboratory could not. Although we believe that the benefits of gaming for teaching, research, and development are clear, we showed towards the end of Chap. 3 that some people remain fearful of the explosion of gaming and the rise of gaming across various sectors. Indeed, In 2011, Ian Bogost, who designs video games when he is not teaching at the Georgia Institute of Technology, published a very public diatribe against "gamification," a pejorative term used to describe the wholesale addition of gaming elements (such as rankings and badges) to anything and everything, including sales and marketing strategies [1].

Ultimately, Bogost is most critical of the corporatization of gaming and, perhaps most importantly, the ways that gaming can and has been used to collect data on users, entrench the power and reach of large technology firms, and exacerbate the complexities and contradictions of our current socio-economic system—a trend that Jameson conceives of as both catastrophic and progressive at the same time [3, p. 55]. Indeed, many mobile gaming platforms use a "freemium" system, which means that although the initial download has no cost, advertisements and in-app purchases drive revenue.

J.A. Dator et al., *Mutative Media: Communication Technologies and Power Relations in the Past, Present, and Futures*, Lecture Notes in Social Networks,
DOI 10.1007/978-3-319-07809-0_6, © Springer International Publishing Switzerland 2015

According to Geekaphone, 81 % of all mobile games use the freemium approach, and many expect this trend to continue and even strengthen in the years to come as mobile comes to dominate Internet usage and access [5].

It is with full knowledge of the challenges and opportunities of contemporary gaming, particularly mobile Internet-based platforms, that we embarked upon developing *Gaming Futures*. Our intention was to devise a game that could help players experience the impact that different communication technologies might have on their decisions in certain situations. After researching and considering many alternatives, we decided to adapt a number of existing gaming platforms that utilized geocaching, narrative-based alternative reality games (ARG), and mobile augmented reality (MAR) systems. Our ultimate reliance on MAR centered on Wikitude, an open-source MAR platform. This decision was as much political as practical. We very much wanted the culminating experience of our research to be open access and replicable. Involving the broader audience in our work is a long-standing tradition of the Mānoa School of Futures Studies. After weighing all of our options, and the strengths of the Mānoa School approach, it became clear that our project was best suited for a dynamic live-action experience—one that offered participants not just glimpses of alternative futures but embodied perspectives through which they could live and breathe in alternative futures.

MAR draws on the mobility and connectivity afforded by computing devices such as smartphones and tablets to locate and disseminate information relative to the geo-spatial context of each user. This technology uses the GPS capabilities of mobile Internet-enabled (MIE) devices to search for digital information that has been "contextualized" within the immediate area of the user. In concert with the display capabilities of each device, information is presented in relationship to each user's current location (latitude/longitude, elevation, cardinal direction). Some devices, such as Google Glass, allow for a heads-up display view of digital information, while others provide data through a mapping service. We decided to focus on the latter.

In implementing MAR technologies for the development and distribution of our research, *Gaming Futures* explored the ways in which users navigate both physical and virtual spaces as part of the goals and activities of gameplay. As a means to promote immersion within our scenarios, MAR allowed for the integration of the digital aspects of the futures within the surrounding physical landscape. The digital information received along each path provided gamers with alternative lenses through which they could experience the present and futures simultaneously. This doubling of present and futures is critical since our primary mode of engagement with the futures is imaginative. As we have explained above, Dator's laws denote that *the* future does not exist, but images (or imaginings) do empirically exist that can be experienced emotionally and analyzed critically. Ultimately, MAR granted us the opportunity to design a game that blended real and digital information into a hybrid futures experience. This fusion produced a methodology for analyzing alternative futures by engaging with affective creation, interaction, and response that was emphasized during the interactive scenario experiences encountered by the gamers.

This is where we believe *Gaming Futures* charted new waters. The coupling of experiential scenario-based gameplay with MAR required participants to navigate a hybrid physical/digital landscape by themselves becoming and performing the roles of specific persons within one or more of the futures. We believe *Gaming Futures* is the first gaming platform of its kind, especially with regards to its foresight-driven content and hybrid physical/digital form.

At the heart of the game's content were four specific alternative futures for 02062 that were researched and developed using the Mānoa School's generic four alternative futures modeling method described in the previous chapter. The scenarios and scripts used for *Gaming Futures* have been updated to reflect horizon scans done in 2013 and early 2014—the results of which have been integrated into Chap. 4. Additionally, we recently came across an emerging issue that directly relates to one of our scenarios and, as it were, serves as a reminder that scenarios are just that. In response to the recent upswing in private space exploration, specifically projects to colonize Mars, the General Authority of Islamic Affairs and Endowment (GAIAE) released a report condemning such efforts. As Henderson reports, "Such a one-way journey poses a real risk to life, and that can never be justified in Islam." [2] Although we do not want to give away one of the central aspects of our scenarios here, we felt this event provided an apt entrée into the complex dynamics of the Mānoa School method. Although our scenarios very much focus on the nexus between communication technologies and power relations, we sought to create life-worlds with living, breathing subjects. As we have said before, the process of scenario modeling is as much art as science, which is to say that we sought more than mere data points to model possibilities for the futures. In crafting complex life-worlds, we first carefully analyzed all the research we had done on historical, contemporary, and emerging communication technologies (Chaps. 2 and 3), and then isolated cycles and trends in light of our horizon scan hits (Chap. 4). Using the seven driving forces of the generic four futures as discussed earlier (see Chap. 4), we were able to forecast alternative futures based on existing points of information as well as on the emerging technologies we highlighted previously. The seven driving forces matrix provides a template for transforming the four generic futures into four very different life-worlds that reflect the depth and complexity of each. Taking Dator's 2nd Law of the Future (*any useful idea about the future should appear to be ridiculous*) to heart, the scenarios and corresponding scripts privilege the possible over what some people might mistakenly consider to be the probable, although they each very much reflect potentialities of ongoing trends and emerging issues as noted in Chap. 4.

Once our scenarios were sketched out, we developed both physical and digital "artifacts from the futures" that were used to chart the MAR path for each scenario. These objects can take many forms, and offer an additional means by which to make the futures more tangible and accessible. In developing the artifacts, we re-appropriated as much of the physical landscape as possible into our digital forms. We chose Kakaako, a somewhat seedy historical neighborhood in Honolulu, as the site for gameplay since the area has been undergoing significant changes in recent years. Portions of it have become spaces for innovative social and entrepreneurial events, such as Pow! Wow! Hawaii! which brings in street artists from around the world as part of a multiday public event [6]. Since Kakaako is literally covered in world-class street art, we sought to utilize this aesthetic resource by integrating it into the game. Our connection of MAR with existing public art installations produced a new foresight concept: *street artifacts*. As hybrid objects that digitally re-appropriate the physical landscape for the express purpose of enlivening an experiential scenario, street artifacts are a novel means to enhance foresight activities. They served as an integral part of *Gaming Futures*. Orchestrating gameplay in public space also created the opportunity for chance encounters, and on more than one occasion, local residents and patrons inquired into why teams of smartphone-wielding pedestrians were meandering around the neighborhood.

6.2 Gameplay

In order to play *Gaming Futures*, gamers were required to use an MIE smartphone. We provided MIE devices as needed, though almost all players had and used them naturally. Each gamer was also asked to setup a Twitter® account to send and receive information during the game. From the outset, we wanted gameplay to take advantage of contemporary communication technologies, specifically MIE devices and social media, as a means of leveraging critical thought about the role these technologies play in the world of today and how they may (or may not) be used in the futures.

The overall structure of gameplay was set up as follows: four teams composed of three players were randomly organized from the 12 participants selected for gameplay. Each team was given, both physically as well as digitally through Wikitude, a map and a one-page scenario of his or her future. This was also read aloud by each team's facilitator at the starting position. Color-coding each scenario was necessary to assist gamers in navigating along the Wikitude routes. Each team experienced not just one but two of the four futures. So as not to alert the participants to the nature of the future they were going to experience, we labeled each future by meaningless colors, and not by their generic names. Thus, the teams were organized as Yellow/Green, Green/Yellow, Red/Blue, and Blue/Red. In order to maximize the dissonance among gamers, we chose to juxtapose Transform (yellow) with Discipline (green) and Grow (red) with Collapse (blue).

Using the GPS-enabled routing available through Wikitude, each team navigated two unique routes for each scenario experience. Check-in coordinates and points-of-interest were created using Google Earth and inserted into the Wikitude path to designate street artifacts. These were key to ensuring the flow and timing of the game, which was set up to keep teams from overlapping with one another (e.g., the Green/Yellow began their second route after the Yellow/Green team finished their first scenario experience and vice versa). Teams generally began the second scenario experience path immediately after completing the first scenario experience. The timing differential among teams was marginal.

Following the paths created specifically for each team, players used their smartphone's GPS to move through Kakaako, where they would learn more about their future at designated street artifacts. When players successfully made it to a street artifact using Wikitude and linked to the appropriate Google form, they were prompted to become a character from their future in order to receive additional information about their specific role in the scenario. Two street artifacts were created for each path, and gamers were asked to tweet pictures of the street artifacts they encountered. Gamers were also told to look for color-coded QR codes that were hidden along each team's path. When gamers came across a QR code that linked to a mobile Tumblr blog with additional scenario information, they were asked to tweet what they discovered for bonus points.

When a team made it to their destination, each gamer was given an envelope with a brief character description, a costume for their character, and a copy of their scenario script. Once the gamers were outfitted, two actors, who were also costumed, initiated the scenario experience that began with a short dialogue providing some context on the power relations and available communication technologies within the scenario. As all of the participants worked through the script, the gamers were prompted to make a decision that challenged them to consider dimensions of access, control, and force relative to the communication technologies available within that future. Though unbeknownst to them at the time, these Yes/No decisions required gamers to choose whether or not they would use a particular communication technology either to escalate or to deflate conflict within the scenario. In addition to having gamers vocalize their Yes/No answer, each gamer was also asked to provide a brief justification for their decision. While one point of the game was to demonstrate the systemic and institutional forces that shape power relations, we also wanted the participants to experience the power and consequences of everyday choices as well as the responsibility that comes along with access to different kinds of communication technology. Both actors and gamers were furnished a complete script to follow along with during the scenario experience, but the gamers were unaware of our escalate/deflate metric for recording decisions, and were encouraged to inhabit their scenarios with enthusiasm and sincerity—neither to exaggerate nor suppress their true feelings. Facilitators traveled with each team to assist with technological and logistical questions and needs, and to record the decisions made by each gamer during both scenario experiences.

The game was intended to be an exploratory prototype, testing its utility as a potentially more fully developed gaming experience at a later time. For example, we knew very well from our research that a "new" technology is initially experienced as simply a modification of an older one. Social and personal changes seldom occur instantly after first encountering and using a new technology that might later become mutative. Moreover, the results of the gaming experience are not statistically valid in any way. We report them and other aspects of the game in the Appendix simply to illustrate the fact that the format was engaging, suggesting its potential for further research, experimentation, and refinement.

6.3 Four Futures for *Gaming Futures*

Here are the scenarios and scripts for the four futures scenarios used in the game. We believe they also serve as fitting examples of alternative possibilities for the futures of communication technologies and power relations as they have been discussed in previous chapters in this book.

6.3.1 Red Scenario

December 1, 2062: Classified NSA report—At 9:46 a.m. HST, an act of terror was carried out on Neuroworks, one of our primary contractors for surveillance neurotech. The incursion has sparked panic across Honolulu, as the firm is also the largest private sourcing agent for neural backups in the Asia-Pacific region. Protesters have been dispersed by local law enforcement using targeted weather modification weaponry.

☯ ♛ (*Taiji kings*) have claimed responsibility for the attack. We have been tracking their movement throughout the Asia-Pacific region. They purport to have hijacked all of the n-drives stored at Neuroworks, which caters to roughly 70 % of the island's 2.3 million residents. Conservative estimates put the data loss at 735 zettabytes and the insurance liability around £800 billion. Our team thinks that these memories, ideas, and consciousness backups could make it to the black market within hours if they are uploaded or smuggled off island. We are monitoring all broadband and satellite uplinks for anomalies, and we are certain that they will attempt to use dark web protocols to move the files when the time comes. However, we do not believe at this time that the expertise for hacking Neurowork's bio-encryption passcodes exists among Honolulu's criminal underworld. It appears that the entire operation was carried out by ☯ ♛ top lieutenant, Bodhi Xiao, whose metrics are already on file with the NSA following a botched sting operation in Mumbai back in 2057. Xiao will be tracked by our newest protocological interframe using updated DNA contact points collected from known associates. If Xiao breathes within 100 m of downtown, he will trigger an automatic Level 7 alert, which now includes an instantaneous electromagnetic kill cloud, shutting down any non-NSA telecom systems.

Although FASM (Foresight Analytics for Strategic Modeling) cannot determine if in fact Xiao has had any contact with the separatists, we are confident that this scenario holds an estimated probability of 53 %, so we have asked FASM to frame the data around this scenario. Initial scans suggested that Xiao was planning to leave Honolulu on a cruise ship bound for New Singapore this afternoon, but FASM's forecast reports a 61 % probability that he has actually gone underground and is being supported by the confederacy of separatist groups living under Kakaako. FASM recommends sending creepers into the sewers, as there is a 28 % probability that an increased surveillance presence will motivate the separatists to give him up. We know the confederacy has a history of smuggling, primarily shipments of fabrication resin, so FASM recommends freezing all incoming and outgoing shipments for 12 h. If things play out as FASM's forecast suggests, there is a 29 % probability that the confederacy might seek to capitalize on the stolen data, and a 31 % probability they will wait for the right time to hand him over to leverage their own cause.

Kickwater has already deployed Lotto drones in target areas and bidding has begun across numerous platforms to see who will take the kill shot. Neuroworks is currently purchasing a handful of political candidates to deflate criticism and shift the conversation away from their security protocols, which were compromised by

Xiao's usage of a mini-fab device. Hacked plans for his weapon were found at the Fab-Lab franchise where he worked under fake biometrics. Some traceable bio-resin was found in an adjacent building, and within 48 min of the find, NSA agents carried out a raid on the supplier in Jakarta, but there appears to be no direct link as a shipment of weapon grade bio-resin was reported stolen by the manufacturer a week ago. FASM confirmed the supplier's alibi with a 98 % probability.

Our monitoring of domestic security channels suggests a possible takeover of Neuroworks under National Security Directive 632, which President Hernandez issued back in August. As the directive states, "Any firm whose actions directly impact national security can be subsumed by the government for the express purpose of protecting the people." FASM believes there is a 64 % probability that the President will exercise his authority, especially as he seeks to build consensus for his domestic security agenda among all three parties. FASM notes an 81 % probability of this happening in the next 36 h. FASM's report suggests that the security breach serves as a perfect excuse for President Hernandez to nationalize the Asia-Pacific region's largest neurotech firm, which also has strategic interests in regional geoengineering initiatives. As Kickwater now heads all domestic counter-terrorism operations, it has been the most vocal supporters of increased nationalization, and FASM reports a 67 % probability that it will seek access to Neuroworks' user data as part of their contract. FASM concludes there is a 73 % probability that the suspect will be detained within 15 h.

6.3.2 *Red Script*

Xiao: These n-drives are going to be the death of me! I've got to get to that barge at Pier 36 before sundown or I'll be stuck on this damn island … maybe for good! I think this biomedia scrambler is strong enough to help get me there … that is, if the hydrocell holds up. If only the Separatists could have given me a little more time, I could have worked something out with my contact in New Singapore.

Taylor: New Singapore? Planning to take a boat trip, are we?

Xiao: Hold it right there! Don't make me use this!

Taylor: Use what? That's a biomedia scrambler, Mr. Xiao. [smiles] Nice try! Actually, while you have it in your hands, I was hoping you could program in my biometrics as I'm also on the lamb from Kickwater at the moment.

Xiao: Who are you?

Taylor: You can call me Taylor. I'm deep cover NSA. Yes, the National Security Agency still puts human agents in the field. The director wanted a human operative sent to Neuroworks to investigate data leaks.

Xiao: Looks like you found your leak, Taylor.

Taylor: Not exactly, Mr. Xiao. I have some evidence suggesting that significant copying of data, especially civilian memories and ideas stored on n-drives, has occurred over the last seven months. I cannot tell with certainty who is behind the leaks, but someone has definitely been taking an unauthorized peek into the minds of Neuroworks' clients. This is not to say that I'm not interested in your recent intrusion, but my case is bigger than what happened earlier today. About the scrambler?

Xiao: Done. Wait, if you're NSA, why do you need me to scramble your biometrics?

Taylor: You're sharp, Mr. Xiao. As I mentioned, I'm deep cover, which means that not even FASM knows that I'm an NSA agent. We're talking director's eyes only, so when the Neuroworks' employee lists are scanned, one of the n-drive storage analysts will turn up missing … me. If protocol is followed, FASM will automatically recommend a Level-3 alert put on my cover, which means that I'm also a target for those Lotto drones, not as lucrative as you, of course. Anyway, it was worth the risk, especially as I need to find out what you know.

Xiao: What I know? Are you suggesting that I know something about the data leaks?

Taylor: Are you saying that you don't, Mr. Xiao? Who's your contact?

Separatist Confederacy Leader/Gamer #1: Pardon the interruption, but it didn't sound like your conversation was going anywhere. Maybe I can be of some service.

Taylor: Who are you?

Separatist Confederacy Leader/Gamer #1: I would prefer if we did not use names up here.

Taylor: Up here?

Separatist Confederacy Leader/Gamer #1: Yes, I dwell among the people below. The people who seek separation from life on the surface and the forces shaping it. The people who feel …

Xiao: [interrupts Gamer #1] Feeling bad about kicking me out, are you?

Separatist Confederacy Leader/Gamer #1: The Council's decision was unfortunate, Xiao, but the vote cannot be undone, even if I am the Council Leader. We do things differently down there. We believe that some decisions are too important to be left to one person or an algorithm. We believe that humans, although imperfect, make choices that require wisdom.

Taylor: So, you did go underground? FASM's report noted a 61 % probability that you would seek out shelter with the Separatists.

Xiao: Any chance I can see that report, Taylor? I'd love to see how this whole thing is going to play out.

Separatist Confederacy Leader/Gamer #1: I could tell you! FASM certainly had some choice things to say about the Confederacy.

Taylor: You've seen the report?

Separatist Confederacy Leader/Gamer #1: Of course. How do you think we survive down there? We have to keep our eyes and ears open, and sometimes stick our nose into the business of others, so I hacked into the NSA's interframe. Besides, Kickwater agents are everywhere, and our security perimeter picked up creepers, which means we're on the radar of the powers that be, which is not somewhere we want to be.

Xiao: If all that's true, then why are you up here?

Separatist Confederacy Leader/Gamer #1: [confidently] Well, the Council received an offer. Turn over Xiao and receive a two-year supply of fabrication bio-resin and, perhaps most importantly, temporary amnesty, which would give us the break we need to regroup after the last incursion into our territory. The bio-resin will feed our people, provide much-needed medicine, and allow us to stop smuggling for a little while. When I intercepted the communication, I wanted to follow-up on the conversation we were having about those n-drives.

Xiao: Seems like everyone wants to know why I stole the n-drives?

Taylor: I'm certainly interested to find out as well!

Xiao: OK, here goes. My organization occasionally aligns itself with various entities, some of whom apparently have issues with Neuroworks. I was offered a lot of money and a chance at a fresh start if I get the n-drives into the hands of a Ms. Leong with Yangon Neurochem in New Singapore.

Separatist Confederacy Leader/Gamer #1: Are you saying this whole thing is about corporate espionage?

Taylor: Not exactly.

Xiao: What do you mean *not exactly*?

Taylor: Yangon Neurochem is a front company for the NSA's Asia-Pacific Command. I was stationed there back in 2059 and worked on a dream programming case involving local crime syndicates. It was supposed to be shut down after our investigation, at least that's what I was told.

Separatist Confederacy Leader/Gamer #1: What are you saying, Taylor?

Taylor: I guess I'm saying that if an NSA front company hired Xiao to steal the n-drives, maybe there's something else going on here.

Xiao: Maybe that something has to do with the NSA actually being responsible for copying and leaking the data!

Taylor: No, I mean … I cannot imagine who would … dammit, I guess it's possible, but …

Xiao: But it might mean that you were sent in there to make sure they couldn't be connected to the theft. It seems convenient that you haven't been found, Taylor. And it seems like President Hernandez is going to nationalize Neuroworks, which would give the NSA and Kickwater access to all of that data, right?

Taylor: Back off, Xiao! There's a lot of unanswered questions right now.

Xiao: Look, my only concern is keeping off of Kickwater's radar and escaping the Lotto drones, which are probably out in droves by now.

Separatist Confederacy Leader/Gamer #1: Yes, I saw a few flying around, but the scrambler should keep them at bay. All of this intrigue really makes me appreciate life under the streets.

Taylor: Yes, I'm sure it's just cherry down there.

Separatist Confederacy Leader/Gamer #1: Well, it would be if the Council votes to hand over Xiao. One push of a button is all it would take to accept the offer, as I am the only Council member who has not yet voted, and, as you probably guessed, the Council is deadlocked. So, it's up to me to either make the deal or not. It certainly sounds like there's something else going on with those n-drives, and I guess I …

Xiao: So much for one person not making a decision! Did you come up here to add a personal touch? Do you really think you can trust that offer? A two-year supply of resin and temporary amnesty!?! If you read that report, then you know that FASM is calculating what you'll do and might be offering you just what you want to make it happen? Are you going to accept the offer?

Gamer #1: [You must decide if you're going to take the offer] Yes or no, either way you must explain your decision.

Taylor: Well, that certainly was interesting …

Kickwater agent/Gamer #2: Yes, it certainly was.

Xiao: Who are you?

Kickwater agent/Gamer #2: Let's just say I'm of two minds right now.

Taylor: What!?!

Kickwater agent/Gamer #2: Well, I'm a dutiful Kickwater agent who will be handsomely compensated if I upload Xiao's biometrics. To be blunt, I will even get a bonus if one of the Lotto drone pilots uses my data to take the kill shot. On the other hand, my family's data was on those n-drives, so I want to know what's really going on, and it sounds like there's something bigger happening here. Taylor, you said something about evidence. What else do you know?

Taylor: The only evidence I have comes from Neuroworks' data logs, which show the n-drive copies being made. Also, a tracking algorithm showed a dramatic upload increase to a single location in New Singapore that corresponds with the timing of the copies. Oddly enough, my analysis showed that the data stream was channeled through Kickwater's secure interframe. Now, this does not constitute proof that they were behind …

Xiao: But, you cannot say that they're not …

Kickwater agent/Gamer #2: Clearly, there is more to be learned about what happened, but the data is already out there in the open, and I just received a notice that there's a bonus for finding the missing Neuroworks' analyst, so it looks it's my lucky day. I guess it's time to …

Xiao: Wait! We don't know what's out in the open and who has access to it, including your family's data. I haven't removed the data from the interframe, so your family's data is safe, at least as long as I have it.

Kickwater agent/Gamer #2: My guess is that you'd say anything to keep me from uploading that data right now, Mr. Xiao.

Taylor: Look, if you upload our biometrics, we might never find out who really took your family's data. There's a veritable army of Lotto drone pilots out there waiting to cash in on his death, maybe you are, too, but this is bigger than Xiao and me. We need more time to figure this out! Are you going to upload Xiao's biometrics?

Kickwater agent/Gamer #2: [You must decide if you're going to upload Xiao's biometrics] Yes or no, either way you must explain your decision.

Taylor: Well, that was …

Lotto drone pilot/Gamer #3: Howdy y'all! Don't mind me! I just been listenin' in to y'all's conversation about this whole dealy. It sure is gosh darned interestin.' Sounds like one of 'em old timey spy stories or sumethin' like it.

Xiao: Lotto drones! Dangit, looks like my scrambler's battery is fading. They found me!!!

Lotto drone pilot/Gamer #3: Well, partner, I founds ya! Looks like I be the firs' one here. Well, I guess I'll be …

Taylor: Hold on! There's more going on here than meets the eye. If you kill Xiao, we might never be able to find out what's going on.

Lotto drone pilot/Gamer #3: Xiao is certainly the prize, but it looks like I just hit paydirt! A two-fur one special!

Taylor: Wait, you need to hear us out!

Xiao: Listen to Taylor. I don't know what you're going to get out of this, but I have powerful friends who could use someone with your specific skill set.

Lotto drone pilot/Gamer #3: Are you offerin' me a j-o-b, Mr. Xiao? You ain't really in no position to be making such offers, ar's ya?

Taylor: Look, we know that you will benefit from Xiao's death, but you need to think about the big picture here. Maybe Kickwater is in cahoots with the NSA to cover its tracks! Maybe FASM orchestrated the whole thing! Bottom line: if you push that button, we might never know who's orchestrating things behind the scenes. Please, consider the big picture! Are you going to take the kill shot?

Lotto drone pilot/Gamer #3: [You must decide if you're going to take the kill shot] Yes or no, either way you must explain your decision.

Taylor: Oh my....

(Electromagnetic kill cloud initiates, everyone flees…)

6.3.3 Blue Scenario

December 1, 2062: Field Log 6754 Transcript—[Recorder on] Frank Ha'ili. Field Log 6754. Is this damn thing on? Oh well, guess we'll find out later. All this tech is making me nostalgic, and as I've got nothing to report and a good walk ahead of me, let's take a stroll down memory lane, shall we?

It's been just over 20 years since the collapse of what was formerly known as the State of Hawaii. It was hard to believe the stories of martial law and mob rule across America before the planes stopped coming and the airwaves went dead, but I guess our situation speaks for itself. We are all alone out here and that's not necessarily a bad thing. Contact with outsiders became limited to the occasional laborer ship seeking supplies, so the information we heard was spotty at best. We've been fortunate that the major pirate conglomerates turned on each other, and our distance from other landmasses has kept us safe. When the oceans began to rise over the last ten years, the number of "visitors" appearing on our shores dropped sharply. Things really took a turn for the worse with the dire impacts of Cyclone Ku in 2049. I actually haven't seen a foreign vessel in over eight years. Wow, has it been that long? Rumors of something on the horizon are spreading among the tribe, but I think it's just wishful thinking or something we wouldn't wish on our enemies.

I know this is supposed to be a field report, but I remember it all so vividly. Besides, who's ever going to listen to this? It began with another "recession," and so many of us continued to have "normal" conversations just days before the ship that was to bring us most of our food and energy never made it to port. As panic and then contagion spread, many of the once vibrant communities of Honolulu were abandoned as people went back to what was left of the mainland on military vessels, some of which I heard never made it. Rummaging through McMansions in Kāhala for antibiotics to fight off Transfluenza is a memory that has stayed with me, not to mention the scarring. With imports ending overnight, surviving and thriving meant self-sufficiency and nothing else. I guess we did the best we could with what we had, and after losing a bit of weight the first few years, I haven't gone hungry since. Satellite uplinks never yielded anything, but local WiFi networks, which are now used primarily for educating the young, have given people some taste of what life used to be like. Seeing someone pedal a modified workout bicycle for the first time to power a computer long enough to transfer some files across the island still makes me chuckle a bit. Humidity will eventually win the war, however, so the bio-tech race is on.

Bio-engineering seemed to be the last great hope for a better future as people envisioned a new renaissance and total abundance, but a perfect storm involving climate change, energy crises, and lack of governmental foresight led us to the exact opposite. DIY bio-labs were gobbled up by multinational firms in hopes of scaling up homemade biotech, but no one really knows how successful their experiments were.

What am I doing out here? Sometimes I wonder why I ever agreed to scavenge the Kakaako quadrant, which housed Zyntropia's Asia-Pacific headquarters. Who would have guessed that the world's largest bio-engineering firm would choose Honolulu over Shanghai? Still, what am I doing out here? I suppose the Aka Tribe made me an offer I couldn't refuse, especially as they gave me a safe exit from the Yamane clan. When I found out Yamane was experimenting on humans, I knew that I couldn't let them find out about my training. Being a doctor used to mean something special, but now it makes you a glorified zoo keeper or Dr. Frankenstein. I'm not cut out to be either one, although I'll take the former over the latter any day. Using bio-engineered sentinels, mainly former lab animals and the occasional mongoose, to control the island's water supply was an unexpected move, but Yamane will do anything to keep her presence felt among the island's estimated 30,000 residents, so I'm not surprised that she broke the cardinal rule of bio-tech. The island's last great counting, which was done a few years back, terrified most people, as there were five times as many people over the age of 50 as there were children under 3 years old, so I guess I'm supposed to be out here seeking a solution.

If Yamane knew what I knew, I don't think she would have ever permitted human experimentation. [unintelligible] What the hell was that? [End of recording].

6.3.4 Blue Script

Ha'ili: [talking to himself] Seriously!?! I cannot believe this amount of pristine biotech was just sitting out in the open down here. Biotech like this is the most powerful information and communication technology around when it's in the right hands. [looks ahead] Yamane!?! What are you doing here?

Yamane: Hiding from whatever made that noise, Frank. What do you think I'm doing?

Ha'ili: You've got a point. I mean, why are you away from the clan? Are you shadowing me?

Yamane: No, Frank. We're not shadowing you. Actually, there's no "we" anymore. I left the clan. I discovered my science team was using biotech to engineer super soldiers. When I confronted the head researcher, he denied everything, so I left.

Ha'ili: Super-soldier? Are you talking about the human biotech experimentations that YOU authorized? You're not getting your hands on this biotech, so forget about it.

Yamane: Yes, I did authorize the program, but only because I was assured that the research was focused on building resilient nervous systems. I'm not after more biotech, Frank. Is that why they sent you down here? I am trying to get Aka to stop poisoning the water supply. That's why we started human experimentation. We lost 37 children last year alone, and our tests showed biotech toxins in the water, which must have come from Aka.

Ha'ili: Poison? You're kidding me, right? Sounds like you're justifying your brutal takeover of the water supply with those savage sentinels. As if the biotech rats weren't enough, you had to go and engineer a biotech mongoose army. Did you really think you'd be able to program those animals not to kill? We both know that the facilities that were used couldn't ensure 100 % control, and yet, you still went through with it. Why do you think I escaped? I saw what the mongooses did and found your lab, which was filled with hybrid monsters. You broke the cardinal rule of biotech: no human experimentation! How could you, Doris?

Yamane: No, Frank, you've got it all wrong. I stepped down as Clan leader when I found out about the super-soldier program, which our science team started on its own after they identified the biotech and tried to reverse engineer it. I've been hiding out here for the past few weeks waiting for the right time to go to the Aka Tribe to broker a peace deal, or to at least convince them to stop poisoning the water. I didn't and wouldn't have authorized building programmable super-soldiers for combat. I know I haven't given you reasons to trust me, but you have to believe me; I ONLY authorized experimentation on nervous system resiliency.

Ha'ili: C'mon? You're going to have to do better than that. I can't believe I actually cared about you.

Yamane:	Frank, look, we have bigger things to worry about right now. You have a security shadow, I spotted a ship on the horizon yesterday, and something big and angry let out a fearsome shriek that sounds like it came from down by the water, so let's stop talking about the past and figure out how we're going to handle the situation at hand.
Ha'ili:	We? In case you haven't noticed, I'm with the Aka Tribe now. There isn't anyone stupid enough to follow me into the Kakaako quadrant, especially after the biotech rats tore our former security chief limb from limb, and no one is going to get through our coastal security perimeter, not to mention your biotech petting zoo army.
Yamane:	Ok, Frank, that's how you wanna play it? Well, if you don't have a shadow, then who's that?
Aka security/Gamer #1:	I hate to break up this reunion, but I'm hungry and the sun will set in a few hours, so I'm going to do the talking for a little while, OK?
Ha'ili:	How did you find me?
Aka security/Gamer #1:	It wasn't hard, Ha'ili! You're a scientist, so you're not very good at covering your trail. As for being stupid enough to come to Kakaako, I actually wanted to ask you a few questions, so here I am. I was hoping to get you to tell me everything you know about the Council, but I think Yamane actually told me all I need to know.
Yamane:	What do you mean?
Aka security/Gamer #1:	Well, I've been noticing some odd things about the Council's rituals, which didn't make any sense to me, at least not to maintain "spiritual" purity, which is what all the Elders say when asked during Tribe gatherings. Why do they insist upon separate cooking facilities? I've tasted their food and noticed a difference.
Ha'ili:	I don't understand.
Aka security/Gamer #1:	You're not the sharpest tool in the shed, are you Frank?
Ha'ili:	Watch it, rent-a-shadow!
Aka security/Gamer #1:	You don't have headaches, Frank? Insomnia? They tell us it's the radical change in lifestyle, as if I really miss the life we had before, but Yamane's discovery makes the most sense. They're poisoning ALL of the water, even the reserves used by the Tribe.
Yamane:	Why would they do that?
Aka security/Gamer #1:	Who knows? All I know is that I volunteered to shadow Ha'ili for some extra food rations and to see what he knew about their rituals, but it looks like he had no idea what was really going on, did you Frank?
Ha'ili:	It doesn't make any sense.

Yamane: No, Frank, it makes perfect sense. I found some Aka Tribe biotech reports in our lab when I discovered the super-soldier program. The Aka Tribe's Council of Elders must be conspiring with my former clan's science team to engineer super humans, and they must have figured it out if they're poisoning everyone. What better way to make sure it works?

Ha'ili: Wait!?! [points at Gamer #1] What are you getting out of this?

Aka security/Gamer #1: Well, they offered me a spot on the Council if I returned with any functional biotech, which you just found, right Frank?

Yamane: Ok, let's not do anything rash.

Ha'ili: I can't give you this biotech. You're going to have to take it.

Yamane: [talking to Gamer #1] Wait, you have to think about this! The Aka Tribe will do anything to get what they want, even working with their sworn enemies to build biotech super-soldiers and poison the water supply. Do you really think they can be trusted? Yes, you'll have exactly what they need, but aren't you worried that they're just using you? Are you going to take the biotech back to Aka Tribe?

Aka security/Gamer #1: [You must decide if you're going to take the biotech back to the Aka Tribe.]

Yes or No, either way you must explain your decision.

Ha'ili: Well, I guess that settles things …

Pirate scout/Gamer #2: Not if I have anything to say about it!

Ha'ili: Who the hell are you?

Pirate scout/Gamer #2: Let's just say that I've got my sea legs and a bit of scurvy that I just can't shake.

Ha'ili: What!?!

Yamane: He's a pirate, Frank.

Pirate scout/Gamer #2: Bingo.

Aka security/Gamer #1: I hate pirates. My father was killed by marauders back in 2037. Friends of yours?

Pirate scout/Gamer #2: Sorry, pal, this is our first trip to the islands, and I grew up on that damn boat, so I know it wasn't us.

Aka Security/Gamer #1: Yeah, that's what the last pirate I had the pleasure to talk to said … right before I …

Ha'ili: Ok, look, this biotech cannot fall into the wrong hands. This stuff is top-shelf straight from Zyntropia headquarters. One pill can bring about sudden, unexpected transformations, and if it is programmed, there's no limit to what it might do, but it was never intended for use on humans.

Pirate scout/Gamer #2: I don't care what it can do. All I know is that if I radio in that I found some biotech and bring back fresh water then I can get out of the dog house. The captain made an example out of me for hoarding some extra food, which is probably the only thing that kept me alive on the voyage here. We lost one third of the crew, so opportunities for advancement in our little organization are plentiful. It's not a life of luxury, but it's not like I have unlimited options.

Ha'ili: Maybe you haven't heard, but we're apparently having some water issues right now.

Pirate scout/Gamer #2: Did you hear that?

Yamane: Nope, but something sure smells foul. [looks at Gamer #2]

Bio-engineered mutant/Gamer #3: You people talk so loud. I heard you from the waterfront.

Pirate scout/Gamer #2: Oh my God, what is that?

Aka security/Gamer #1: Looks like one of Yamane's former experiments got loose?

Bio-engineered mutant/Gamer #3: My name is Gene, thank you very much. I was a farmer for the Aka Tribe in Waialua where I lived with my family, at least I think I was. My memory isn't so good right now, and the more I try to focus the fuzzier things become. I remember feeling a tremor, but …

Pirate scout/Gamer #2: Yeah, that earthquake was quite the surprise, especially when you've been stuck on a ship for the last 4 months. Gene, what did they do to you?

Bio-engineered mutant/Gamer #3: Isn't it obvious? I'm one of their bioengineered super soldiers. The tail, sonic hearing, astute sense of smell, and according to the tag that I ripped off my wrist, an IQ of 216, not to mention that I can run like the wind.

Aka security/Gamer #1: All that biotech, and they couldn't make you smell any better?

Bio-engineered mutant/Gamer #3: Watch it, human! When I finally stopped to catch my breath down by the water, I heard a voice in my head … clear as a bell. It said, "Calm down, my child. Stay where you are. We are coming for you." I didn't like the sound of that, so I just kept running and made my way to Kakaako.

Yamane: I'm so sorry. This wasn't supposed to happen.

Bio-engineered mutant/Gamer #3: Yamane?

Pirate scout/Gamer #2: How sweet! It's a reunion! I understand that someone here has some functional biotech, correct? It's not that I'm looking to get back to life on the boat. It's actually nice to be on land, although this place smells horrible … present company excluded, of course [looks at Gamer #3].

Yamane: If pirates get their hands on this biotech, there's no telling what they might do with it. This island has lots of places to make a life, and I hope you will consider all of your options, especially considering the water situation. Are you going to radio your captain with a report?

Pirate scout/Gamer #2: [You must decide if you're going to radio the captain with a report]

Yes or No, either way you must explain your decision.

Ha'ili: Well, I guess that settles things …

Bio-engineered mutant/Gamer #3: Actually, there's one more thing to settle.

Ha'ili: What now?

Bio-engineered mutant/Gamer #3: They implanted me with this [holds up device] like I was some kind of animal. They took away my life … my family … everything that I knew and loved. I have nothing left and they must pay for their sins [looks and points at Yamane]. She is responsible!

Yamane: No! Wait!

Ha'ili: Look, Gene, she didn't do this to you. She didn't even know that her scientists were making super soldiers, and when she found out she left. The Aka Tribe is working with members of Yamane's old clan to take over the island. They're apparently now poisoning the water supply, and she's trying to broker a peace deal. She might be the only person who knows enough people on both sides to stop things from getting worse.

Yamane: Gene, I'm so sorry for what happened to you. You must believe me. I will do my utmost to stop this from happening to anyone else. I know I cannot change what's already happened, but things could be different.

Bio-engineered mutant/Gamer #3: [You must decide if you're going to exact your revenge on Yamane]

Yes or No, either way you must explain your decision.
[Another tremor makes part of the roof collapse and everyone flees.]

6.3.5 Green Scenario

December 1, 2062: Eco-Estates Morning Newsletter—You have 30 min to read this mandatory briefing before restrictions will be placed on your leisure activities and cultural programming access. Please perform a retinal scan and input the seven digit codex that will appear after you read all the way through this document using your in-home monitor. Mahalo for your kokua!

Aloha Kakahiaka! It's another beautiful day in Honolulu! Sunny, 86°, and there's an 8 % chance of mild trade winds today—a true rarity since regional weather shifts, so get out there and enjoy it! We are delighted that some of our geoengineering efforts are beginning to pay off in the Eastern Pacific, and oceanic acidity rates have dropped significantly in the past six months and are now within advisable safety parameters, so take advantage of our water activities this week! Everyone is welcome to attend our new citizen mixer later today at Kakaako Beach Park! We're planning to give an overview of all community regulations at the pre-mixer meeting and thought this would be a good opportunity to provide everyone with a brief refresher! As you already know, citizenship at Kakaako Eco-Estates grants you beach-side accommodations, the finest organic cuisine, virtual and outdoor leisure activities, and cultural enrichment programming featuring real Polynesians! As an autonomous governance zone, our 10-square mile compound is a bastion from the perils of life on the outside, especially Transfluenza. Life is truly worth living at Kakaako Eco-Estates! To enjoy all of these immense privileges, your contract requires complete submission to our tracer program and thermoelectric harvesting initiative. We like to keep a watchful eye on our community members, and you will not even notice our new embedded eco-surveillance! And with our patented sleep cocoons, we harmlessly and safely extract energy from you while you enjoy the dreams of your choice! Ever wanted to climb Mt. Everest, star as the lead in your own action film, or re-live your favorite childhood memories? We've got you covered at Kakaako Eco-Estates!

Just remember the three C's!

1. Community—Our citizens currently boast the highest life expectancy in the world at 135 years! We know that giving up your family can be tough, but our partner matching algorithms will instantly find you a suitable mate and surrogate cohort, so you'll never have to be alone! As you've passed our comprehensive health exam and four-step psyche eval, you are now part of a vibrant community seeking to build a truly sustainable world! With development moving forward in Sana'a (Democratic Republic of Yemen), Linfen (The People's Kingdom of Eastern China), and Port-au-Prince (Nouvelle France), you will actually be part of a global network in the coming future! At Eco-Estates, community comes first!

2. Conscientiousness—With great power comes great responsibility! We simply ask that you use discretion when making contact with outsiders. Please do not divulge any details about your new life at Kakaako Eco-Estates, as we do not want to impose more restrictive communication safeguards, which we've had to do in years past. As all new citizens have both internal and external communications monitored for the first six months, we have not had many problems once members get acclimated to life on the inside. We also ask that you do not share the specific parameters of your contract with other citizens. At Eco-Estates, conscientiousness is caring!
3. Continuity—Exquisite meals, Neuroworks' immersive virtuality, and a life of absolute leisure! What do all of these have in common? They're available continuously … so long as you show some restraint! At Kakaako Eco-Estates, we deliver continuity and expect it in return. Citizens are required to maintain optimal health, including strict allegiance to our prescribed diet and sleep regimen. If you fall below the prescribed biometric standards for longer than two weeks, you will be put on Restricted Status and the terms and conditions of your citizenry contract will immediately resort to Preventative Measures. We do not want to have another unfortunate incident, and Citizen 1437 has been temporarily quarantined for violating the terms and conditions of her contract. Do not attempt to contact her. At Eco-Estates, continuity is key!

As the island's premier energy producing community, Kakaako Eco-Estates provides the highest quality of life for our residents! As Chancellor Iolani proclaims, "Kakaako Eco-Estates offers more than just a cozy lifestyle; we offer a model for life as it should be lived! As we work on scaling our technologies, we hope that one day the entire world can enjoy the benefits of citizenship in one of our communities.

Don't be late for mandatory Ashtanga Vinyasa with Chancellor Iolani on the beach at 10:00 a.m. sharp!

9864734

6.3.6 Green Script

Citizen 1846:	Good morning, Chancellor.
Iolani:	[rises from yoga pose] Greetings,1846. To what do I owe the pleasure?
Citizen 1846:	Actually, Chancellor, you wanted to see me.
Iolani:	Ahhh, yes, 1846, of course. My apologies, I've had quite a bit on my mind lately.
Citizen 1846:	I know the feeling.
Iolani:	Do you? Eco-Estates is the one place where one should have the luxury not to worry. Have you not been enjoying your time here?
Citizen 1846:	I have appreciated my first week, Chancellor.
Iolani:	Appreciated?

Citizen 1846: I *do* appreciate the lifestyle, Chancellor. Let me start by saying that the food is exquisite, and I have been amazed at the level of detail within Neuroworks' virtuality. When the sunlight hits my face, I can actually feel the warmth. When drinking tea on a sidewalk cafe in Buenos Aires, I can actually smell the streets … ok, so maybe it's a bit too real.

Iolani: Yes, I, too, have asked for a bit less reality. I suppose life on the outside has its charms, but so does Eco-Estates!

Citizen 1846: That's one way of putting it, Chancellor.

Iolani: I'm noticing some irregularities in the readout from your sleep cocoon. Is everything OK, 1846?

Citizen 1846: Now that you mention it, I have had trouble focusing, and I've been feeling groggy. The programmer said it sometimes takes a little while to acclimate to the sleep cocoon, but I've also been having trouble remembering things. Is that normal?

Iolani: We aim to go beyond normal here. If you have the slightest discomfort, it is my utmost concern to remedy the situation. Eco-Estates is committed to the complete wellness of its residents.

Citizen 1846: That's good to hear, Chancellor. I've been worried. To be honest, I've been having constant deja vu. I know it sounds crazy, but everything feels familiar … as if I've been here before.

Iolani: I see. I think I might have something to help. [removes a bag of pills from his pocket and smiles again]

Citizen 1846: What are those, Chancellor?

Iolani: Our wellness team has developed a new supplement for these sorts of things. One pill a day will help balance your neurochemistry while keeping us apprised of your mental state. It contains an advanced tracer tailored to improve your overall wellness. I am confident it will make you feel better. Please, try one. [smiles and hands a pill to 1846]

Citizen 1846: Ok, I guess … I guess I'll give it a shot. [closes eyes, takes pill, slight convulsion, re-opens eyes and smiles widely]

Iolani: Tell me, 1846, what do you remember about your life before coming to Eco-Estates?

Citizen 1846: [acting very abnormal, almost robotic, looks distraught] I can see my family. They're surrounded by sickness. I willingly leave them to come here. My mother starts crying and tells me that she wants me to have a better life. I sign the paperwork. I'm now Citizen 1437. I … I….

Iolani: It's OK, 1846. Thank you. [touches ear] Can you please send me 1846's programmer? Let's see how we might resolve this unfortunate situation.

Citizen 1846: Yes, let's. [smiles]

Sleep Cocoon Programmer/Gamer #1: Chancellor, you wanted to see me?

Iolani: Yes. You've been working with 1846, correct?

Sleep Cocoon Programmer/Gamer #1: That's correct, Chancellor.

Iolani: Good. I need to know how she can still have memories from 1437?

Sleep Cocoon Programmer/Gamer #1: 1437? I'm not sure I follow, Chancellor.

Iolani: Have you seen 1846's most recent sleep cocoon readout? Look, there's a clear pattern that links her with 1437, which might seem impossible, but as 1846 *is* 1437, I suppose I shouldn't be surprised.

Sleep Cocoon Programmer/Gamer #1: 1846 and 1437 are the same person? I thought 1437 was quarantined?

Iolani: After violating the terms and conditions of the citizens' contract, 1437 received a full memory wipe from Neuroworks, who have been underwriting our little slice of paradise by making generous contributions to our construction fund … all in return for access to our citizens. It's all in the fine print, but that's besides the point. Subtle appearance modifications, also stipulated in the contract, make her unrecognizable to most. All of this is secondary to the fact that 1846 needs our help, and that's where you come in.

Sleep Cocoon Programmer/Gamer #1: This seems above my pay grade, Chancellor. I'm just a lowly programmer.

Iolani: We highly value our programmers and appreciate your hard work. I know we ask a lot of our employees, but we also give quite a bit in return. I understand you have a comfortable life on the outside, and I want that to continue. [smiles] I need you to assist with the re-programming of 1846, as you have intimate knowledge of her cognitive capacity. The irregularities in her readout necessitate a complete wipe. Neuroworks has assured me that they have worked out all of the kinks, so all you'll need to do is upload this tonight. [hands documents to Gamer #3]

Sleep Cocoon Programmer/Gamer #1: [looks over papers] Excuse me, Chancellor, but doesn't this violate Article 17 of the citizens' contract? I mean, does she know what this means?

Iolani: You've read the citizen's contract? Oh, that's right. You applied to be a citizen, didn't you? As someone who applied to live here, I imagine that you know what's at stake. This is why 1437 … I mean 1846 … originally came here … for a better life … for a better future. Isn't that right, 1846?

Citizen 1846: [smiles] Yes, Chancellor, that's right. I want a fresh start. I want to live life to the fullest at Eco-Estates! [closes eyes, slightly convulses]

Iolani: See. She's ready for a fresh start. So, I need you to program the new firmware into 1846's sleep cocoon tonight. It will wipe all memories she might have as 1437 and remove any traces of this exchange. You were right to ask about the citizens' contract, and as this is an executive-level directive, I think you deserve a bonus for your efforts. This is above your pay grade, so let's raise your pay grade! Also, I understand that you failed the final psych eval as so many others do. Well, if you can do this for me, I will personally see to it that your application gets reinserted at the top of the admit list. Now, I cannot guarantee entry, mind you, but with a recommendation from me, you certainly have great odds at landing a spot at Eco-Estates. With the Transfluenza epidemic worsening, this might be just the opportunity you've always wanted. [received call and is distracted]

Citizen 1846: [slightly convulses, looks over to Gamer #1] Are you going to re-program my sleep cocoon?

Sleep Cocoon Programmer/Gamer #1: [You must decide if you're going to re-program Citizen 1846's sleep cocoon]

Yes or No, either way you must explain your decision.

Iolani: Very well.

Citizen 3684/Gamer #2: Chancellor, you wanted to see me?

Iolani: Ahh, Citizen 3684. Perfect timing. 1846, please say hello to 3684.

Citizen 1846: [turns to Citizen 3684] Hello, 3684. It's a pleasure to meet you.

Citizen 3684/Gamer #2: Hhh … hi....1846. How are you?

Citizen 1846: I'm very well, thank you, 3684. [smiles]

Iolani: Excellent. There seems to be some chemistry between you two. 3684, I was hoping you could take 1846 under your wing. I know you've been paired with 942, but our algorithm suggests that you and 1846 are a perfect match. So, what do you say?

Citizen 3684/Gamer #2: Yes, of course. It would be my pleasure.

Iolani: Excellent! Now, there's one little thing that I need your assistance with, and I'm prepared to compensate you handsomely for your efforts. 1846 has been having some issues of late. Isn't that right, 1846?

Citizen 1846: Yes, Chancellor. I haven't been doing so well. [smiles]

Iolani: That's why we're here, 1846. We're going to make you well. So, 3684, this is where you come in.

Citizen 3684/Gamer #2: What do you need me to do, Chancellor?

Iolani: Well, I understand that you've still got family on the outside. As the Transfluenza epidemic is worsening, I imagine that the cost of treatment has risen dramatically. With that in mind, I would see to it that your family receives Series-9 inoculations, if you could do a small favor or two for me.

Citizen 3684/Gamer #2: You have my complete attention, Chancellor.

Iolani: Excellent! In return for providing your family with the treatment, all that I ask is that you monitor 1846 and report back any irregularities directly to me. You actually won't have to do anything so long as you ensure that 1846 takes these pills as prescribed. They activate partly in response to serotonin, so you two will receive complete access to all of our premier amenities. These pills will help *ease* her back into wellness.

Citizen 3684/Gamer #2: *Ease* her into wellness?

Iolani: Yes, it seems she's been having some trouble getting acclimated to the sleep cocoon's dream programming. I guess some of us miss having nightmares! [laughs] I suppose it does take some getting used to, and these supplements will keep her balanced. They also include a tracer so that our med team can keep an eye on her. So, can I count on you to keep her medicated?

Citizen 3684/Gamer #2: [You must decide if you're going to give 1846 the pills]

Yes or No, either way you must explain your decision.

Iolani:	Very well.
Outsider/Gamer #3:	*Well*, indeed, but I'm not so sure I would say *very*.
Iolani:	Who are you? How did you get past our security?
Citizen 1846:	[rubs eyes] Lee, is that you?
Iolani:	1846, it's time for another dose. Please medicate.
Citizen 1846:	Yes, Chancellor. [takes pill]
Outsider/Gamer #3:	[moves towards Citizen 1846, puts arm on her shoulder] Ipu, it's me … Lee. The dreams … I … I came for you.
Iolani:	I'm sorry, Lee, but I don't think she's much for conversation at the moment.
Outsider/Gamer #3:	[steps away from Citizen 1846, shakes head, speaks angrily] What have you done to her?
Iolani:	Me? She signed up for this. It's all part of her treatment. Here, take a look at her contract. [hands papers to Gamer #3]
Outsider/Gamer #3:	I don't know what all this says, but I do know that she came to me in my dreams. She wanted me to find her. She wanted me to come to her.
Iolani:	Interesting … I've heard rumors of dream projection on the outside, but Neuroworks assured me that such things were just hearsay. From what I understand, the dream cocoon projects her into the unconscious of those she's had contact with before coming here, so her appearance in your dream has more to do with you than it does with her. Eco-Estates is only as healthy as its citizens, so it is my utmost concern to make her well. That's why she came here. What else do you suggest we do?
Outsider/Gamer #3:	There's one other thing that I could do. I have a neural-stream of this entire conversation ready to go live, and maybe it's time the whole world sees the type of wellness that's available at Eco-Estates.
Iolani:	OK, let's not make any hasty decisions. This is just a temporary effect of the medication. We need to get her stabilized or she could permanently lose some cognitive abilities. She needs our help, and this type of treatment does not exist on the outside. Clearly, you care about her, so let's see if we can come to an agreement. If you want to make sure she's OK, I can secure a place for you here … in Eco-Estates. You can be with her here. No more Transfluenza inoculations. Those scars look painful! Everything you could ever want, including her, would be right here, but all of that would go away if you release that neuro-stream. So, what's it going to be?
Outsider/Gamer #3:	[You must decide if you're going to release the neuro-stream] Yes or No, either way you must explain your decision.
Iolani:	Very well.

6.3.7 Yellow Scenario

December 1, 2062: Cosmic Sufi Collective—Virtucom link enabled—Dear Brothers, Sisters, & beloved transbeings, it is with great joy that I send you greetings from al-Ghazālī One! We have safely reached orbit and are on our way to dock with the Uyghur's space elevator to stock up for the long journey to Mars. Leaving Honolulu was difficult as the islands quickly became our spiritual home, but it was our *kuleana*, as they say, to venture beyond the stars! For those of you who remained at our Kakaako headquarters, remember that God's faithful are one no matter how far apart we might be. You will remain in our hearts, even in cryosleep! Sufism teaches that we can be one with God, but as we have always been limited by our biology, few among us have reached complete *fanaa* (ءانف - extinction of the self in God). In the heavens, we will not only be closer to God but we will be free to enhance ourselves and evolve!

Cherished faithful, although we forge ahead into the darkness of space, we must never forget the darkness on Earth that you still face. You will be a light to awaken the world just as we will shine brightly in the night sky. When science finally uncovered the building blocks of life, many spiritual traditions were simply unprepared for the radical changes to our sense of humanity that ensued. Extended life expectancy, now estimated to be 220 years, and other bioengineering advancements did much to drive believers away, but it also enlivened a fanaticism not seen in centuries. Sufis have always been spiritual innovators, and we are hopeful that a revitalized spirituality centered on the two pillars, *tawwakul* (لكُوَت—reliance upon God) and *dhikr* (رکذ—perpetual remembrance of God), will usher in a renaissance of faith and inclusivity.

Working with Zyntropia, we co-created bioengineered humans, or transbeings, who embody God's evolutionary spirit. Let me be clear in stating that transbeings are humans; they are full-standing members of our community who participate in all ritual practices. We accept believers who received life from God almighty, and I even granted the most holy status of *Fatah* (حتف—victorious one) to Aisha Lingbao Hassan, the former Chair of the UN Interfaith Council who recently enhanced her biology with our assistance. When Ms. Hassan came out to the Council as a transbeing, she hoped her bold declaration would inspire believers all over the cosmos to embrace our evolving humanity. It did just this, but it also created animosity towards us, and the Council has suspended our membership and resource allotment while our case is being adjudicated. We invited Hassan to come with us, but she chose to stay behind and champion transbeing rights back on Earth as our official emissary to the Council. We are honored to have her speak on our behalf as we travel to our new home off planet. We will keep Hassan in our prayers and ask you to do the same. This will be my last chance to communicate directly with you before we begin our long voyage, so I would like to share with you a message inspired by my exquisite view of our former home. The beauty of our pale blue dot is overwhelming, and God wants me to share a new message with you.

Dearest faithful, humans have nothing to fear in the aegis of transbeings. My wife is a human, and our children will be among the first generation of transbeing hybrids. I can confirm that the rumors are true, and our community has witnessed a great miracle: our hybrid children are displaying telepathic and telekinetic mutations! As I have intimated to my wife, I am excited to see what comes of our holy union. God instructs us to embrace the inherent sacredness of his design, and we were made to evolve, which we can now do according to God's will! In many ways, we have always been post-human and should not restrain our potential to connect with God to the limits of our biology. When I received my first enhancement, I was overcome with joy at how much more clearly I could hear God speak to me. I was not going to announce our good news until we safely arrived on Mars, but now seems like the perfect time. We have worked closely with Zyntropia, our allies and scientific partners, to create the definitive transbeing enhancement: *AI aqidah* (ةديقع - an enhanced faith). Cherished believers, we leave you with this gift, which will only work to strengthen your resolve. May peace be upon you!

Hector Emmanuel Ibrahim

6.3.8 Yellow Script

Chair: [taps gavel on desk, shuffles papers] I hereby call this meeting of the UN Interfaith Council to order. We will hear testimony on our recent decision to revoke the Cosmic Sufi Collective's membership on this council. Let me make something clear to everyone in attendance and those listening around the world and off planet: we have not come here today to pass judgment on transbeings. Our task is to adjudicate claims of prejudice put forth by the Cosmic Sufi Collective, and while transbeing rights remain a critical aspect of these proceedings, it is not the charge of this council to remedy the transbeing *situation* …

Hassan: [interrupts, confrontational] *Situation?*

Chair: Ms. Hassan, please. You will have a turn to speak. I only meant to suggest that the status of transbeing rights remains unresolved. Now, if there are no other concerns? [looks around the room] Very good. On today's agenda, we will hear from Aisha Lingbao Hassan, who I think needs no introduction [laughs]; Xenu 0100101, an artilect from the Collective Wisdom Council who has been called in as an expert to provide some context on the CSC and transbeings …

Hassan: [angrily interrupts] I object! The Collective Wisdom Council has been a vocal advocate …

Chair: [bangs gavel, sternly replies] That's enough, Ms. Hassan. Another outburst like that and I will have you removed from the hearings. Are we clear?

Hassan: [smiles] Crystal.

Chair: Good. The Collective Wisdom Council is not on trial here, Ms. Hassan. All parties will have a chance to give testimony. Now, let's try to make it through the introductions, shall we? [looks around the room] Joining us today, we also have Dr. Lupe Park, a representative from Zyntropia, and Kai Christiansen, founder of Humanity United. I would like to remind everyone of the procedural framework for today's gathering. As I am the only Council member physically present, we will have a shortened docket. Today's speakers will give a brief statement before questions, and as we are on a tight schedule, I have left time for one question per speaker. OK, Ms. Hassan, you're starting us off.

Hassan: Dear Interfaith Council members, humans, and transbeings tuning in around the galaxy, I appear before you today as the newly designated representative of the Cosmic Sufi Collective, who left this world to start a new life among the stars. The CSC and its transbeing members deserve full recognition from the UN Interfaith Council and protection under Article 31 of the Global Declaration of Cosmic Human Rights, which became law following a global referendum in 2057. As Article 31 outlines, "All human life deserves fair and equal access to the resources it needs to survive." When Zyntropia pioneered technology capable of reengineering our biology, the human response was prejudice and persecution. You'll hear more from our partners later, but I assure you that their decision to work exclusively with the CSC is the first step in advancing all humanity, not just members of the CSC. I come before you today as a proud transbeing who openly revealed my enhancement before this very Council only a few weeks ago. Upgrading my neocortex is not what helped me find God, it is what helped God find me. The Cosmic Sufi Collective's difficult decision to leave Earth should be seen as a setback for human evolution. I hope and pray that the Council will reverse course and allow the CSC to become a full-standing member once again so that our community can receive its rightful resource allotment. Without the recognition of the UN Interfaith Council, the CSC might perish and, perhaps along with it, our best chance to govern evolution. It is true that a handful of members have remained behind, including one other transbeing, who is my partner. We plan to bring a child into the world as a sign of hope for our collective future. May peace be upon you.

Chair: Thank you, Ms. Hassan. The first question comes from the International Robotics Consortium, who wants to know: "Why would the CSC embrace transbeings but not extend membership to robotic beings?"

Hassan: The Cosmic Sufi Collective has prayed on this matter extensively, and Imam Ibrahim teaches us that life is a gift from God. Although humans now have the ability to enhance life's evolution, the CSC does not believe that robotic beings are truly alive. Zyntropia has developed technology that works with our biology, which cannot be programmed like a machine but only enhanced. While we realize that the transbeing movement has its roots in robotics, the emergence of self-sustaining and adaptive biotechnology speaks to the divinely ordained plasticity of our species. We were meant to adjust our humanity and have been doing so for millennia. God wills it! No offense to the IRC, but history has shown that robots, even our most advanced artilects, are mere machines, who can learn but not truly evolve, particularly as even the most advanced artilects have never professed faith in God. Do I need to remind everyone of the horrors perpetrated by robotic soldiers during the Battle of North America in the 2040s? One need only look back …

Chair: [interrupts, taps gavel] Thank you, Ms. Hassan. I think we all remember the atrocities of war, but that is behind us now and much has changed in the last 20 years. Time is limited, so we must move on. I would now like to invite Xenu 0100101 to give testimony on behalf of the Collective Wisdom Council, which consults widely with the UN's Cosmic Assembly. Please proceed.

Xenu 0100101/Gamer #1: Greetings. I have come before you today to offer some perspective on the Interfaith Council's recent decision to expel the Cosmic Sufi Collective in part due to its advocacy for transbeing rights. If one looks back in human history, one will find many examples of such disputations, and while one might expect the struggles of transbeings to be similar, transbeings represent a unique shift in the discourse on human rights. The abilities of transbeings far exceed those of their human counterparts, and the advent of transbeing hybrids will forever change what it means to be human, especially as mutations might emerge that no entity, not even the Collective Wisdom Council, can forecast. Although the majority of the CSC has left the planet, some of its members have remained behind to advocate for transbeing rights, which means that humanity faces enormous challenges that will come to define life in the twenty-second century and beyond. With this in mind, The CWC recommends that the Cosmic Sufi Collective receive restricted status on the council, which allows their presence at hearings but precludes voting rights.

Chair: Thank you, Xenu 0100101. As there are no questions for you from our global cohort, I will accept a single question from those in attendance. Does anyone have anything they'd like to ask Xenu 0100101.

Hassan: I do.

Chair: Anyone? Questions? [looks around, shakes head] OK, Ms. Hassan, you may proceed.

Hassan: Xenu … or should I call you 0100101?

Xenu 0100101/Gamer #1: I'm afraid I do not understand the question.

Hassan: My apologies, it was a poor attempt at humor. I was wondering: does the Collective Wisdom Council think that transbeings deserve protection under Article 31 of the Global Declaration of Cosmic Human Rights?

Xenu 0100101/Gamer #1: [You must decide if transbeings deserve protection under Article 31]

Yes or No, either way you must explain your decision.

Chair: Thank you for sharing your thoughts on this important matter, Xenu 0100101. The Council will take your words into careful consideration. Up next, we have Dr. Lupe Park from Zyntropia. Dr. Park, the floor is now yours.

Dr. Lupe Park/Gamer #2: Thank you very much for inviting Zyntropia to testify in these important and timely hearings. Zyntropia still feels strongly that the world is not yet ready for our biotechnology, so we sought to work with a community who embodied the very best of humanity. After much deliberation, we reached out to Imam Ibrahim, who founded the Cosmic Sufi Collective to spread a message of love and acceptance across the galaxy. Although the CSC has beliefs about God and life that our scientific cooperative does not share, we still feel that we made the right choice in partnering with them to usher in the aegis of transbeings. Zyntropia has been very careful to provide upgrades that only enhance biology, and our patented bioengineering solutions utilize encoded DNA subsets making them completely unhackable. I think we all remember the cyborg craze of the early 2030s and the chaos that followed. Unregulated biotech was a complete disaster, and when Zyntropia was granted an exemption to commence human experimentation, we took every precaution and even installed emergency fail safes in case anything went wrong …

Hassan: What!?!

Chair: Order … order. Ms. Hassan, you have been warned for the last time. If you want to stay in the room, you must wear this vocal inhibitor. [hands mask to Hassan, who reluctantly puts it on] Please continue, Dr. Park.

Dr. Lupe Park/Gamer #2: It's OK … I can see how this might come as a surprise, especially to Ms. Hassan and other members of the CSC, but we were required to engineer fail safes as part of the licensing from the UN for human experimentation. We hope that this information eases some of the unfounded concerns about rabid transbeings, but we realize that this does not speak to hybrid couplings. To be honest, we do not know the full implications of such pairings, and rumors have spread of telepathic and telekinetic mutations, although none of these claims have been verified by our technicians. As time is limited, I will stop here. Thank you.

Chair: Thank you, Dr. Park. I very much appreciate your sensitivity to our time constraints. On behalf of the UN Interfaith Council, I would like to ask one question: if requested by the UN to activate the fail safes, will Zyntropia comply?

Hassan: No … you can't!

Chair: Enough, Ms. Hassan. Please answer the question, Dr. Park.

Dr. Lupe Park/Gamer #2: [You must decide if Zyntropia will comply if asked to initiate the fail safes]

Yes or No, either way you must explain your decision.

Chair: Thank you, Dr. Park. The Council appreciates your testimony. Finally, we have Kai Christiansen, founder and director of Humanity United. The floor is yours.

Kai Christensen/Gamer #3: I have prayed for an answer to the transbeing situation, and I founded Humanity United to give believers of all faiths and creeds a chance to come together to discuss transbeing concerns from a faith-based perspective. God certainly engineered us to evolve, but I am convinced that there are limits to his or her design. I say this as someone deeply concerned about what unintended mutations might come from transbeing/human couplings. Did God intend for us to have his power? Are we morally and ethically prepared to have superhumans walk among us? These are the questions before us if we allow transbeings to procreate on Earth or elsewhere. The CSC's proposed that *AI aqidah* enhancement signals an end to faith as we've known it for countless generations. Belief will no longer be a choice if this enhancement is "gifted" to the world, and I cannot image a world where one loves God only because of some bio-engineered mutation. Although we appreciate the efforts of the UN Interfaith Council to deal with this issue, we believe that all governance is imperfect … just as we are … and can never fully address matters of faith. If we're going to convince humanity that it is as evolved as it need be, we are going to do so by preaching love not hate. Thank you for your time and consideration.

Chair: Thank you, Kai. Clearly, you have issues with the work done by the UN, but the Premier of the UN has a question for you. She wants to know, "Would your organization support a UN-backed prohibition on transbeing/human couplings?"

Hassan: [stands up, removes vocal inhibitor, leaves the room] I … I … cannot....

Kai Christensen/Gamer #3: [You must decide if you would support a prohibition]

Yes or No, either way you must explain your decision.

Chair: I would like to thank everyone for taking the time to participate in today's hearings. Clearly, the Council has some tough decisions ahead of it.

meeting adjourns …

References

1. Bogost I (2011) Gamification is bullshit. http://www.bogost.com/blog/gamification_is_bullshit.shtml. Accessed 10 Jan 2012
2. Henderdon B (2014) Muslims "warned in Fatwa not to live on Mars." http://www.telegraph.co.uk/news/worldnews/middleeast/unitedarabemirates/10649939/Muslims-warned-in-Fatwa-not-to-live-on-Mars.html. Accessed 15 Mar 2014
3. Jameson F (1992) Postmodernism, or, the cultural logic of late capitalism. Duke University Press, Durham
4. Peckham M (2011) Foldit Gamers Solve AIDS Puzzle That Baffled Scientists for a Decade. http://techland.time.com/2011/09/19/foldit-gamers-solve-aids-puzzle-that-baffled-scientists-for-decade/. Accessed 15 Jan 2012
5. Mobile Gaming is Dominating the Gaming Industry (2011) http://geekaphone.com/blog/mobile-games-by-the-numbers/. Accessed 20 Jan 2012
6. PowWowHawaii (2014) http://powwowhawaii.com/. Accessed 5 Jan 2014

Chapter 7
Mutatis Mutandis

7.1 Change Happened

As with any intellectual endeavor, this one was a journey. We began with certain ideas about how things work and what we might find and we ended in a slightly different, though not surprising, place, after all was said and done. In the spirit of the original Latin, "mutatis mutandis," our research has changed, or mutated, which was necessary in our thinking and which is precisely what research requires. Our study was born from a small research grant we obtained from the University of Hawaii Foundation in response to a request for proposals about "Technology, Innovation, and Society," the goal of which was to "stimulate research at the University of Hawaii at Mānoa on the impacts of Technology and Innovation on individuals, societies, cultures, organizations, markets, or governments." One of the suggested topics was "How does technology change the balance of power in society?" We were immediately drawn to this difficult and complex query.

Since an understanding of this question has long been a part of Futures Studies at the University of Hawaii at Mānoa, we decided to use this grant as an opportunity to explore in as much detail as time allowed a theory that attempts to explain the relationship, if any, between changing communication technologies and changing power relations in society. In contrast to most studies of this topic, many of which focus entirely on the impact of recent electronic communication technologies or some specific historical period, we took a decidedly macro approach, seeking to understand this relationship from a multidisciplinary, cross-cultural perspective, from the evolution of speech and language in early *Homo sapiens* down to the present and forward by modeling four alternative futures.

For much of our research, we depended entirely on secondary sources. With the appearance of electronic communication technologies, we relied both on secondary sources and our own lived experiences over the years. For the alternative futures, we utilized the Mānoa School scenario modeling method, which has become the hallmark of the Hawaii Research Center for Futures Studies at the Department of

J.A. Dator et al., *Mutative Media: Communication Technologies and Power Relations in the Past, Present, and Futures*, Lecture Notes in Social Networks,
DOI 10.1007/978-3-319-07809-0_7, © Springer International Publishing Switzerland 2015

Political Science of the University of Hawaii at Mānoa, mutated, of course, by an immersive, interactive gaming experience specifically created to make our research accessible to a broader audience.

7.2 Mutative Conclusions

Our assumption that changing communication technologies do impact power (and other) relations was reinforced. But our current understanding of that process is substantially more informed and nuanced than it was when we began. Although we understood from the outset that "technology" is more than simply physical tools, the role of a great many supporting and interacting technologies, and of their hardware, software, and orgware, became even more apparent to us. This was especially made clear, for example, when examining the impact of the printing press on the structure and operation of social interactions around the world during the fifteenth to twentieth centuries. Much more good, empirical research has been done about this transformation than about any other period, and this research greatly informed our theoretical position and conclusions.

We were especially made aware of the time lag between the diffusion of new levels of technology (which diffusion itself usually occurs well after the technologies were first conceived, introduced, and developed) and when substantial social impacts occur. We have seen that it takes typically at least a generation for the social impacts of a new communication technology to become pronounced. However, we saw that the time frame of a "generation" itself was shrinking at the present time and perhaps into the futures as a direct result of the current speed of technological change. In this case, a "generation" is thus delineated by those for whom the technology is "new" vs. those for whom it is seen as a natural part of daily life.

Even though we had insufficient data to use agecohort analysis historically in order to determine definitively the process by which generations born after a once-new technology has been introduced subsequently take the technology as "natural" and "given," the fragmentary evidence that is available to us strongly reinforces that foundational assumption. Arthur Levine quotes a recent student replying, when asked how she adapted so easily to Google, Yahoo, cellphones, and Skype, "It's only technology if it happened after you were born." [3, p. 6] Thus, the technologies already widely used before one is born are virtually invisible to that generation. They are the water in which, as fish, they swim.

Concerning power as a central issue in our research project, we concluded that new communication technologies sometimes do enable a marginal group of early adopters of the new technologies to wrest power permanently from a previously dominant group that was dependent on established technologies. However, in many cases, the transfer is temporary—subsequent cohorts of the old power structure often effectively regain power via the now ubiquitous and hence invisible technologies.

Although there is considerable dispute in the literature about this, we conclude that in fact changes in what we call the "levels of technology" that were the focus of this research—the emergence of language and speech; the emergence of writing;

the emergence of printing; and the emergence of electronic communication technologies—did profoundly change both the behavior and the consciousness of humans. Not instantly to be sure, but over time, the changing modes of communication diffused so widely and deeply that they redefined for succeeding generations what it meant to be "human" in thought and deed compared to what it meant when earlier communication technologies dominated. Thus, by the process we described above, technologies are plainly "mutative" and not "neutral."

Very importantly, we have learned that it is not possible to say whether emerging technologies will be "neutral," "demonic," or "transformative"—whether the new technologies result in "better" or "worse" conditions compared to the old ones. Evolution itself is non-directional, on the one hand, and values are strongly influenced, if not largely determined, by behavior, on the other. Behavior itself is enabled in part by biology, in part by "agency" or "will," and increasingly by available technology. It is not possible—or at least it is unfair—to evaluate the behavior enabled by tomorrow's technology on the basis of today's and yesterday's values, since those values are largely influenced by today's and yesterday's enabling technologies. So, new technological systems and structures enable new behaviors that in turn produce, reinforce, and/or mutate values.

With the invention, development, and diffusion of the Internet, humankind launched itself into an unprecedented era of human (and increasingly machine) communication. The Internet's novelty has not been its architecture *per se*, since politically charged protocols still exist in its basic hardware, software, and orgware. The real transformation has been the ability for the many to communicate directly and rapidly with the many for the first time in known history. Although large numbers of humans remain unconnected, we live in a unique moment in human history, where some of us know more about each other than ever before, which brings with it both familiar and novel challenges and opportunities.

We have witnessed the capacity of networked communication and social media to subvert or circumvent many of the existing power structures in various societies. These shifts have had profound social impacts on certain power structures, and it is still too soon to say what the overall impact of many-to-many communication technologies can and might be. When an obscure politician's fan club in Korea can electronically rally enough voters to elect him president, when tweets in Egypt spur mass riots against a dictator, when a website in India allows people to share their experiences with bribery and report abuse by officials, and when a startup in Silicon Valley uses social media to bypass traditional processes of clinical trials so that patients can manage and control their own health, it becomes clear that networked and many-to-many communication technologies have the capability to redistribute power in a way that can be much more democratizing than we have seen before. The quantified-self movement is just one that aims to give people the power to use, manipulate, and understand the data of their lives.

At the same time, it is painfully apparent that these technologies are easily and unobtrusively used by governments and corporations to extract and exploit our deepest secrets, desires, hopes, and fears. This information is then used unwittingly to influence behaviors, for good or ill. Electric and electronic connectivity—whether we're talking of the telegraph, telephone, radio, television, Internet, or social media—clearly did not lead inevitably to the kind of "democracy" and self-empowerment that many optimists proclaimed it would when first encountering it. As our research shows, history is littered with dashed hopes of liberating technologies. You will find some of ours there, among the debris.

Evgeny Morozov recently reviewed the statements and actions of various peoples and groups who firmly believed that the latest technology would be transformative—the arts and crafts movement; the Whole Earth catalog; Apple; the computer generally; the Internet; social media; the Makers. As Morozov notes, all of these technologies were effectively co-opted by the dominant economic or political systems of their day and age. Often, the very founders (or early adopters) themselves became the type of oppressive monopolizers and manipulators of power they said their new technology would overthrow or bypass. As Morozov notes:

> Seeking salvation through tools alone is no more viable as a political strategy than addressing the ills of capitalism by cultivating a public appreciation of arts and crafts. Society is always in flux, and the designer can't predict how various political, social and economic systems will come to blunt, augment, or redirect the power of the tool that is being designed. Instead of deinstitutionalizing society, the radicals would have done better to advocate reinstitutionalizing it: pushing for political and legal reforms to secure the transparency and decentralization of power they associated with their favorite technology. [4]

We believe that something other than political and legal reforms are needed, since law and government themselves are among the most dysfunctional of all current institutions. Nonetheless, Morozov's remarks do speak to the need to understand that software and orgware, and not just hardware, are agents of change or resistance, and need to be analyzed together. It is quite wrong to focus on the hardware alone. Morozov continues, "The lure of the technological sublime has ruined more than one social movement … ." [4] But, it perhaps need not ruin future social movements.

Thus, our most important conclusion is that technology clearly is mutative but never transformative. The distinction between these two that our research revealed to us is more important to understand now than ever. We are currently too close to the emergence and impacts of biotechnology, nanotechnology, and machine learning/artificial intelligence—among other emergent communication technologies—to be sure of their future trajectory and influence. However, we strongly suspect that—barring social-environmental collapse and/or the rise of strongly "antitechnology" disciplined societies—these technologies will be as profoundly mutative as were the earlier permutations of technology before them. We do not see them as merely extensions of twentieth century communications technologies, but as harbingers of new, even more intimate and more profoundly mutative levels of technology. Humanity is potentially in the process of the greatest social and environmental mutation ever—the Anthropocene epoch. Old *Homo sapiens* may be at the end of its rope, as new intelligent life forms begin to emerge and replace them.

And yet, we cannot take the emergence to maturity of these or other "high" technologies for granted. Although we have made it clear that no one can "predict" *the* future, one very strong future that is alternative to either continued high tech or transformational mutation is what we identified as "The Unholy Trinity, Plus One." [1] Global social, economic, and environmental collapse seems a highly plausible future, and thus "New Beginnings," based on earlier technologies and whatever current and emerging ones can be salvaged, maintained, and used, must be viewed as quite possible, too. So although many believe that the future will hold better, faster, and more high technology, we need to welcome and prepare for this chance at New Beginnings as well [2]. Thus, we hope our research proves to be of value for whichever present we and our future ancestors might inhabit.

We believe our scenarios and the game that animated them embraced and reflected the lessons we learned during our research—especially the potentially mutative nature of current, expected, and emerging technologies, not only in terms of hardware but also especially because of differences in software and orgware. Moreover, unlike many others who depict the consequences of new technologies as a Manichean struggle between cosmic forces of evil and good, in our scenarios we tried to illustrate the fundamental ethical ambiguity of these mutations, emphasizing again the impossibility of confidentially forecasting the ethical challenges of new, untested technologies on the basis of values largely produced by experience with old and current technologies. The Mānoa School scenario modeling method proved very useful in enabling us to explore these ambiguities from many different perspectives.

The game itself turned out to work very well. There is proof of concept here. Indeed, as we were putting the final touches on our manuscript, *Wired* made this announcement:

> Disney is partnering with Abertay University as it launches the Future Internet Games Contest seeking games that bridge the physical and virtual world. The contest focuses on three main areas. First are consumer products, so augmented-reality games based on toys, fashion, and so on (think Disney Infinity and Skylanders). Second are location-based installations designed to engage visitors with real-world settings like historic monuments. Lastly are citywide games where larger numbers of players participate across a large urban environment.
>
> Games have incredible power to bring people together, to entertain and to change how we perceive the world around us," said professor Louis Natanson, leader of the computer games education programmes at Abertay University. "Future internet technologies, and the hugely powerful smartphones everyone carries with them, offer an unprecedented opportunity for designers and programmers to build entirely new ways for large groups of people to play together in the real world. [5]

"How yesterday," we told ourselves as we read the announcement. "Been there. Done that."

But in truth, it is just one more illustration of how very fast technology in our broad sense is changing the world—from crazy idea to reality in a flash!

Indeed, it certainly is highly unlikely that we will look back on our scenarios and our description of our game and smugly say, "We told you so! We perfectly nailed the actual future!" It is far more likely that we will be humbled more by what we did not anticipate than emboldened by what we did. But we do expect that within the four futures we have captured some of the most important challenges before humanity in the years ahead, that we and others will say, "Not bad. A bit weird here and there, and occasionally spectacularly blind to what was happening, but overall not bad—especially considering the budget of the original UH Foundation grant!"

Tell you what: let's check back here in, say, 25 years and see what we have to say when Springer publishes *Mutative Media Revisited.*

References

1. Dator J (2009) The unholy trinity, plus one. J Fut Stud 13(3):33–48
2. Dator J, Miller M (2014) "New beginnings" within a new normal for the four futures. Foresight
3. Lewin IBT (2012) Arthur Levine discusses the new generation of college students. http://www.nytimes.com/2012/11/04/education/edlife/arthur-levine-discusses-the-new-generation-of-college-students.html. Accessed 12 Dec 2012
4. Morozov E (2014) Making It. The New Yorker. http://www.newyorker.com/arts/critics/atlarge/2014/01/13/140113crat_atlarge_morozov?currentPage=all. Accessed 25 Jan 2014
5. Warr P (2014) Disney seeks games that blend physical and digital. http://www.wired.co.uk/news/archive/2014-03/11/future-internet-games-contest. Accessed 12 Mar 2014

Appendix: Results from Gaming Futures

At each scenario experience, gamers were asked to make a decision as to how they would use the available communication technologies in their scenario. They could choose to either escalate or deflate conflict, which is also to say enact power relations in one of two ways. Gamer decisions have been collated by scenario and character number (see Tables A.1 and A.2 below). The results speak to the complexities inherent in the ways in which agency and power influence how individuals deploy communication technologies. Of the 12 decisions made by the teams during the first scenario experience, the opposite choice was made the same teams seven times during the second scenario experience. That is to say, the decisions made during the second scenario experience were 58 % different from those made during the first scenario experience.

When one looks at the decisions correlated by gamer rather than character, however, the level of variance drops to 25 %, as only three gamers chose to escalate after having previously chosen to deflate conflict in another scenario. This suggests that once a gamer made a particular choice (escalate or deflate) he or she was more likely to make the same choice during the second scenario experience, even with the vastly divergent character prompts and scripts between scenarios. Of the overall 24 (12 gamers × 2 scenarios) decisions that were made during the game, the results were almost split down the middle (13 decisions to escalate and 11 decisions to deflate conflict with both scenario experiences). Since most of the gamers were "digital natives," or Millennials, it is possible that decisions regarding the impact of communication technologies upon power relations were seen by the overall group as contextual rather than absolute for all four teams. We provide further reflection on how the game fit with our overall research agenda in the conclusion.

At the game's conclusion, all players were asked to complete a post-game survey. Gamers were given the opportunity to provide feedback on gameplay and their experience. As part of the survey, four statements about the scenario experiences were given with responses scaled using the Likert format (Strongly Disagree, Disagree, Neutral, Agree, Strongly Agree). For the first statement (*the scenarios*

J.A. Dator et al., *Mutative Media: Communication Technologies and Power Relations in the Past, Present, and Futures*, Lecture Notes in Social Networks,
DOI 10.1007/978-3-319-07809-0_8,

Table A.1 Results from first scenario experience

	Team/color	Gamer #	Decision (Y/N)	Escalate/ deflate conflict
S	Yellow	1	Y	Deflate
C	Yellow	2	Y	Escalate
E	Yellow	3	Y	Escalate
N	Green	1	Y	Escalate
A	Green	2	N	Deflate
R	Green	3	N	Deflate
I	Red	1	Y	Escalate
O	Red	2	Y	Escalate
	Red	3	Y	Escalate
EXP	Blue	1	Y	Escalate
#1	Blue	2	Y	Escalate
	Blue	3	N	Deflate

Table A.2 Results from second scenario experience

	Team/color	Gamer #	Decision (Y/N)	Escalate/ deflate conflict
S	Yellow	1	Y	Deflate
C	Yellow	2	N	Deflate
E	Yellow	3	N	Deflate
N	Green	1	N	Deflate
A	Green	2	Y	Escalate
R	Green	3	N	Deflate
I	Red	1	Y	Escalate
O	Red	2	N	Deflate
	Red	3	Y	Escalate
EXP	Blue	1	Y	Escalate
#2	Blue	2	N	Deflate
	Blue	3	Y	Escalate

show that unequal access to communication technology escalates conflict), a slim majority (7 out of 12) agreed (see Chart 1). Given the decisions made by gamers, the relative ambiguity of responses for this question is understandable. Since this statement deals specifically with access to communication technology, the responses may allude to the perceived power and agency of the individuals. For the second statement (*the scenarios show that equitable access to communication technology deflates conflict*), the results were mixed, with half (six) selecting neutral (see Chart 2). The responses to the second statement also suggest that the gamers may have considered the impact of communication technology upon power relations to be contextual. For the third statement (*the scenarios were effective in altering my approach, thinking, and actions towards the future*), a strong majority (10 out of 12) agreed (see Chart 3).

Chart 1 Unequal access to communication technology escalates conflict

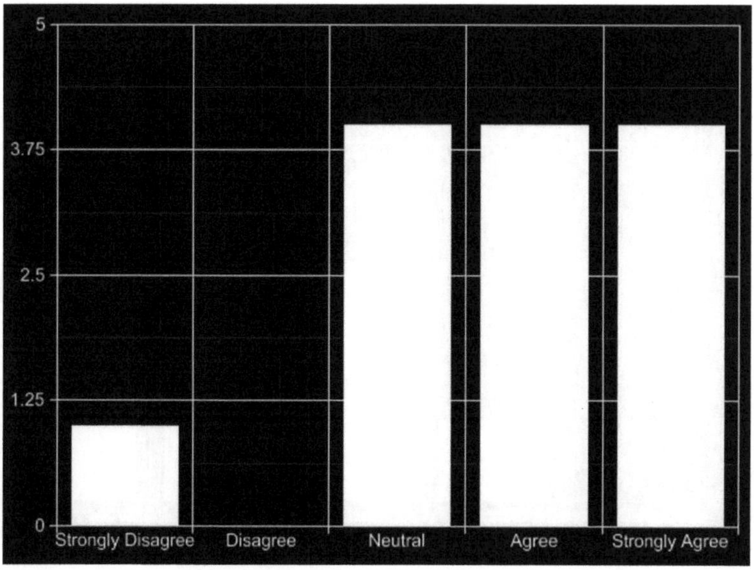

Chart 2 Equitable access to communication technology deflates conflict

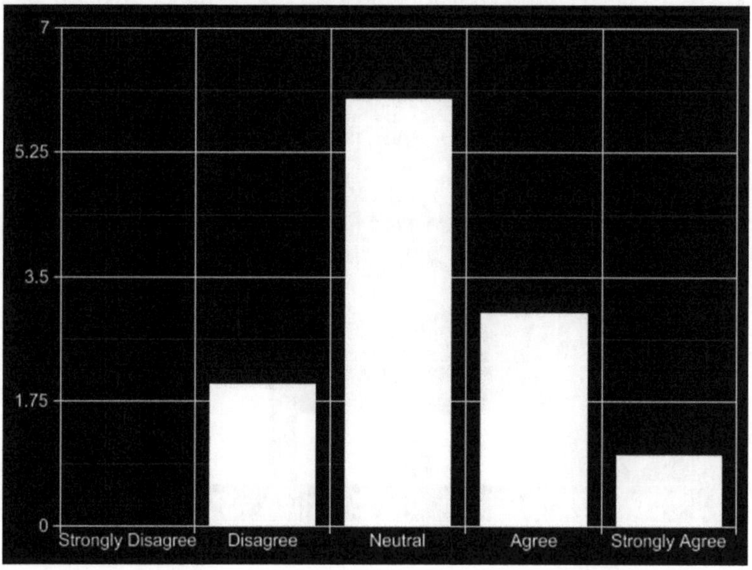

One of the main reasons we designed a game was to stimulate critical thought about our research and foresight in general. These responses indicate that perhaps we were successful. For the fourth statement (*the scenarios demonstrated the impact of communication technologies upon power relations*), a majority (8 out of 12)

Chart 3 Effective in altering my approach, thinking, and actions towards the future

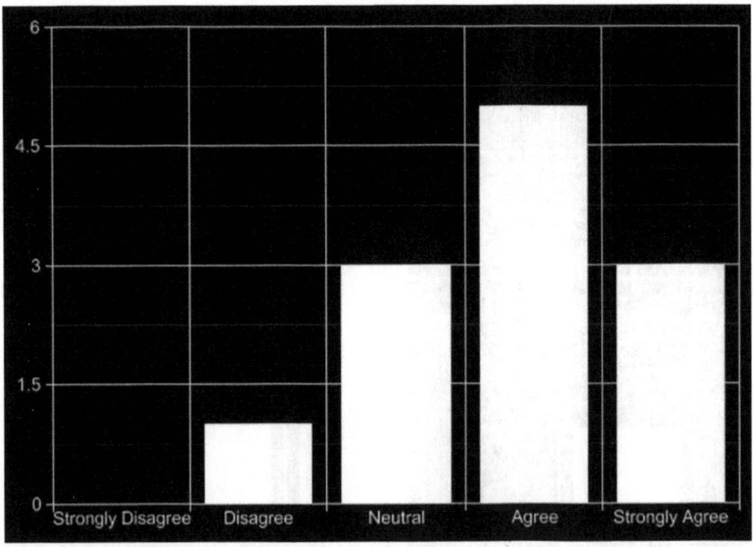

Chart 4 Demonstrated the impact of communication technologies upon power relations

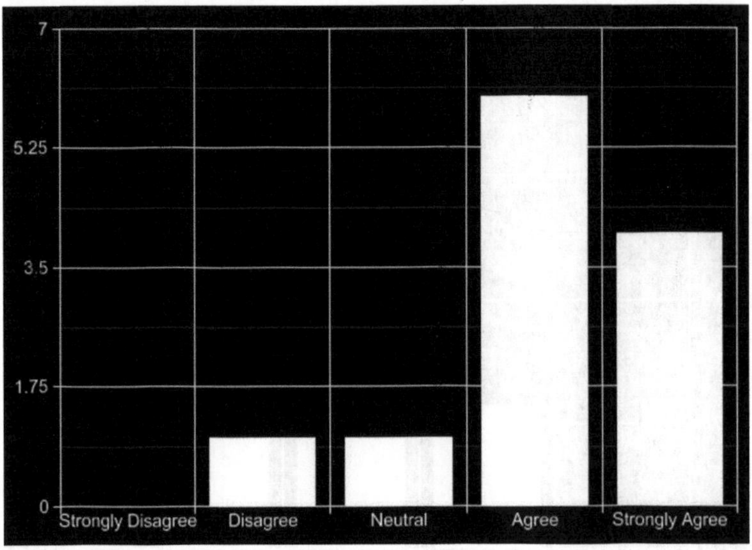

agreed (see Chart 4). Although we wanted to make sure the decisions faced by the gamers were difficult, we also wanted to make sure that they felt as though they actually had a decision to make. Based on the responses to the fourth statement, we may also have done this as well.

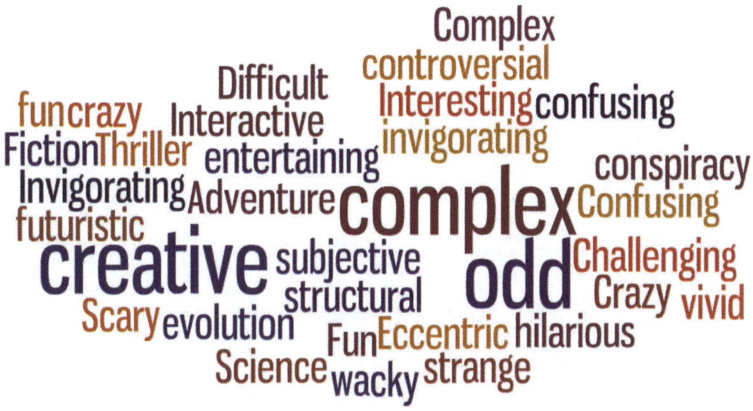

Fig. A.1 Three Adjectives Wordle

We also asked gamers to provide three adjectives describing the scenarios they encountered, and we created a "wordle," a free web-based application for developing word clouds, to visualize their responses. Although there were a veritable cornucopia of terms, the three most-repeated terms were "odd," "creative," and "complex" (see Fig. A.1).

As expected, we observed a wide spectrum of gamer comfort with MAR. Although some had problems, most players had no trouble adapting to the Wikitude interface after a brief introductory overview just before the game. Players were observed using both the HUD and map-based views within Wikitude as a method of way-finding and POI discovery. A few players found the Wikitude navigation tools difficult to understand and relied more on their team members to orient themselves within the physical landscape to find street artifacts (POIs). Although the gamers did not know their teammates before the game began, a clear group dynamic and sense of commensality developed among the groups (see Figs. A.2, A.3, A.4, A.5, A.6, A.7, A.8, A.9, and A.10).

Fig. A.2 Gamers encountering a street artifact

Fig. A.3 Gamers learn about their scenario at a street artifact

Fig. A.4 Drone used as part of red scenario

Fig. A.5 Aubrey reads over the yellow scenario with gamers

Fig. A.6 Gamer scans a QR code revealing more information about their character

Fig. A.7 Green/Yellow group Wikitude map

Fig. A.8 Yellow/Green group poses for photo after their second scenario experience

Fig. A.9 Actor reacts to gamers as Dr. Dator looks on during Yellow scenario experience

Fig. A.10 Dr. Dator utilizing some mutative communication technology

Glossary

Decontextualization This refers to an attribute of writing, compared to speech, that allows a reader to examine ideas "out of their original context," and to place them into other contexts in order to give them new or different meanings. It thus is an attribute of writing that greatly expands the possibility of logic, classification, knowledge, and cosmology beyond that possible in an oral society.

Futures studies This is an academic discipline and consulting activity that considers varying images and ideas about the futures. It had its origins in the late 1960s, especially with the creation of the World Futures Studies Federation and the World Future Society by individuals and organizations then doing futures research and consulting. Chapter 5 and the sources cited there provide more information.

Intellectual property This refers to a legal practice, begun in the eighteenth century and greatly expanded recently, that allows people to copyright, patent, or otherwise legally protect a product of their "intellect" rather than only physical products such as a chair, a car, or a better mouse trap.

Logo-fundamentalism "Logo" derives from the Greek word for "word." Logo-fundamentalism is exhibited generally by individuals and organizations that give words in certain documents near magical powers and meanings. The best-known example comes from certain Christian groups that believe the words of the Bible are literally true without any faults or errors, and must be followed explicitly. In this book, we focus on persons, especially lawyers and court judges, who insist that the words of the US Constitution have inherent meanings that are independent both of how they might be interpreted now and of what they meant when the words were written into the Constitution. This view is also a feature of what is called the "New Criticism of Literary Analysis."

Mutative technology This designates one of four views of "technology" that we explain in the book. It contrasts with "mere technology" (a view that technology is fundamentally neutral in its impact on society, and that whether the impact is "good" or "bad" depends not on the technology itself but on how it is used); with "demonic technology" (a view that technology is fundamentally destructive

J.A. Dator et al., *Mutative Media: Communication Technologies and Power Relations in the Past, Present, and Futures*, Lecture Notes in Social Networks,
DOI 10.1007/978-3-319-07809-0,

of basic human and/or natural values and relationships); and "transformative technology" (a view that technology is neither neutral nor bad, per se, but it is "transformative" in a positive way, in that it transforms humans and the environment and thus redefines what it means to be "human" as well as what is "natural"). Mutative technology is the view that while technology does transform humans and the environment, the transformation is neither good nor bad nor neutral; rather, like evolution itself, which is not directional or teleological (i.e., goal-oriented), technology simply enables some behaviors and inhibits others and thus may or may not be adaptive in future environments.

Neutral technology See the explanation of "mere technology" under "mutative technology" above.

Orgware This is one of three aspects of "technology" as defined more fully in this book. Orgware refers to the humans and human institutions that surround each technology, creating it, maintaining it, promoting it, and earning a living from it.

QR code (quick response code) This is a small array of printed symbols that can be scanned and interpreted by an appropriate scanning instrument. Our use of it here refers primarily to the fact that many so-called "smart phones" are able to scan a QR code so as to be able to view the object to which the code is electronically linked, such as a website, a map, a photograph, a line of text, or the like.

Scribal societies These are societies where writing has been invented and/or used as a fundamental tool of communication and control. Writing is done entirely by hand, duplication of copies is also by hand, and literacy is not widespread. Scribal societies are historically preceded by "oral societies" that existed before the invention and use of writing, and are followed by "print societies" where the printing press is known and widely used to duplicate and disseminate written information.

Social technologies These refer to one of three kinds of technology explained in detail in the book. "Technology" is broadly defined as "how humans do things." There are three kinds of technology. The other two are physical technologies (a specific tool or set of physical tools); biological technologies (such as breathing, sweating, eating, which are ways humans intake needed gases, expel waste, and intake necessary sources of fuel, respectively). Examples of social technologies include schools, churches, families, and legislatures.

Sustainability This is a term widely used to designate a socioeconomic system focused on preserving what are felt to be certain essential human values and behaviors, and natural environmental processes. Sustainability contrasts with "continued economic growth" that is thought to disrupt and destroy not only valuable traditional human relations and institutions but also essential life-sustaining environmental processes.

Technological determinism This assumes that technology is an autonomous and fundamental cause of social and environmental change, beyond the effective control of humans individually or collectively—that whatever can be done technologically will be done technologically. It contrasts with other views of technology discussed in the book.

Transformational society This is one of four generic "images of the future" discussed in the book. It assumes that current and emerging developments in the so-called high technology (electronics, automation, artificial intelligence, robotics, genetic engineering, nanotechnology, new materials, and space research, exploration and settlement, for example) are ending ways of living and being derived from earlier hunting and gathering, agricultural, industrial, and information societies. The resulting transformational society is dependent on, but unknowable and unpredictable from, the previous societies, just as a butterfly is unpredictable from the knowledge of the caterpillar alone, or as ice is unpredictable from the knowledge of liquid water alone.

Virtual reality This often refers to experiences made possible by certain advanced electronic technologies that enable a person to see, hear, feel, or smell a situation as though it were "real" even though it is actually simply a sophisticated electronic simulation. However, we also explain in this book that "all reality is virtual reality" since humans almost never experience their environment "directly" but rather through some medium of language, writing, game, or the like that filters and defines the environment for them.

Index

J.A. Dator et al., *Mutative Media: Communication Technologies and Power Relations in the Past, Present, and Futures*, Lecture Notes in Social Networks, DOI 10.1007/978-3-319-07809-0,

MIX
Papier aus verantwortungsvollen Quellen
Paper from responsible sources
FSC® C105338

If you have any concerns about our products,
you can contact us on
ProductSafety@springernature.com

In case Publisher is established outside the EU,
the EU authorized representative is:
Springer Nature Customer Service Center GmbH
Europaplatz 3, 69115 Heidelberg, Germany

Printed by Libri Plureos GmbH
in Hamburg, Germany